I0815259

ADVANCE PRAISE FOR

Vineyard Melody

"*Vineyard Melody* is a harrowing story of escaping a toxic marriage, but more than that it's a powerful testament of following one's dream, especially when that dream leads to the French wine country. Namratha Stanley is a marvelous storyteller and hers is a story we can all toast! Santé!"

—Susan Blumberg-Kason, author of *Bernardine's Shanghai Salon* and *Good Chinese Wife*

"Namratha's story is so inspirational, so real, and written from the heart. Forget about *Eat, Pray, Love*...and drink in the world, fight for your future. Her journey is a battle cry to all women—no matter what country they are from. She is brave, strong, and her voice sings off the page. She brings us, the reader, on an emotional ride from Bangalore to Bordeaux with many twists along the way. No spoilers... But, ultimately , her story is about a mother's love for her daughter and doing whatever it takes to create/blend a new beautiful life...one grape at a time. Cheers! Raise a glass! To Namratha! Cheers to new starts and second chances!"

—Samantha Verant, author of *Seven Letters From Paris, The Lucky Widow*, and *The Private Chef*

"I've never read a story like this one. The author's life within a stifling marriage in India, and her literal journey to break free, is only part of the book. She arrives in Bordeaux, France, determined to start over and then send for her daughter, who's still in India. I rooted for her as she rescued her daughter as she learned the wine business and eventually became an international success in that field. This is a wonderful read, with plenty for book clubs to discuss as well."

—Gabi Coatsworth, author of *Love's Journey Home*, *A Beginner's Guide to Starting Over*, and *A Field Guide to Library Ghosts*

"This memoir is a reminder that even in the darkest moments, a new beginning is possible—and in Namratha's case, in the world of French wine. People love to know the story behind the wine label—but few stories are as inspiring as Namratha Stanley's. From an abusive home to personal freedom, she uncorks a tale of strength, hope and second chances. Be sure to pour yourself a glass of Solicantus to toast her success."

—Suzanne Mustacich, author of *Thirsty Dragon*, co-host of *The Wine Podcast* and *Wine Voices*

"A story of resilience and reinvention. A woman who dared to dream beyond the borders she was born into and reinvent herself in the sun-soaked vineyards of France. A gorgeously told story to sip and savour."

—Janice MacLeod, author of *Paris Letters*

"From a restrictive and abusive marriage to the enchanting world of wine and vineyards, Namratha Stanley's memoir is a powerful story of resilience, strength, and the unbreaking love of a mother."

—Lyn Liao Butler, bestselling author of *The Fourth Daughter*

"Namratha Stanley humanizes the wine industry, offering a peek into the darkest cellars, historic vineyards, and esteemed auctions. But the delight of such a life is tinged with trauma and struggle, which she ultimately, happily, triumphs through."

—Amy Thomas, author of *Paris, My Sweet* and *Brooklyn In Love*

"What price would you pay for love? In *Vineyard Melody*, Namratha Stanley searches for freedom as she grapples with her controlling husband and her in-laws' expectations and strict rules. Trapped in traditional married life in India, her wings were clipped—but when she immerses herself in Bordeaux's wine community, she sprouts a vibrant new set of feathers and learns how to soar on her own. Moving and inspiring, Stanley proves it's never too late to reinvent yourself and live life on your own terms."

—Kristin Vuković, award-winning author of *The Cheesemaker's Daughter*

"All expat stories I know are tales of radical reinvention—Nam's more than most. She has found her voice through winemaking. Readers will admire her courage and passion."

—Elizabeth Bard, author of *Lunch in Paris, Picnic in Provence,* and *Dinner Chez Moi*

"I have read many memoirs of survival and transformation, but few have moved me like *Vineyard Melody*—a story of a mother who fled twelve years of violence in Bangalore to build a wine business in Bordeaux's vineyards, all while separated from the daughter she was fighting to save. What strikes me most is the impossible mathematics of her sacrifice: four years apart, learning French in secret, entering a male-dominated industry as a woman of color, all to create a life worth bringing her child home to. Namratha's voice carries both the weight of those who came before her—women who couldn't escape—and the fierce hope of those who will come after. This book is not simply a memoir—it is a gift of courage, a light for those still searching for their way forward, and a testament to the power of love and perseverance."

—Kiersten Hathcock, co-founder of the National Institute for Law and Justice, award-winning entrepreneur, and author of *Little Voices*

Vineyard Melody

How One Woman Rebuilt Her Life, One Grape At A Time

NAMRATHA STANLEY

A REGALO PRESS BOOK
ISBN: 979-8-89565-293-0
ISBN (eBook): 979-8-89565-294-7

Vineyard Melody:
How One Woman Rebuilt Her Life, One Grape At A Time

Cover Design by Jim Villaflores
Grape Wreath Art by Samantha Verant

Publishing Team:
Founder and Publisher – Gretchen Young
Editor – Adriana Senior
Managing Editor – Caitlin Burdette
Production Manager – Kate Harris
Production Editor – Rachel Paul

As part of the mission of Regalo Press, a donation is being made to the Mukul Madhav Foundation (MMF), as chosen by the author. Find out more about this organization at https://www.mmpc.in/.

Regalo Press
New York • Nashville
regalopress.com

Published in the United States of America

1 2 3 4 5 6 7 8 9 10

For my daughter, Shloka—

&

For every woman who has ever felt trapped, silenced, or unseen—
This book is for you. May it remind you that you are stronger than you know, that freedom is always possible, and that your story is worth telling. Your journey, no matter how difficult, holds the power to change not only your life but the world around you.

&

For the men who uplift us, support us and believe in us—
Thank you for standing by our side. Your respect, kindness, and belief in our strength undoubtedly make our world a better place.

"A real connoisseur does not drink wine,
but tastes of its secrets."

—Salvador Dalí

Contents

Contents

Author's Note

A few years back, I embarked on a beautiful journey of writing this memoir. I didn't know where to begin or how to give voice to all that life had unfolded before me. I knew in my heart that I must write. With time, this book became my space for reflection and healing. I hope that in these pages, you find echoes of your own story and, perhaps, a reminder that we are all artists of our own lives, capable of shaping even the darkest moments into something meaningful.

This book is based on my personal experiences and recollections. While every effort has been made to convey the emotional truth of my journey, memory is inherently subjective, and different people may remember the same events differently.

To protect the privacy of individuals, I have changed names and altered or omitted some identifying details. I've condensed timelines so this book doesn't become a thousand and one pages. Certain scenes have been reconstructed or condensed for narrative clarity and flow, but the essence of my experiences remains intact. Conversations have been paraphrased based on how I remember them. I don't intend to harm or defame any individual in these pages. It is a deeply personal account of my life, written from my perspective, and is shared in the hope that it may offer support, inspiration and solidarity to others.

This memoir is not only a window into my world but a testament to my struggles, my successes, and my transformation, which has led me from the lowest point of my life to self-discovery and freedom. Thank you for taking the time to walk this path with me.

—Namratha Stanley

Prologue

Tom Mullen watched as I poured my wine into two Riedel glasses. I placed the bottle back on the garden table, but this time closer to him, so he could inspect it. The golden swirl on the label glittered in the bright afternoon sun. I smiled. It had taken me a good four months to design the label and give it a fitting name. I then glanced at the paper on my lap, prepared for possible questions the American journalist would ask.

Why did you choose France? Why not America or any other country?

It was not just for the love of Monet, Louis de Funès, or the sexy president Macron that I had moved. The country was fueled by a combination of the best cheese, bread, and, of course, wine. Its architecture and landscapes were a sort of drug that mesmerized and haunted me, even in my dreams.

Oh, and I couldn't forget the most vital reason: Liberté.

Freedom.

Or would I confess that I had voluntarily loved and married someone who had turned my life into a living hell for more than a decade?

That, against the expectations of his family and culture, I had decided to save myself?

"Are you ready?" Tom asked as he held his phone close to me.

I wasn't ready. I would never be. I was about to discuss my most painful memories—ones that I had buried in a trunk and thrown into the far end of the ocean.

"Yes," I said, brushing my fears aside.

"Three, two, one, and start," he said and pressed the record button. "Namratha, your journey is very inspiring. Could you tell me what made you leave India to become a wine entrepreneur in France?"

I took a deep breath and began.

***

That evening, when I returned to my apartment, I was exhausted. I dropped my tasting bag on the floor and sat next to it. Shloka's photo was hanging on the wall to my right. I looked at her as doubts flooded my mind. Would I be able to make up for all those years without my daughter? Would I be able to rebuild my bond with her? We spoke daily, but it was not the same as living together. She had just turned thirteen, and I could sense that her hormones were all over the place. I was balancing being a friend and a mother from five thousand miles away. But how would it be in real life?

I'll find out in a week, I thought, and smiled.

I had waited four long years to move her to Bordeaux, but this last bit of waiting was making me impatient. As for Shloka, would she be shocked to meet the new me? She had seen me as a haggard-looking mom who had no skills outside of cooking, cleaning, and chauffeuring. Now I was forty, with a new wine business that made me optimistic in a very exciting way. I looked trim and confident in my business suits.

Wine had changed me entirely. I felt uninterested in conversations if they weren't about wine. My library consisted of books that spoke only about wine. My cellar housed nothing but wine. I couldn't think of any other gifts to give people on special occasions. I was living in the world's most beautiful region, far away from my husband, Moksh. I had dared to take one bold step, and I had broken free. This was my reward. The universe had laid a beautiful path in front of me.

In the corner, an easel was mounted with a large white canvas. The time was perfect. I quickly inspected the wine bottle in my tasting bag. There was a little left after the interview with Tom.

This should do, I thought as I grabbed the bottle, stood, and went to the kitchen, turning on the radio on the way. I took a glass from the shelf and emptied the wine into it before returning to the living room. The radio was now playing "La Vie en rose" by Édith Piaf. The *mélange* of her voice, a glass of red, and a blank canvas felt magical.

I drew a curved line from one end of the canvas to the other. After a sip of wine, I dipped the thinnest brush into the golden oil paint and ran it along the same line. It left a beautiful, glittery trail. Then I blended magenta with a tiny dash of black. It became the same color as the liquid in my glass. I stroked the canvas, swirling the thick Leonardo brush next to the golden line. Finally, the wine label that I had designed was coming alive on canvas.

Soon my eyes began to droop. I looked at the clock. It was almost 4:00am.

I should go to bed, I thought, then perked up when I remembered that tomorrow would be another day closer to being with Shloka. I smiled, stepped back, and took one last look at my painting.

***

The next day, I was awakened by the buzzing of my phone. It was Tom. I sat up and rubbed my eyes before answering.

"Namratha, good morning. Your interview is up on *Forbes*."

"What do you mean, *Forbes*?" I asked.

It can't be, I thought with a start. Surely he wasn't referring to the magazine that featured CEOs and billionaires?

"I've sent you the link. Take a look," he said.

I thanked him, hung up, and quickly clicked on the link he had sent.

"How This Woman from India Created a French Wine Label," the title read.

"Oh my God, I'm in *Forbes*!" I exclaimed to the empty room.

I hadn't realized Tom was interviewing me for an article on *Forbes*. He had only mentioned that he wrote for a lifestyle magazine. I tried to let the news sink in, but how could my brain process this piece of information? I was sleep deprived. My eyes were groggy. My body, covered in pink pajamas, wanted to sink back into the cozy comforter. Instead, I resisted, threw back the blanket, and jumped out of bed.

My mind must be playing tricks on me, I thought as I walked into the living room. *Only famous people are in* Forbes.

I sat on the couch and opened the link again. It was real. *I* was in *Forbes*.

Suddenly, it dawned on me that Moksh would probably read this interview. Would he regret losing me? Or would he plot against me?

On the bright side, if it were not for him, I wouldn't be here. He was a perfect example of a man who'd torment you until you harnessed the inner strength you didn't even know you had. Then you'd save yourself and achieve things you never dreamed of.

In the article, Tom had beautifully captured my strength and determination to succeed, despite my obstacles. I read on.

"'In the initial stage of marriage, they asked me not to work. But I said, can I study? My husband was okay with the idea of me being a student. He said that it was not for him to decide but I needed to ask permission from his parents.'"

I closed my eyes and journeyed back to my earlier life, then further back to my childhood in India. It flashed across my mind like a movie trailer.

***

The late summer of 1988 ushered in balmy days in the little town of Pondicherry, India. My memories are filled with the sounds of lush waves, shrieks of excited children, and flocks of cawing birds wheeling far above the sea.

During school break, my sister, Megha, and I were packed up and shipped off to our aunt's, who lived by the sea with her husband and two children, Sara and Raghav. Little Sara was the crowning achievement in the family. Unlike most couples during those times, Aunt Anitha and Uncle Daniel had longed for a girl. Almost a decade after their first child, Raghav, was born, the family welcomed a tiny miracle: Sara.

If Aunt Anitha wasn't at the nearby school teaching, she would be baking delicious cakes for us. Uncle Daniel would take us down to the beach and let us play as long as the sun shone bright.

On one such evening, we walked along with our colorful sand kits. It was a day I would never forget. Our little feet raced up and down the shore, gathering seashells in small buckets. When the heat became unbearable, we dove into the cooling sea, tumbling and falling against the force of the crashing waves. I remember a giant wave suddenly knocked me over, stinging my eyes. I coughed heavily as I tried to expel the salty water from my mouth. I retreated and started to build sandcastles on dry land.

"Let's go, kids! Pack up!" Aunt Anitha soon announced.

She had finished icing her cake and had come to take us back to her home. Megha helped Uncle Daniel collect buckets and spades that were scattered around.

The light dimmed by the minute, and I knew darkness would soon fall. It was time to return home, eat, rest, then come back again the next day. But my eight-year-old soul wanted nothing more than to stay longer at the beach.

I glanced at my cousin Raghav, still close to the water. His gaze was fixed on something at his feet. *What was he staring at?* Then he beckoned to me.

I stood, dusted the sand off myself, then walked toward him, straining to see what he pointed at. Something had washed ashore. It looked like a bag.

When closer, I finally saw what had caught his attention. Next to his feet lay a small figure.

I threw my hands to my cheeks and gasped with delight. "A doll!"

Her little face shone in the dim light. I picked her up, then dropped her instantly. My heart sank at the sight of her bloated belly and discolored skin. A clip was fastened to her umbilical cord. I looked at my cousin as my mind raced and my pulse quickened. He nodded to confirm what I feared.

How could this happen? Who would kill a baby? Tears welled in my eyes and spilled onto my cheeks. This was terrible. I ran to inform my aunt and uncle. Uncle Daniel went to inspect, but a big wave soon swallowed the corpse. Aunt Anitha took us back home.

***

Later that evening, as we gathered at the table for dinner, we discussed the gruesome discovery that had left us all in shock.

"She was so beautiful," I said. "I thought she was a doll."

"Her face was calm, like she was in deep sleep," Raghav added.

Aunt Anitha was pale. "Unfortunately, this is common practice. Sad, but true."

Tears filled my eyes again. Common? My heart was breaking. All I could do was sit helplessly with my hands in my lap.

She continued. "None of the authorities have managed to crack down on sex-selective abortions, and no hospitals are held responsible for dumping little bodies into the sea. It's horrible."

"I wish she was alive. We could have brought her back home, and I would have a sister," said Sara in a sorrowful voice.

"Aunty Anitha, if we had found the baby sooner, could we have saved her life?" Megha asked.

I looked at Aunt Anitha, who didn't respond. I couldn't read her expression.

Uncle Daniel finally put down his newspaper and came to join us for dinner as his wife ladled a delectable vegetable curry over the hot, steaming rice on our plates. I had forgotten how hungry I was until I inhaled the aroma of curry. I only hoped I could stomach the food after what I had experienced that day. I sat up and tried to push the memory of what I'd seen out of my mind as I began to eat. When my uncle spoke, I knew he was trying to lighten the mood and change the subject.

"Do you all want to go to Auroville tomorrow?" he asked as he took another serving.

"I want a baby sister to play with." Sara wasn't going to let anyone dissuade her from her thoughts.

"Why would someone hurt a little baby?" Raghav asked.

Aunt Anitha looked at Uncle Daniel.

"Maybe it was a ghost," Sara gasped. "It must be the work of Annabelle the evil doll! She doesn't like babies."

"She's right behind you," Raghav shouted as he grabbed the back of her neck. We all shrieked and laughed, momentarily forgetting the reality that had forced us to stray far from our childish comfort. Uncle Daniel shushed us.

"Annabelle?" Aunt Anitha said. "There's no such thing as Annabelle—or ghosts, for that matter. It's the work of some heartless people who sadly discard unwanted babies into the sea."

"Unwanted? Who wouldn't want a little baby girl?" I said in disbelief. It was unthinkable to even hear the word "unwanted." We were, of course, living in a different world, far from the harsh realities of life.

Sara began to cry. Uncle Daniel soon took her in his arms and comforted her.

"Why would a baby be unwanted?" Megha asked again, growing anxious.

"It's unfortunate that some parents do not want to have a baby girl. They think a girl is a burden and a lifelong responsibility."

"What?" the three of us chorused.

"But our parents didn't do that, and we're girls," I said.

"That's right. This kind of thing happens in some towns and villages. It is less frequent in the city. A girl brings a ton of value to the family, but some don't understand that. They perceive a girl as more of a problem than a source of joy. You are all too young to understand this now." She sighed. "But you must remember, in spite of it all, the world is still a beautiful place."

We nodded. Right then, nothing seemed beautiful to me.

"Now, who wants some delicious mango ice cream for dessert?" Aunt Anitha asked, again trying to lighten the mood.

***

Over the next few years, I didn't bother with questions, as I was too busy living my childhood, but I hadn't forgotten. Then, as I grew older, the veracity of that memory became starker and couldn't be brushed aside. In everyday life, I observed the social boundaries placed upon women, the hardships of mothers, and the prejudices against girls. The disparities bothered me, the social norms bewildered me, and the memory saddened me.

Over time, I understood why a girl's life was less valued. She would be a liability, and her safety would be a burden to her family, so she would be married off young—sometimes to a man much older than her. Her life skills were taught in the kitchen. School was an option for a few, but never a necessity.

Huge sums of money and gifts had to be paid as dowry so she could start the journey of being a wife, a personified slave to her husband and his family. If she did produce only girls for her beloved husband, it was her fault, never his. She then would be labelled a curse to the family—and in many villages, even banished. Her parents would be shamed for producing an incapable and unfit daughter.

A son was glorious. He would work to bring back earnings and carry the family name forward.

Who sets these norms? Why? When and where did all of this begin? Was it because the Bible said Eve was made to keep Adam company? And Eve was the perpetrator, who offered the forbidden apple to Adam? Or was it because, through evolution, men were physically stronger, and thereby played the role of guarding and hunting, while women stayed home to cook and care for children?

Did this lead to more power in the hands of men, while subordination became the fate of women? Haven't times changed? Hasn't there been a paradigm shift? Haven't the roles evolved? Shouldn't the thinking change?

I'm Namratha, and this is my story.

CHAPTER 1

The Wedding

Bangalore, India
October 2004

They say marriages are made in heaven. Mine too, maybe, had been decided there and destined to take place on Earth in a magnificent Hindu temple in the city of Bangalore in India. Every stone laid there could tell a story of a couple who began their journey of togetherness. Our story was next. The priest had consulted the position of the stars and chosen an auspicious day and time to unite us. This was it. My big day!

I was rushed to the dressing room to be draped in a saree. My two best friends, Susan and Pooja, walked by my side, and my sister, Megha, led the way. In the corner of a hall, a man stood on the last step of the tallest ladder I had ever seen. He was decorating walls ornately with orange and yellow marigold flowers, symbols of good fortune. A teakwood *mandap* elaborately decorated with white roses sat in the middle of the grand hall. Moksh and I were to walk around the fire and tie the knot later that day. The noise from all the final preparations was drowned out by the melodies that came from the musical instruments—*nadhaswaram* and *thavil*—played live by the best maestros, who were commissioned by my father. They sat on an elevated platform at the far end of the room. No South Indian marriage was complete without their music. I had witnessed many such weddings since I was little—it was hard to believe that it was finally my turn.

Like a typical South Indian bride, I dressed in a beautiful red *Kanchivaram* silk saree adorned with gold weavings. The previous night's henna had cast its magic and left beautiful dark brown designs deep in my skin. Susan and Pooja hung necklaces around my neck and attached matching *jhumkas* to my ears. My sister, Megha, carefully slid glass bangles that I had chosen from an old bangle seller's trunk onto my wrists.

"Ouch," I said as the hairdresser tugged on my hair.

She had braided it and was trying to roll fresh jasmine flowers around it. My mother, Ambika, placed a red dot—a bindi—on the middle of my forehead. It symbolized the Indian woman. She then covered my head with a traditional red and gold organza *chunri*.

"Ambika," a voice called from afar.

"Coming," my mother shouted, wiping the sweat off her temples with a tissue.

Just before hurrying out of the room, she paused, took a long look at me, and kissed my forehead.

"Darling, you look nothing short of an Indian goddess."

"Thanks, Mom," I said and smiled.

The hairdresser held a mirror in front of me. I peered into it with amazement. I couldn't believe this day had arrived. I was finally marrying the man of my dreams: Moksh.

Moksh and I had met at a family event and fallen in love. I wasn't sure if it was his bewitching smile or his charming ways that had captivated me. I felt special every time his deep, dark hazel eyes looked at me and celebrated my existence. I found him very attractive. With Moksh, life was fun and adventurous. He would take me to new places, sometimes sneaking me out of my parents' home to a nightclub, swinging me to the beats until dawn. Moksh had recently started working for his father, but he made sure he spent his evenings and weekends with me. We discussed everything: our jobs, our dream house, our children's names, their schooling, our grandkids, our retirement, and countless other things.

As I walked to the *mandap* accompanied by my parents, I spotted Moksh. He was dressed in a white silk *dhoti* with thinly woven golden borders tied around his waist. A similar-colored shirt and a silk scarf complemented his light brown skin. The princely white and gold turban that sat on his head made me giggle. It was the first time that I had seen him in traditional dress.

When we reached the *mandap*, the priest asked us to sit facing each other with a fire between us on a platform, under a pavilion. Suddenly, I felt anxiousness take over me as scenes from the previous month flashed across my mind.

"After we marry, will you see me off when I go to work every morning, like my mother does for my father?" Moksh asked.

I laughed and said, "Only if my job allows that."

After four years of hospitality studies, I looked for a job. A well-reputed five-star hotel chain offered me a position in Delhi, but I declined it and looked for work in Bangalore in order to stay closer to Moksh. I loved him deeply, and I would never let anything or anyone keep us apart.

Soon, I succeeded in another interview and landed a job as a junior chef in a hotel close to home. The salary was decent. I was elated. I broke the news to Moksh, but he had different plans.

"I'm going to speak to my parents about us this evening. We both are twenty-four. It's about time we tied the knot."

I hugged Moksh. I couldn't be happier. It was easy to see our future together. I had a job, and I was marrying the man I loved. Life looked perfect from every angle.

Both our families readily accepted our decision to wed, as we were distant cousins and had the same circle of relatives on my mother's side. After a few exchanges, the heads of our families decided that the wedding would take place in a few months. My mother got busy with shopping for sarees and jewelry; my father did the rounds to finalize the venue and the caterers.

One evening, just a month before the wedding, my parents met Moksh's parents to discuss the last few arrangements. When they returned home, they seemed disturbed and had a worried look on their faces.

"I cannot believe that they would do this at the last minute," my mother fretted.

"What happened?" I asked, feeling nervous.

"They do not want you to work after marriage," my father, Arvind, replied.

During the conversations at Moksh's house, Patil had disclosed to my parents that he would not ask for any dowry or gifts, but in turn, he wanted a stay-at-home daughter-in-law. My parents were upset. The wedding was so close. The invitations had gone out. All the shopping was done. Advances had been paid to the caterers, musicians, priests, and others.

"That's impossible!" I waved my hand in disbelief.

"They are being unreasonable," my father ranted. "I don't trust them anymore."

"Financial independence is very important, sweetie. You will feel secure and free when you earn for yourself. My time was different, but you shouldn't give into pressure."

My mother's words made sense. She and my father had fallen in love and married in a different era. While my father worked, my mother stayed home to care for my sister and me. She was smart and intelligent but felt undervalued, leaving her frustrated throughout her life.

Both my parents knew how deeply I loved Moksh. They knew I would be devastated without him.

"We are not happy about this, but will support you in whatever decision you take," my father concluded.

I knew I had to ask Moksh to convince his parents to let me keep my job.

After a few days, Vasumati and Patil spoke to me.

Moksh had tried to negotiate with them about me working. It hadn't gone very well.

"Are you sure you want to marry our son?" Patil began. "If you do, then you must not work."

"But how would my working affect anyone?" I asked, feeling frustrated.

"Listen to me carefully. After you marry, we will be responsible for your safety and well-being. It is not in our culture or tradition to let a woman go out to earn. It will bring us shame. Our family has a certain status in this society. Allowing women of the house to work shows that we are weak and incapable of taking care of the vulnerable."

"There are thousands of women who go out and work every day. It's really not dangerous," I protested.

"I can assure you that we will look after you well and provide you with everything. Our son will keep you happy," Vasumati said as she ran her hand over my head.

"I understand, and I really appreciate it, but at the same time, I need my identity," I said, trying to keep my voice from rising. I knew I couldn't afford to upset my would-be in-laws if I wanted to be with Moksh.

"Then you will have to rethink about marrying my son. Either you choose to work and give up on this marriage, or you agree and live happily married to Moksh," Vasumati concluded.

I felt as though none of this made any sense.

Later that evening, Moksh consoled me and asked me to consider his parents' request. He seemed to have changed all of a sudden; he no longer saw how important this job was to me.

"You'll be earning peanuts," he said.

"It really doesn't matter. It's the experience that counts," I said, feeling positive.

"Can't you sacrifice this much for me? My parents are so generous. They are so happy to have you in the family and are making all of the arrangements for our big day. They have accepted you with open arms. We'll have a beautiful life together, I promise."

I loved him very much, but I couldn't bear to see myself in the role of a housewife. I imagined long, lonely days of cooking, cleaning, and waiting for Moksh to come home from work.

"I'll be happy working, Moksh. It's better than sitting at home and going crazy." I paused before continuing. "I only want you and your parents to understand my position and make an exception."

I didn't want to hurt Moksh, but somehow, I felt my insistence would not mix well with the stubborn beliefs I was being forced to accept. I turned around to see Moksh tear up. I had never realized the pain I was causing him.

"Fine," he finally relented. "I'll talk to them after our marriage about the job, since you insist. I'll tell them you need something to keep yourself busy."

Moksh had sounded convincing. However, would he really be able to go against his parents' wishes after we married? Would this damage his relationship with them? I felt terrible to have put Moksh in a difficult spot. I could not bear to think of a life without him. I hoped he loved me enough to fight for my freedom.

My thoughts vanished as the priest handed us offerings of puffed rice and clarified butter to throw into the fire while he chanted the mantras. Hindu wedding ceremonies usually have a number of rituals and customs, each emblematic of old traditions. Moksh's mother, Vasumati, was insistent that all of them were performed, including a ceremony where my parents sat on the floor and washed Moksh's feet in a large bowl with their hands. Moksh was perched on the chair with an uncomfortable look on his face. I didn't understand why this was important. Some of these age-old rituals didn't make sense to me.

It seemed like the longest morning. I glanced at Moksh, who was struggling to keep his eyes open. The priest finally directed us to stand and handed the holy *mangalsutra* to Moksh.

"This thread is a symbol of marital dignity and chastity. It is a promise from a husband to his wife that they will always live happily together," the priest said, looking at us.

Moksh smeared kunkum, a red powder at the top of my forehead with his thumb and held up the *mangalsutra*, a yellow thread painted with curcuma paste featuring a small ornamental golden disc. Once all the ceremonies were performed, this thread would be replaced by a thick gold chain for everyday use. Moksh fastened the holy thread around my neck with three knots.

The crowd roared and cheered as the drums and trumpet sounded. Moksh and I looked into each other's eyes, momentarily drowning out the commotion around us. Finally, we were husband and wife.

The priest then asked us to take the wedding vows by circling around the fire seven times. Moksh held my hand tight while we walked the rounds that symbolized our eternal journey together. The priest chanted once again.

"May god give you an abundance of food, of strength, of wealth, of happiness, of children, of cattle, and of devotion...."

He handed us both garlands made of jasmine flowers that we hung around each other's necks. He then concluded that our marriage was regarded as consecrated and irrevocable because the vows had been taken in front of the fire God.

Then the evening's grand reception party began. Blaring lights focused on Moksh and me. We cheerfully stood on an elevated space while five hundred guests walked up to us and wished us a happy life together. The camera had immortalized our memorable day. I was very eager to spend the rest of my life with the one and only man I loved—who loved me equally as much.

The same evening, I was ceremoniously welcomed into Moksh's home. His mother, Vasumati, brought out an ornamental plate that contained betel leaves, a red powder called *kunkuma*, and a burning lamp. Moksh held my hand as his mother moved it around our glowing faces in a circular motion to perform the *aarti.* Instructed by Vasumati, I kicked a medium-size tumbler of rice grains into the house, splattering it all over the floor. Then I carefully stepped onto a plate that consisted of liquid *kunkuma* and took a few steps with stained feet to leave red footprints on the ground.

While I gracefully walked on the white marbled floor, contradictory thoughts reeled through my mind.

How could I suddenly make this my home? Shouldn't there be a transition period into this new life?

I never thought I would have these emotions surface as I walked into Moksh's house. A feeling of anxiety swept over me that day when I had to bid goodbye to my parents.

CHAPTER 2

The Family

Bangalore, India
November 2004

Cling, clang, clatter.

It had been a couple of weeks since I had sacredly stepped into Moksh's family household, and I could hear the sounds of dishes in the kitchen just below my bedroom. It was six in the morning. Terrified, I jumped out of bed, dressed, and hurried downstairs. The clanking died down as I entered the kitchen.

"Did you sleep well?" asked Vasumati.

"I did, thank you."

"I've decided to make rava upma for today's breakfast. Here, chop these fine," Vasumati said in a sweet voice.

I would give anything not to chop onions so early in the morning, but I had no choice but to obey without a fuss.

"That wretched cook hasn't turned up today. I'll make sure to cut her salary this month. She needs to learn a lesson," Vasumati fretted, as the morning suprabhātam—a collection of holy hindu hymns—echoed in the background.

"Here, take these, wash them clean, and then chop the coriander fine—and the tomatoes, too. Cut and dice them small like this." She demonstrated on the chopping board. I strained to see through the tears from the onions.

"Rani... Raniii.... Where has this lazy girl disappeared? She was supposed to water the garden and come back to grate coconut by now. Rani... Raniii.... She deserves a beating for this."

Vasumati's voice trailed off as she went looking for Rani, the live-in help. I had watched these types of melodramatic soaps on television and had always believed their scenarios to be exaggerated for entertainment value. But this was real, and I was now a part of it. My mother had managed to feed us without a fuss over the years, so I didn't quite understand why this kitchen felt like Gordon Ramsay's Hell's Kitchen.

"I hope you have a beautiful baby soon." Kanakamma, the housekeeper, stopped in the midst of her work and moved her hands in a circular manner on either side of my head, then cracked her knuckles on the sides of her own head in order to give me her blessings.

"Thank you, Kanakamma." I blushed.

"Madam is coming. I better get going." She sped off to mop the floors of the three-storied building.

Kanakamma had never been to school. She had worked her entire life in people's homes earning a meager salary, most of which her parents saved for her dowry. When they married her off, her drunk husband had gambled away all of it. Her life had changed after the birth of her granddaughter. She aspired for her granddaughter what she'd never had: an education. She worked as a housekeeper in five different homes to cover the cost of school fees, struggling hard to give her granddaughter a decent life.

"I'm so sick of everyone in this house! If I don't keep an eye on them, nothing will ever get done," Vasumati's voice echoed.

I walked towards the living room in a hope to help calm Vasumati, but stopped when I heard my father-in-law, Patil's voice.

"She's still a young girl, let her be. Why are you yelling at her early in the morning?"

I peeped and saw him lighting a lamp in the God's room. Vasumati was pacing the living room holding a basket of fresh flowers.

"Now it's my fault, is it?" Vasumati's tone changed. "I've been running this house for so many years without taking a break. Do I get any appreciation?"

"Relax, don't get angry about everything. We now have a daughter-in-law in the house. What will she think? Please serve me breakfast. I have to go to the office in five minutes."

As angry as Vasumati was, she would never let her husband leave on a rumbling stomach.

I decided to head back to the kitchen and continue with the chopping. After about five minutes Rani rushed into the kitchen and pulled out the old, heavy, iron wedged coconut grater. Tears rolled down her tanned cheeks as she sat there grating the freshly cracked open coconut on the long serrated edges. She would turn sixteen in a week. A few years back, her father had died in an accident near their village. Afterward, her brother had been sent to live with her uncle's family, her older sister had been married off, and Rani was brought to Vasumati, as her mother couldn't afford her schooling. Vasumati had readily accepted her to keep at home for petty jobs.

"Please don't cry, Rani," I whispered.

Rani looked up with tears in her eyes. "I wish my father was alive."

I felt helpless. I was new to this family myself and didn't dare correct Vasumati. I hugged Rani and told her everything would be all right, and that she could come and talk to me anytime she wanted.

Moksh entered the kitchen. “I’m leaving with dad to the office today. Could you please pack my breakfast? I’m quite late.”

“Sure,” I said and searched in the new territory for a tiffin box.

“Here, madam,” said Rani, handing me a box, a spoon, a hand towel, and a bag. She had been well trained by Vasumati.

“Rani… Raniii….” Vasumati called from downstairs.

“Coming, madam.” Rani sprinted off in fright.

“Finally, we are alone,” Moksh said, hugging me tightly. “I love you so much. I still can’t believe we’re married,” he said, grinning. “I’ll try to come home early tonight. Maybe we could go out for dinner.”

I looked into Moksh’s eyes. His shoulder-length hair tied into a pony complemented his light brown skin. I blushed and kissed him. The morning drama was behind me now, and I looked forward to the evening with Moksh.

***

It was half past three when Rani knocked on my door.

“Madam, big madam is calling you. The photographer is here.”

“Tell her I’ll come in five minutes.”

I changed and went downstairs. The photographer handed over two big albums and left.

“Come, sit next to me. Let’s look at them together,” Vasumati said.

There was great excitement in her voice. As she turned the pages, it was clear that the photographer had captured some beautiful moments at the wedding. There were pictures of Moksh and me performing different rituals.

“You look like a real princess.” Vasumati ran her hand down my hair.

“Thank you,” I said.

“Ohhh, your father-in-law looks so young in this picture. I must show him this evening.”

We both laughed and enjoyed the moment together. "You look beautiful in that pastel green *Banarasi* saree," I said.

Vasumati grinned. "I had another saree in mind, but in the end, I chose to wear that one."

I could see so much of her in Moksh, while Aarav, his brother, resembled his father.

"If only I had gotten two more hours of sleep the previous night, it could have made me look so much better in these pictures," she sighed.

Both sides of the family had gone to great lengths to get Moksh's and my big day right. They had carefully handpicked five hundred invitees for the day, many of whom we had never seen in our lives. To our parents, this wedding was a special occasion to reconnect with old friends and family, who had disappeared over time.

"Madam, look at these photos of you wearing colorful bangles," Rani said.

Lean and angular, Rani sat on the floor looking at photos from the pre-wedding album. After the morning fiasco, she had returned to her normal chirpy self. In the picture, I was dressed in a peach-colored *lehenga* and blouse. I held out my arms that were covered in myriad colors of glass bangles up to my elbows. This was the first day of the wedding rituals. An old, frail man with a long white beard had tottered into Vasumati's home carrying a big steel trunk filled with all sizes of glass bangles.

"Each color has a significance," he'd explained. "Red represents energy and prosperity. Green, good luck and fertility, blue denotes wisdom, yellow for happiness, white for new beginnings, and orange for success."

He had put the silver and gold bangles into a different box since they were higher priced and symbolized strength, fortune, and prosperity. The closest of the women in the family and friends circle had been invited for the ceremony that evening. While beautiful music played in the background, the man handed out bangles to the invitees, who then lovingly slid them onto my arms. By the end of the evening, his trunk was nearly empty. Vasumati paid him and packed him up with enough food to last him a few days.

"I don't understand how the old man made a living just selling bangles on the streets," I said.

"It's tough. But I'm sure he is doing what he likes best. Just like me." Vasumati smiled.

I wondered what she was referring to—her cooking, or her yelling? I looked at Rani, who had a smirk on her face. The pictures were very colorful. I felt lucky that, in my generation, there still existed in small parcels these simplicities of bygone days. I sighed as I turned to the next section of the album, which had images of the decorated house.

Vasumati and a few aunts had performed a ritual before tying a branch of the plantain tree to one of the gateposts. Above that stretched the marriage canopy, a sheet of woven coconut leaves that went all the way from the entrance to the portico. Festoons of mango leaves decorated the top of the ornamental front door.

"Do you know why we have a ceremony just to decorate the house with mango leaves and banana leaves at the entrance?" Vasumati asked.

I shook my head. I had never studied this at school, nor had my parents emphasized such traditions while Megha and I were growing up.

"Mango leaves are considered auspicious in Hindu customs because they represent the goddess *Mahalakshmi*, who prevents negative energy from entering the house and protects it from evil spirits. These same leaves are also associated with prosperity and happiness. You see, Lord Shiva and Parvathi married under a mango tree, and so it's considered sacred. Now, there's a scientific reason behind it too—the leaves are believed to purify the house by absorbing excess carbon dioxide and giving out oxygen," Vasumati said.

She took pride in her knowledge of Indian customs and traditions. Another photo showed Rani smiling brightly in front of a *rangoli* she had drawn at the entrance of the house.

"Rani, this color suits you well. I'll be going to the store this evening; I shall bring you another beautiful dress in red to wear on your birthday," Vasumati said sympathetically.

Vasumati was sharp-tongued and a tough taskmaster. She behaved like a tyrant at times, and everyone at home wished they were out of her sight. It was young Rani who usually bore the brunt of her anger. As for me, I witnessed her anger all mornings. Since the very first week in this house, I'd understood that Vasumati wouldn't tell me, but expected me to know, that I needed to be in the kitchen before six o'clock to help her every morning. The clanking of the vessels was always a clear indication of her discontentment, and the intensity of the noise grew with every passing minute until she saw my face.

Other times, she was tender and kind-hearted. These extreme emotions left everyone, including me, on edge and perplexed most of the time. Vasumati and her sister were brought up singlehandedly by their mother. After Vasumati married Patil, he'd tamed her to his convenience. Despite that, her inborn nature lurked just below the surface, especially early in the morning.

"Gosh, I look hideous in these pictures," I exclaimed. "Ugh... thankfully this was not a big ceremony."

My face and arms were colored in a yellow paste. My mother had prepared a paste made with curcuma, yogurt, sandalwood, and gram flour, then rubbed it onto my skin before a ceremonial bath. I was a bit anxious about looking like a mango candy on my wedding day, so I'd asked my mother to tone down the yellow in the curcuma mixture.

"It's a very old tradition. You must follow. The mixture will make your skin glow," my mother had said.

"Mom, somehow I feel like a goat being prepared for sacrifice," I'd said, and we'd both laughed.

I missed my mother terribly. During the wedding, my parents had blessed us with all the happiness in the world. As much as they were delighted that I was getting married, I knew they felt a huge sense of loss in their lives. My sister, Megha, had married and left their nest a long time back. With me gone, their home would be empty, a new reality for them to accept.

"It's been two weeks already. I must visit mum and dad this weekend," I said.

"Yes, it would be nice to see your parents again. But first you must ask permission from your father-in-law."

My face paled. Sudden doubts flooded my entire body. I had no idea where that came from, or why I needed permission from my father-in-law. It seemed ridiculous, but then, I had never given it thought before.

"Why do I need permission?"

"Your father-in-law is a very nice person. He'll never say no. But it's better to ask him once, as he's the elder in the house, and no one does anything without his permission," Vasumati insisted. "Let me call him. He needs to take his medicine anyway. If I don't remind him, he'll forget." Vasumati picked up the phone and dialed the number.

"Hello, did you eat lunch? What about your tablet? Good! One more thing, your darling daughter-in-law wants to visit her parents this weekend." After a long pause, she said, "Sure, I'll let her know," and hung up the phone.

"He's asked me to pack sweets for you to take along." Vasumati smiled.

I exhaled, relieved.

"And he said you must not go alone. You must take Moksh with you every time."

I went cold. I couldn't travel freely? This couldn't be happening. It didn't seem right. I had always had the freedom to ride my scooter everywhere. My father had strict rules about the hour Megha and I returned home, but he never bothered to know where we were during the day. It was my mother's duty, and she had complete trust in us. So much so, that one Saturday afternoon, Megha and I rode for two hours to the other end of Bangalore to meet a three-and-a-half-month-old lioness called Sheeba. She was being looked after by a veterinary doctor and his mother at their house. My sister had come to know of this information, and we had taken off together without telling our parents.

Eager to play with little Sheeba, we entered the vet's modestly sized home in a residential area of Bangalore, but we were shocked to find what appeared to be a full-grown lion sitting in their living room. The doctor explained that the mother had abandoned three cubs after giving birth to them. Out of them, only Sheeba had survived. However, she needed special attention, as she was severely malnourished. The doctor's family received a call from the Bannerghatta Zoo to help with Sheeba, and they had agreed to care for her for a short time before releasing her into the wild. My hands trembled with fear while I gently caressed the cub. My sister bravely sat next to the partially blind lioness and played for a while before we returned home.

The next day, we divulged our little adventure to our mother, who was shocked. She told us that we should never do such things by ourselves and that we must always take her with us.

I was fifteen, and Megha was eighteen at that time. Those kinds of restrictions—to protect us—made sense. But I could not understand why Vasumati and Patil would establish unnecessary rules.

"Madam," Rani said, "Moksh sir loves you a lot. Look, the color of your henna has changed into deep dark brown."

I stopped listening and stared at a picture of myself in the album. Two women sat squeezing green paste out of a cone into thin lines that beautifully covered my arms and legs in elaborate designs. Thoughts crowded my mind. Why must I get permission to see my own parents? Why would they restrict me? I knew then that Moksh and I needed to have a long talk.

"The *mehndi* ceremony was my favorite day. It was the first time I saw Vasumati madam dance," Rani continued without realizing how upset I was.

"My head's hurting. I think I'll go upstairs and get some rest before Moksh returns." I really needed some time alone. Was this how traditional families worked? I couldn't believe it. I had seen Moksh go about the town freely during our courtship. I never realized that women were treated differently in this house.

"Rani, go and quickly make some tea for madam," Vasumati commanded.

"I don't want tea, thank you." I hoped my voice didn't tremble too badly.

"What happened, darling? Did I upset you? But this is the way I've been living in this home all my life. Even at this age, I ask permission to step out of the house. Didn't Moksh ever tell you this?"

"I was not aware of these rules," I said, feeling disappointed, and left the room.

***

Later that evening, in the car on our way home from dinner, I confronted Moksh. "You had promised me before the wedding that you would take care of me, and that, once married, you would convince your parents about me working. What happened to that promise?" I knew my voice sounded frustrated, but Moksh needed to know exactly how I felt. "It's turning out to be a whole different story after the wedding. I am now being restricted from seeing my parents. It's not fair! Why didn't you tell me about these ridiculous rules?"

Moksh cut in. "Who's restricting you? They're only asking you to let them know where you're going and when. It's for your own safety. I don't see any problem with that. In fact, my parents are nice enough to ask you to take sweets along. If they really wanted to restrict you, they would have told you not to go."

"Moksh, I understand you defending your parents. And yes, I appreciate them sending sweets and all, but that's not what I need, nor my parents for that matter. I miss them and want to spend time with them. Besides, why force you to come along with me? Don't they trust me? What have I done wrong?" I demanded.

"Look, love, my parents are very traditional. They just expect small things from us. If we do those things, it will make them happy. My mother has never left home without asking my father's permission. It's been like that forever."

"That's exactly the problem. Don't you see? They expect the same from me. I'm sorry, but I need my independence, Moksh. I would like to meet my parents or friends whenever I want. I cannot have anyone controlling my life."

"Don't make a mountain out of a molehill."

Moksh's voice held an icy tone. The car went silent. I had made him mad at me. How was I ever going to convince him to help me?

I hadn't realized our relationship would change to this extent after marriage. I felt alien in this new world of Moksh's. If this was just the beginning of our married life, I feared I could not live the rest of my life this way. I felt trapped.

All I did was wake up to help Vasumati in the kitchen, then prepare the God's room for Patil to light the lamp. I served hot breakfast to Moksh before he left for work, then had breakfast with Vasumati, which usually wasn't pleasant. Then we went shopping for groceries and vegetables. In the afternoons, I lay in bed wondering what I was doing with my life, waiting for Moksh's return home. As happy I was to be with him, I also felt that this wasn't the life I wanted. I had sacrificed far too much for love and doubted I could do much more.

***

It had been only a few weeks since the wedding when Moksh drove me to my parents' home. En route, he adopted an appeasing tone.

"Sweetheart, I've been thinking about you visiting your parents on your own. I'll talk to dad. I know it's quite unfair for me to tag along with you all the time. Besides, I don't have much to converse with them about. I'm happy to visit them once in a while."

"I appreciate you being thoughtful about this, Moksh. My parents will always be happy to see you. You are like a son to them, you know that."

It was our first time visiting my parents since the wedding. Migo, the family dog, greeted us with his loud barks at the gates and wouldn't leave our side. The moment we entered the house, a waft of delicious aromas enveloped us. We looked at each other and inhaled deeply. My mother had prepared some of my favorite dishes. After a scrumptious lunch, I helped her clear the table. When we were alone in the kitchen, she asked how I was doing.

"I'm great, Mom. Just a little bored, but I'm sure I'll figure out something to keep myself occupied."

"Time is precious, baby, don't waste it. Learn something new. Maybe you could do a course on interior designing. There's the Deco Institute that's not too far away from your place."

"That's a brilliant idea, Mom! I'll call the Institute first thing tomorrow and see if they have any seats available."

"If you can't work, you can always study, darling." She arranged the tray with a teapot and four teacups. "Are you happy, my love?"

"Yes, Mom, I'm very happy. Please stop worrying about me." I tried to assure her, yet, despite my words, I realized I had paid a high price for this happiness. Did that feeling of emptiness have something to do with my dull routine? I was idle enough to become a household ornament. My mother was right. I would be better off studying.

***

The next day, I went online to check for interior design institutes. There was one near the home. I called to ask if there were any seats available. The lady on the phone answered all my queries; they had spots available for the next batch of incoming students, and classes were to begin in a month. She sent me an online brochure, which I then printed and took to Moksh and Vasumati, who were in the living room.

"It's a good idea. If your father-in-law agrees, I could join too," Vasumati said.

I was surprised to hear these words. I had least expected Vasumati to be in agreement with my plans. She never wanted me to be independent, partly because she was never herself allowed by Patil to work or study. I felt she was seeking her own freedom through me. Everyone knew it was Patil who had the final say in the household. Nevertheless, Vasumati was the last person I wanted to spend time with. I still smiled in agreement and hoped it would persuade her to convince her husband.

"I'm not sure dad will approve of it. Try asking when he is in a good mood," Moksh added.

I felt relieved there was no objection from Moksh or Vasumati. The ball was in Patil's court. As if on cue, he strode into the living room.

"Our home is sparkling with our new daughter-in-law."

His comment was welcoming, and he looked at me affectionately. I wondered if the time was right. He did seem in a good mood. I gave Moksh a glance and he returned with a nod.

"Nam has something to ask you," Vasumati interjected.

"Tell me, darling. What is it?"

"Vasumati and I were thinking of joining a three-month course in interior designing," I said. "It's not far from the house. Here's the brochure."

"That's really unnecessary. Look around the house—there's so much to decorate here. Tomorrow, Vasumati and you must go shopping to decorate *this* house. The couch in the hallway needs to be changed. This room needs a new carpet. It would be good to have some indoor plants and some new paintings. Here, take my card." Patil held out his credit card. "Oh, and Moksh, please send the driver back home as soon as he drops you off at the office tomorrow, so these two can start shopping early," Patil instructed Moksh.

I noticed that Vasumati did not look disappointed. She had known that Patil would never agree to this. She had perhaps tried every way to gain her own freedom over the years and had encountered stiff resistance. If Patil had given in to my wishes, it was likely that Vasumati would have declared a war in the house.

"But the point of joining the course is to learn something new so we can do an even better job," I cut in. Someone had to make a convincing argument for us to attend the classes.

"Dad, it's good for Nam and mom to do something different," Moksh chimed in.

"If that's the case, then why not help us with office work? They can learn something new and be of help too. I have to travel to Delhi next week. Nam, could you please see about the best flight available and the times?" Patil avoided further discussions. Before anyone reacted, he turned to Moksh and changed the subject.

"Yourself and Aarav must join me on this trip to Delhi. There is a government tender for fifty thousand semiconductor sensors. We need to speak with Mishra from the electricity board to secure this order."

Patil was a thoroughbred businessman. He had built his entire empire from nothing. In his forties, he married Vasumati, his dream girl, who'd given birth to two boys soon after. Patil was overjoyed. He trained them young to be the inheritors of his multiple businesses. Vasumati was very dear to Patil. She served him well, though she detested the fact that he controlled everything in her life. She ladled hot food and waited patiently next to him to give him a second serving if he desired.

Religion had always been a priority for Patil. He lit the lamp in the God's room every morning before he left for work. The staff were alert and quick-heeled whenever he was around. Rani accompanied him, carrying his briefcase to the main entrance, where the driver received it and placed it in the car and promptly opened the door for him.

***

A few months passed. It seemed like the life Moksh had promised me was just a mirage. My chaotic mornings in Vasumati's kitchen hadn't changed, and my boredom had turned into loneliness. I began to feel desolate and bereft. I spent most of my time with Vasumati and the staff. Moksh seemed content with the fact that I was always there for him, whatever time he returned home.

One evening, Patil invited some friends over for dinner. Vasumati was stressed, as usual, and had started spitting fire in the kitchen. I decided to lay covers on the table and not argue with her.

"Nam, you look better in traditional Indian clothes. Please do not wear trousers, jeans, or western dresses henceforth. It's against our culture," Patil commented.

I froze. There was only so much I could tolerate. Before I opened my mouth to speak, Moksh protested, "Dad, that's Nam's personal choice."

"I know, Son, but it's better to keep up our culture and tradition," Patil persisted.

Moksh didn't push at all. After all, he was still under his father's reign. Patil commanded respect, and going against his wishes would be very consequential. Moksh and his brother Aarav's lifestyles were supported by their father, who had conveniently never let them become financially independent. Both sons had high regard for their father, as Patil had singlehandedly created an empire.

Patil's comments upset me terribly. I lay awake that night, pondering. It felt like my life was spiraling uncontrollably into a deep dark void. I felt suffocated by the endless rules that were being imposed on me. I could feel the pain as if each feather was being slowly clipped from my wings until I was trapped in a golden cage. The beautiful life I had once envisioned with Moksh seemed like it had faded into the darkest of winters.

I tossed and turned restlessly while Moksh peacefully slept next to me. My eyes flooded with tears that rolled down my cheeks and stained my pillow. I couldn't stand living in this house anymore, nor could I bear losing Moksh. I had given up my freedom for his love. However, this had gone too far. It was time I took matters into my own hands.

CHAPTER 3
The Alliance

Bangalore, India
June 2005

The following morning, I walked calmly to the kitchen. Vasumati, unaware of me standing behind her, continued the clattering of the kitchen vessels to wake me up. I grabbed an empty pan from a shelf and flung it on the floor. Vasumati turned towards me. I could see the color drain from her face. The pan slid and came to a halt. There was a dismayed silence until I spoke. "That's *enough*! From now on, if anyone in this house makes a noise, there will be twice as much noise from me."

Vasumati stood still. She had never imagined I would react this way. There was a look of shock on her face. After a few minutes, she stormed out of the kitchen and went straight to Patil. I could hear her at a distance, ranting to him.

"I'll talk to her; please calm down," I heard Patil say.

But he never confronted me. He left for his office in a hurry. Maybe because he was late, or maybe because he wanted to avoid being in a sticky situation. From that day on, things were never the same between Vasumati and me. She was vexed for a little while but eventually took note of the abrupt change in my docile nature. She stopped dictating terms and viewed me as a worthy adversary. Perhaps it was an improvement in her boring life. I no longer succumbed to the wishes of Patil either. Over the course of a year, I gradually started living life on my own terms—within the boundaries of the house. I cared less about comments made at me and went about my daily routine.

***

On our first anniversary, Moksh decided to surprise me. He brought home a tiny little four-legged fur ball. We named the month-old puppy Casper. I fed him, played with him, bathed him, and took him on long walks. We became inseparable. He was a high-energy dog. It was tough keeping him busy and out of trouble. We played tug-of-war, and I always let him win. Hide-and-seek was another one of Casper's favorite pastimes. When Rani covered his eyes, he would sit and patiently wait for the count of ten. Then he would race off, looking for me in every nook and cranny of the house. His fawn-colored tail swung left to right as his wet nose twitched rapidly, looking for my scent. I hid behind doors, under the couch, and even inside closets. It was surprising that he never got sick of it, even if I kept picking the same hiding spots over and over again. When he found me, I gave him a big kiss, a tight hug, and his favorite doggy treat.

With Casper around, Moksh spent more time at home. He snuggled between us at night, occasionally nudging Moksh out of bed. In the morning, Casper's damp nose gently kissed my face and nudged my arms to wake me for his morning walk. If I didn't wake, he would bay until I put on my shoes and fastened his leash around his neck. He also spent several evenings playing ball with Moksh's twin brother, Aarav. The two shared a special bond. Vasumati and

Patil were hesitant to accept Casper into their lives, but in due time, they gave in to his unconditional love. At six months, Casper had become a handsome, full-grown Labrador. He was the darling of the house. The only person he shied away from was Moksh's grandmother, Padma Devi, who stayed in a room on the first floor of the house. She was still strong and healthy at ninety, but she would never allow Casper anywhere near her for fear of tripping and falling over him. She always used a stick to scare him off.

Rani and I often took Casper to the nearby park, where he smelled the ground and lifted his leg to leave his scent every ten seconds as he walked along. He barked at little dogs while quietly walking past bigger ones. Unlike other watchdogs, Casper guarded the house only when he wasn't fast asleep or finishing off his big bowl of kibble. He was not very welcoming of strangely dressed men either. As it happened, on one occasion, he almost chewed off Pandit Krishna's *lungi*. Krishna was a traditional South Indian Pandit who was known to the family for many years. He had come home with a proposal for Moksh's brother, Aarav. He was dressed in a white *lungi*, a simple length of white cloth wrapped around the lower half of his body, and a half-sleeved shirt on top.

Casper took offence.

"Grrrrrrr..." Casper growled and tugged, holding a part of Krishna's *lungi* in his mouth.

"Ahhhh...help, help!" Krishna cried, holding an envelope as high as possible in his right hand while desperately clutching his *lungi* with the other hand to prevent it from falling off his oversized waist.

I rushed to his rescue.

"Madam please, hold him. I'm very scared of dogs," Krishna pleaded.

"Casper... Casperrr... stop it... stop it right now." I grabbed his collar and pulled him away on time. I soon fastened a leash and tied him to the nearest post.

"Please don't untie him until I leave," said Krishna in his quivering voice.

"I'm so sorry; there's nothing to worry about now. Please come inside, Pandit Ji," I said apologetically.

Krishna had brought photographs of three girls in their twenties, whose stars matched with those of Moksh's brother, Aarav.

"Can I have some water, please?" Pandit Ji asked, panting once he was seated in the living room.

Vasumati quickly gestured to Kanakamma to fetch a glass of water.

"Here, madam, please take a look at the girls in these photos. As you requested, I've checked the *kundali*, and all three perfectly match Aarav sir's. They all come from very good families and live in small towns in the north of Karnataka."

"The girl in this photo seems fine. What's her name, Pandit Ji?" Vasumati asked.

"That's Bhavika. She belongs to a big family in Hubli—a very soft-spoken girl. She has just completed her diploma in computers. She does not have any career ambitions and will be happy to stay at home. You might know her aunt, Deepa Gowtham, who is Sapna madam's husband's sister."

"Oh yes, I know Sapna. I might have met Deepa at some party, but I cannot recollect her face. The ultimate decision is Aarav's, though."

Vasumati observed the other two photos.

"Pavitra and Niti both are from well-known families in Dharwad," said Krishna.

"Niti's got beautiful features, doesn't she?" Vasumati asked as she turned to me for my opinion.

I was quite aware of arranged marriages. My parents themselves had suggested a doctor living in America and a young man from

Dubai come see me, but I had refused, saying if I did marry, it would be someone I loved.

Isn't it odd to choose a girl in a picture and live the rest of your life with her? *It might just work—who knows.* I kept my thoughts to myself. I wondered if any of the three girls in the photos would be a part of this family soon.

Moksh's brother, Aarav, was the noninterfering kind and had found peace in music. He had never even uttered a girl's name, so the idea of him choosing one from three photographs was odd. Nonetheless, he didn't disappoint his parents. Patil and Vasumati both had done some investigation of the chosen girl and her background. Soon they made arrangements to go see Bhavika and meet her family.

***

On a mild October morning, we hopped into an eight-seater van. Patil settled in with Vasumati; Aarav and his two sisters sat in the front. Moksh and I sat in the middle, along with Vasumati's sister, Varuna. She was suffering from motion sickness and had taken sleep medication to manage the journey. I silently looked out my window at the crowded streets where vendors sold their produce on the sides of busy roads. Mongrels searched for any morsel of food they could find while trying to avoid moving vehicles.

"Ravi, drive carefully," Vasumati said loudly when the driver narrowly avoided crashing into a man on a bicycle.

"Don't worry madam; I have thirty years' experience driving these roads," he said.

"Shut up and drive, Ravi. Don't argue with the boss," Patil said mockingly.

***

He soon changed the route and merged onto a highway that was wider but filled with heavy trucks ferrying merchandise to different states. They made a lot of noise with their blaring horns. After driving for a while, we finally arrived at the countryside. Geometrically carved green patches appeared in succession. I could see toiling peasants working with their tools, tending to crops on cultivated parcels of land. I rolled down the window and smelled the fresh, unpolluted air. Scattered hills posed serenely in the background, diminishing from view as the driver accelerated. After four hours, we turned onto a narrow lane that led into a small town.

Heaps of hay stacks were lying next to cattle that were fastened with ropes to trees on the sidewalks. Little chicks marched behind their mothers who clucked and moved away from the middle of the street as they heard the sound of our motor. Red tractors, not cars, were parked in front of homes. Goats tied to posts made loud bleating sounds as we entered the vastly walled grounds.

I noticed two of the latest models of SUVs from Volkswagen and Volvo parked inside the premises. My eyes then fell upon one corner of the house where cows were being milked. Next to it was a large brick wall with fresh, round-shaped dung pasted onto it. Not far away were neatly stacked discs of the same dried dung piled up to the roof. Varuna finally woke from her slumber.

"I can't stand this smell," she said as she took a perfume bottle out of her handbag and sprayed it all over her.

Bhavika's parents came to welcome us as we got out of the van. We greeted them and proceeded to follow them into the freshly painted house. I saw Aarav, the groom to be, scanning the surroundings, hoping to catch a glimpse of Bhavika, whom he had seen only in a photograph. I wondered if she would qualify to be his future wife. The family was the richest in the village. They had acquired their wealth over several generations and had many acres of agricultural land cultivated into crops for export.

We settled on comfortable couches in the living room. A slender girl in a magenta saree walked in, carrying a tray with several glasses of fresh homemade buttermilk. The room went silent.

"This is our beloved daughter, Bhavika," said her father as she served the drinks.

"She's lovely," Vasumati commented.

"And very obedient," Bhavika's mother, Indira, added. "She will fill your house with joy."

"We will be very fortunate," Patil said politely.

There was an odd pause before Bhavika's father, Ramanand, asked, "Would your son like to speak with my daughter? We're traditional people, but we certainly try to adapt to modern times."

The whole room looked toward Aarav. He nodded.

Patil tried to gesture to Moksh, but he was in deep conversation with the bride's brother.

Then, all of a sudden, Patil said, "Nam, could you accompany Aarav please? It's good if he speaks to Bhavika before we make our final decision."

Oh God, why me? I had never done this sort of thing before—still, I obeyed. Aarav and I followed Bhavika to a different room. I sat next to the couple, who smiled at each other, but hesitated to start a conversation. A few minutes passed in silence. Then I asked the bride-to-be what she had studied. Bhavika answered computers, Aarav's favorite subject, and the couple took off from there, discussing hobbies and interests. I still worried how two people who barely knew each other could make such an important decision that would affect their entire lives.

I excused myself and joined the others, who were now discussing assets in possession of each family.

"We have five factories manufacturing semiconductor sensors. We make most of the parts in our company, but those that we cannot, we import from China and assemble. Three of our units are in the city, while the others are near the outskirts of Bangalore, Goa, and Mysore," Patil said.

"Whom do you supply these to?"

"Eighty percent are government orders, and the rest are private."

"Great! Do you get enough support from the government?"

"Yes, fortunately. Venkatesh Hegde, the late chief minister, was of help."

"His secretary, Chidanand, is a good friend of mine. We grew up in a village not too far from here. Please don't hesitate to ask me for any help relating to government orders," Ramanand offered.

Patil's face lit up. And just like that, the subject changed to politics.

The ladies chatted amongst themselves to find possible connections of people they knew in common. Turns out, they knew a lot of them after all. As Pandit Ji Krishna had mentioned, Deepa Gowtham was Bhavika's aunt, who lived in the heart of Bangalore and didn't miss a game of rummy in the evening at the ladies' club. Her brother was married to a Punjabi called Sapna Baweja, who had gone to the same school as Vasumati and her sister Varuna. Patil's uncle had married Indira's distant cousin, and so on.

Aarav blushed while he made his way back into the room. The mood was very cheerful and happy. After some delicious homemade sweets, Patil and Vasumati thanked Bhavika's parents for their hospitality and told them they would make their decision soon. The following day, the verdict was declared. Patil was content with the family, and Aarav agreed to the wedding. The engagement was to happen within a month, and the marriage would take place by the end of five months. The atmosphere in the house turned joyous. Both Vasumati and I worked in harmony to get things going for the grand day. Our relationship was finally settling down. From wedding invitations, to gifts, sarees, and jewelry shopping, Vasumati asked my opinion. Not only had we learned to live alongside each other, but we had also started to bond with each other.

There were things to be taken care of on the home front. Kanakamma was given the responsibility of making the house sparkling clean, while Rani was put to work wiping every door and window in the three-storied house. The cook, Revathi, was glad that Vasumati spent less time in the kitchen belittling her forty years of cooking experience.

***

Pandit Ji Krishna came home again to discuss the exact date and timing of the wedding that had been chosen by Bhavika's parents—this time wearing trousers. He had called Vasumati while still standing outside the gates of the house to make sure Casper was not around. Pandit Ji was the mediator between both parties and had taken the initiative to arrange everything that was required for the rituals. Once the actual date and time was agreed upon, elaborate invitations were printed and distributed along with silverware, and Kanchipuram sarees were gifted to close family members as a token of appreciation to attend the function and bless the couple.

In no time, the couple had exchanged rings, since Aarav and Bhavika had both willingly accepted the decision of their parents. Meanwhile, Moksh became very busy with a project at work. He seemed perturbed with his father. He preferred to unwind with his friends in the evening before returning home. Exhausted from the day's activities, I had no energy left to wait for him. I felt upset, as the only time we spent together were weekends amongst friends. As our couple time became close to nonexistent, I started feeling the emptiness in our relationship. Even though I knew he loved me deeply, he had transformed into someone I hardly recognized.

One night, Moksh returned home at an even odder hour than usual. He was infuriated for some reason and pulled me out of bed.

"I need to talk!" His voice echoed in the calm of the night. Restless and irritable, he paced up and down the room.

"Tell me, Moksh—what's wrong?" I asked in a concerned voice, moving closer to him.

"I can't take this anymore. It's too much pressure at work." His complaint sounded bitter.

"I understand, Moksh. We'll find a solution soon. Don't worry."

"No, you don't understand. You never understand.... Nobody understands. I hate *everybody*," he bellowed, then punched his fist into a mirror on the wall.

I tried to stop him, but he grabbed my hair and swung me to the floor. My body landed a few inches away from the shards of glass. Having woken up to the noise, Vasumati, Patil, and Aarav barged into the room. Aarav held Moksh, preventing him from hurting me further.

Vasumati helped me up and took me out of the room.

"What happened?" Vasumati asked. Her voice was filled with concern.

"I don't know.... I really don't...." Unable to stop myself, I burst into tears.

"Don't cry, sweetheart. Everything will be fine," Vasumati said, wiping the tears from my face. "Are you hurt?"

Tears continued to roll down my face. "I'm okay," I said even though I felt pain in my head and my body.

None of this made any sense. I had never seen Moksh enraged like this before. Why was he so angry? What had happened between Patil and him at work? Why did he hurt me? Thoughts cascaded through my mind. What did he want from life? Why had he changed? Did he not love me anymore?

Vasumati and I both heard Moksh's voice reverberate from upstairs.

"Get out of my room! I can't stand anyone in this house! Leave me alone!"

Vasumati led me to an empty room on the first floor. "Please sleep in the guest room tonight. I'll ask Rani to keep you company until you fall asleep."

"I'm fine. I don't want to trouble Rani," I replied.

Moksh's ninety-year-old grandmother panted as she came out of her room. Upon seeing us, she began chanting prayers while holding the *Rudraksha Mala* in her hand.

"Don't worry, child; everything will be alright soon. It's just a bad hour. I'm chanting to ward off the evil," she whispered in a shaky voice. Then she disappeared.

I lay in bed that night and tried to recollect how my relationship with Moksh had become so strained. Moksh was not the same man I knew before marriage. He had changed. His deteriorating relationship with his father made things worse. His drinking and smoking habits seemed to intensify. It almost felt like I was an acquisition to him rather than a wife. I didn't hate him for that, but I had tried my best to adjust to this new life he had offered me. In the first two years, our relationship was like the seasons, changing from time to time. There was so much love that we felt closer than ever. At other times, there was a void that could not be filled. Something had drastically changed. Moksh was more stressed and avoided coming home early. He hardly spoke to me about his problems.

"It's nothing concerning you," he'd say whenever I asked. It was hard for anyone to make sense of the situation. My thoughts gave me no relief.

The following morning, Patil called for me.

"Are you fine, Nam?" he asked.

"Yes, I'm better. Thank you."

"Please forget whatever happened last night. Moksh is not a bad person; he just needs a little time to get back to his real self. I'll try to talk to him today. It's mostly my fault—he's upset with me. We have a lot of things going on in the office with all of the government orders. He wants to do things his way, but he doesn't understand that he's inexperienced. If we lose an order, our competitors will overtake us."

I nodded. After all, Moksh was under Patil's thumb. I knew he couldn't make independent decisions as long as he worked in the family business.

"Speak to him. Speak to him in good words; correct him with love if need be and not by force."

"I don't see how I can make a difference if he's upset with things at work," I said.

"You're his wife; he needs you more than ever now. I'll do my best, but it's all in your hands. You need to keep him calm and give him peace of mind when he comes home," Patil continued. "Keep this to yourself. Please, don't let it leave the walls of this house. I'm trusting you to keep our family's dignity in this society."

I nodded again.

"Do you need anything, Nam?"

"No, nothing. Thank you," I said, almost voiceless while I stood there weak and desolate. There I was again, nothing but a mere pawn in Patil's big empire.

"Stop bothering Nam," Vasumati said as she strolled into the living room. "Speak to Moksh. He's getting out of control."

I just wanted to leave to a place where nobody knew me. Away from all this drama.

"Come, sweetheart. Let's go to the market to get some fresh vegetables and fruits," Vasumati said, running her hand on my head.

I felt grateful that Vasumati was on my side for once. She had called me sweetheart for the first time. This was a big step in our relationship.

"Rani...Raniii...bring the shopping baskets and the keys to my car."

On the way, Vasumati picked up her sister, who also wanted to shop at the Sunday market. She briefed her about the previous night's events.

Varuna grimaced. "I don't understand why Patil doesn't split the factories between Moksh and Aarav. At least they can make their own decisions. They're not kids anymore, you know."

"My husband loves to be in control of everything and everyone. He will never allow that. He's afraid that if the children become financially independent, he will lose power. I've been married to him for thirty-eight years, so I understand how his mind works. He has made me his puppet. I'm so sick of his ways."

"He's ruined your life, and now he's doing the same with the kids," Varuna said.

There was a lengthy silence before I spoke. "I was thinking of going to my parents' home for a few days."

"It would be good for you, but I'm not sure Patil will agree. We have lots of work to finish. The wedding is just around the corner," Vasumati said.

I knew I was trapped. I felt miserable. I didn't know how to get out.

"Don't worry. I'm here for you if you need to talk about anything," Varuna said kindly.

At twenty-six, I was still too inexperienced to deal with the complex characters of this family. I wanted nothing more than to go back to the comfort of my mother's care for a while.

Should I tell my parents about last night?

They would certainly be furious with Moksh and would even want to meet Patil and Vasumati to confront them. Would Patil be upset if I broke his trust? Would Moksh be put to shame? What if Moksh changed his ways? Would I cause my parents to worry unnecessarily about my well-being?

Probably, I thought.

The same evening, Moksh apologized.

"I don't know why I acted that way yesterday. I'm really sorry to have put you through hell. How could I raise my hand to you? I'm ashamed!" he said in remorse. "It's better if I take a week's break from work. We'll spend time together. I'm so sorry. Please forgive me?"

I saw tears forming in his eyes, and I couldn't bear to witness Moksh cry. I forgave him immediately. We reconciled and soon became busy with the wedding arrangements. Bhavika's parents finalized the venue for the two-day event. Caterers were called and menus were shortlisted. A band of musicians were also selected to entertain the guests on Aarav and Bhavika's special day.

Somehow, I still felt traumatized. I did not understand how or why Moksh raised his hand to me. So much was happening around us, but I could not stop replaying the events of that horrific night in my head. I decided to confide in my two best friends, Pooja and Susan. Pooja was the oldest among her siblings. Both of her parents were doctors and insisted she become a doctor too. Pooja resisted, but finally gave in and became a physiotherapist. Susan, on the other hand, was an only child. Her parents had given her the freedom to make her choices, be it in life, education, or choosing a life partner. Susan married her childhood sweetheart and settled not far away from our current home.

Over the years, we had joked together, laughed together, cried together, sang together, and danced together. Some even called us "the Three Musketeers."

Both Pooja and Susan had noticed changes in Moksh's behavior after we married. I revealed my insecurities to the girls over coffee one evening.

"What? How dare he? You should have called the cops straight away!" Susan exclaimed.

"Suzy, it's easier said than done," Pooja said calmly. She had been brought up in a traditional family herself, so she fully understood how families like Moksh's worked.

"What a jackass! Did you tell your parents?" Susan persisted angrily.

"Nope. I didn't want to cause them unnecessary stress. Moksh has promised that this will never happen again. Besides, if I tell my parents, they will be worried forever."

"Hmmm..." the girls chorused, unconvinced.

"We've both been working on our relationship since then, and things seem to be falling into place."

"Nam, we are always here for you. Please don't hesitate to walk into my place at any hour," Susan said.

"Call me and I'll fly to wherever you are," Pooja said, and we chuckled.

"I don't know what I'd do without you both." I could not be more grateful for my two best friends.

Later, I returned home, feeling hopeful things would be better.

***

The wedding day finally arrived. It was a great show of pomp and splendor. The guest list included many of the bride's father's political contacts. Patil was overjoyed, since his business connections were getting stronger. The wedding was a big success.

Bhavika started her new life with Aarav. The couple began their getting-to-know-each-other phase. They did little things to make each other happy. Bhavika baked a cake; Aarav brought her flowers. They went to the cinema twice a week and never missed a meal together. Their relationship soon blossomed into love. Bhavika smoothly transitioned into Vasumati's kitchen too. She obviously didn't have the same problems I had. By the end of my first year of marriage, I had set the tone in the kitchen and made sure there was some sensitivity to a younger woman in the house. Vasumati soon began comparisons. She joked with her sister, Varuna, about who among the two of us qualified to be the better daughter-in-law. I ignored it. Despite how things were shaping up at home, it was good to have Bhavika around. Now that Vasumati was occupied with her, I took the opportunity to do something more useful in life. My baking skills were still my greatest strength, and I had been one of the brightest students of my culinary school. For the final exam, I produced a marvelous Tiramisu that the judges raved about, and I received top scores for my work. But this skill was of no use in Vasumati's traditional South Indian kitchen.

I started home baking. At first, I made cakes. Then, truffle-filled chocolates for birthdays of close friends and family. I designed a menu that described the cakes and types of chocolates I could provide. Even though Patil did not encourage my baking, he did not prevent me from taking orders either. He most likely thought it was a temporary activity. Casper sat by my side and wondered why I didn't play ball like I used to.

"Sweet Moments," I said aloud, and Casper turned to me with that perplexed, questioning look that always brought a smile to my face. He had saved me from loneliness.

The word spread in no time, and baking orders poured in from clients other than family and friends. Finally, I started to see revenue. I bought Moksh an Omega Seamaster watch as a gift and reinvested the rest of the money into better packaging. Diwali, Christmas, and Valentine's Day saw orders up to a hundred kilos in chocolates. I found myself wrapping chocolates until the wee hours of the morning. I felt content; I was an entrepreneur, and I had a burning desire to take this business to the next level. For that, I needed a commercial space and staff to handle the day-to-day operations. I started to create a real, working business plan.

To my delight, life brought back all its goodness. After that terrible night, Moksh felt remorseful and made every effort to be the man I had fallen in love with. Sometimes he'd even help me wrap chocolates in colored foil in his free time, but always said that I was trying to start a business that wouldn't last. I ignored his remarks. Casper was always a help, licking cream and sugar off the kitchen floor. I finally felt content that I had succeeded in attaining a work-life balance.

One afternoon, I was icing a cake when my head started to spin. Our neighbor had ordered one of my specialties: a chocolate truffle cake with orange fruit filling. I quickly gulped down some water.

I've been working too much. I need a good rest after this order, I thought as I carefully garnished the iced cake with chocolate-dipped oranges.

"Please bring me the cake box," I instructed Rani, who usually assisted me out of pure curiosity.

Rani quickly returned with the box in her hand. I slid the cake into it and sealed the top. I could feel my hands tremble as I carefully lowered the box into a carry bag. I felt like I could throw up. Suddenly my phone began to ring. I took it out of my pocket and answered.

"Guess what?" Susan's excited voice echoed from the other end.

"You got a promotion?" I asked.

"How did you know?" She chuckled.

Susan was career driven. I knew that moving up the ladder meant everything to her, so if there was any good news from her end, it was obvious what kind of news it was.

"We need to celebrate," I said enthusiastically as I climbed the stairs to reach my room.

"Let's go for dinner tonight. I'll call Moksh and ask him to bring you."

Before my "yes" came out, the muscles around my upper body began to tighten. My throat started to expand as I felt pressure rising up my stomach. I dropped the phone, held my mouth tightly with my hand, and ran toward the sink.

CHAPTER 4
The Nanny

Bangalore, India
October 2006

After about fifteen minutes, I was still feeling sick. Susan called back, asking what was wrong.

"I'm not sure. Maybe something I ate today didn't agree with my stomach," I said.

"You're pregnant!" she said confidently. "Let's get you tested."

I grappled with the words. Susan was probably right. I had missed my period and not realized it in the rush of things.

Susan picked me up soon after, and we went to see a doctor close by. She checked my vital statistics before giving me a little box to pee into. The urine test results came after what felt like an eternity.

"It's good news. You're into your fifth week," she said.

Susan couldn't contain her excitement.

"Congratulations!" she exclaimed and hugged me.

"You must take good care of yourself. Please avoid all heavy work. The more you rest, the better it is for the baby. Here, these are some light exercises you could practice to keep yourself and the baby in good health," the doctor said, handing me a little booklet.

"Will do, Doctor. Thank you," I managed to mumble despite the overwhelming emotions that were surging through me.

I called Moksh as we walked out of the clinic.

"Moksh! You're going to be a father soon," I said and waited for his reaction.

"What? What do you mean?"

"I just got tested. You're going to be a dad, Moksh."

"Oh my God, I can't believe this. I love you so much, Nam," Moksh exclaimed on the other end of the telephone.

"I know! I can't believe it either."

Even as my words faded and I cut the line, I felt a storm brewing inside me. I was overwhelmed with uncertainty. My life would be very different from now on.

I will have the responsibility of a child. What if that awful night when Moksh turned violent repeats again? What if my relationship with Vasumati turns sour again?

Susan saw me tense and immediately hugged me. "Everything will be fine," she said.

"I'm not sure if I'm ready," I said, feeling worried.

It had been two years since I tied the knot with Moksh—nevertheless, I still felt unsettled. Maybe it was because I was insecure. My financial dependency on Moksh felt like chains attached to my feet. My mother was right. She had advised me before the wedding that having a job was very important, but it was too late now. I felt trapped. I had sacrificed everything for love. Now, with a baby on the way, I worried whether I would be a good mother with all the constraints I had. I felt hopeless.

"Of course you're ready. You have everything going for you, girl. Moksh, Casper, and now this bundle of joy. And of course, amazing aunts, who will spoil your little one rotten," Susan comforted me.

"Ohhh...Suzy, my baby and I are blessed to have you and Pooja around." I hugged her.

***

Moksh called Vasumati and Patil to break the news. I called my family, and they were elated. Then there was a ripple effect. Word spread, and our phones didn't stop ringing that evening. Moksh decided to throw a party at our favorite rooftop restaurant. He invited our closest group of friends. The table was set for eighteen, and it overlooked the busy city of Bangalore. Susan didn't leave my side and made sure I was fine throughout the evening, and Pooja and her husband came with a bouquet of flowers.

"Have you thought of a name for the baby?" Pooja asked as we sat at the table.

"Vasumati will be summoning Pandit Krishna after my delivery to figure out the appropriate letter with which to begin the name. It needs to be based on the time of birth and the position of the stars. Until then, we will call him Pranam if he's a boy or Shloka if she's a girl. Pranam symbolizes the first three letters of each of our names, and Shloka means fearless," I said. Moksh and I had discussed our choice of names on our way to the restaurant. "I really don't care about the gender of the child. All I want is a healthy baby. If I have a girl, I'd dress her in the most stylish outfits. And if the baby is a boy, I will avoid generations of period pain in the family," I said and chuckled.

Moksh sat to my right at the table and held my hand, kissing it from time to time. I wanted this special moment to last forever. Susan's eyes caught mine. She smiled reassuringly, and I chided myself for overthinking. This was the real Moksh, the Moksh I knew. I looked at him in total admiration. He was telling his friend Supreet that he was on cloud nine and that he still couldn't process the fact that he was going to be a father. I tried to take in everything that was happening around me.

***

Later that evening, when we returned home, Patil and Vasumati were watching television in the living room. Patil started a conversation with Moksh about business while Vasumati walked me to my room. She told me not to bother going downstairs for anything.

"Whatever you need, I'll get Rani to ferry it to you," she said.

Casper conveniently placed himself beside me.

"You must not have Casper sleeping in your room from now on."

I looked at Casper, whose ears had straightened at the mention of his name. He moved his eyes in a funny manner between me and Vasumati, attempting to understand why he was the subject of the conversation.

Both of us laughed at him.

"He's such a rascal," she said as she closed the door behind her.

***

In the following weeks, I meditated and practiced the light exercises the doctor recommended. Before long, I was eating the healthiest foods. All of the "blah" vegetables went in without a fuss. Broccoli, bitter gourd, milk, yogurt, kale, spinach, and all the stuff that people around me said was good for the baby. Vasumati and Varuna frequently went shopping together and indulged in purchasing tiny little outfits in anticipation of the baby. When they came home, Padma

Devi, Moksh's grandmother, warned, "It's bad luck to buy clothes for an unborn child."

Vasumati countered, "Those are superstitions. In this age, it doesn't really matter. Look, we've bought white and yellow cotton bodysuits, and they are organic and gender neutral. They can be used for a boy or a girl. I shall ask Rani to wash them until they are soft enough for the baby to wear."

"It will be a boy; I'm praying every day," Padma Devi said, laughing. "Patil will be very happy to have a grandson."

As Padma Devi's words sunk in, the memory of the dead baby on the beach resurfaced. I wondered if my baby would be born a girl or a boy. If I had a daughter, would she be accepted by the family? If not, what would I do?

My thoughts faded as Casper's barks filled my ears. Pregnancy was a delight with him keeping me company. I would keep one hand on my belly and try to speak lovingly to my baby while he peacefully sat beside me. I wondered if he sensed my pregnancy. *Dogs always have a way of knowing and understanding everything,* I thought. Whenever I looked into his eyes, I saw a whole universe in them.

He had become extra protective and loving. He waited for me to wake up rather than baying at me to get out of bed, even though weeks of morning sickness had disrupted his walks. Unlike before, when he barked to get my attention to be let out, he now sat patiently outside the bathroom, waiting for me to finish making horrible retching sounds. He'd lay down next to my bulging bump, reassuring me that he would protect us both. Often sniffing my tummy, yapping, and growling while the little baby inside me squirmed with excitement, reacting to the sounds.

"You're my first baby," I'd say affectionately, cuddling him.

***

Into my second trimester, my tummy grew in size as I continued to run my little business from home. During this time, I took fewer orders and focused more on my baby and our well-being. It was a tradition that a young mother, after her delivery, spent the first three to five months at her parents' home. To that end, my parents were happily making all arrangements to receive me and the baby.

Sadly, I couldn't take Casper with me for those months. The mere thought of leaving him really bothered me. Rani promised to care for him. I still worried. To add to that Moksh's problems with his father resurfaced. He appeared to be deeply troubled, and I feared the repetition of that dreadful night. *I must stay calm and not think about negative things. It's not good for the baby*, I convinced myself. Moksh eventually stopped going to work. He stayed at home, sleeping most of the day, keeping awake at night, and pondering. His ideas never matched with his father's. Moksh wanted the factory to be run in a certain manner. It was difficult to convince Patil, who was old-school and stuck to his already-established ways. The huge generational gap between them made it difficult for them to understand each other and work together.

"My dad's unreasonable; there's no point arguing with him every day," Moksh said whenever I asked. What Moksh failed to see was that Patil didn't need him. He didn't need a son who threw tantrums. Aarav was the more patient one, obeying every word his father spoke. I tried desperately to change Moksh's mood, but I saw him slipping further into depression.

I turned to Susan and Pooja for some consolation.

"Depression? How's that possible? He appears cheerful when he's around us," declared Susan.

"It's difficult to say. This could be temporary. Don't stress too much," Pooja assured me. "He's got a baby on the way. He's going to have to pull up his socks and restart work."

"That's true. Fatherhood might change him entirely." Susan sounded so positive that she had me quite convinced.

***

It was the last day of the prenatal classes. I was due in one month. Our educator decided to take our group of eight to the birthing ward. I waddled like a penguin on swollen legs, curious to understand what the grand finale would be like. As we walked through the hallway of the upper floor of the hospital, a shrill voice came from one of the rooms, where a woman was screaming in apparent agony. Alarmed, we glanced at each other. The educator was quick to assure us it wouldn't be that bad, and the woman was to be given an epidural soon. As if that wasn't enough, she showed us the birthing chair, demonstrating how high we must place our legs on it so that the baby could easily slide out. I was overwhelmed with fear.

"Husbands and parents are allowed to stay with you during birthing," the teacher assured us. I felt a bit of relief upon hearing this, as I imagined Moksh standing next to me, holding my hand and cheering while I pushed our baby out. However, I returned home horrified and wished I hadn't attended that session.

From then on, the sounds from the birthing ward started to haunt me. I cringed at the thought of laying on that chair, screaming in anguish. I ached for Moksh to hold me, caress me, and tell me that everything would be alright. But he refrained from speaking too much. It felt like he was unaware of time. It was hard to say if he could distinguish between day and night. If he wasn't out with his friends, he'd be watching television, listening to music, or living in his thoughts. His eyes sank deeper, giving him a sickly appearance.

I was certain he needed professional help, but he brushed away the idea, saying, "I'm not depressed. I definitely don't need to see a doctor. You're overthinking. I just need some time for myself, that's all."

Everyone in the family had tried in vain. I suffered in my own way, not knowing how to help Moksh or myself. I felt trapped between the past and the future.

"The baby is losing weight—that's not a good sign," the obstetrician said with a worried look on her face. "Twenty-one days to go; you must take good care. Eat well."

"I'll do my best, Doctor," I said, then went back home to find Vasumati in a fit. She had demanded that Revathi, the house cook, serve lunch to Moksh while she went to the supermarket with Rani. Revathi had tried to wake him up a few times by knocking on the door to his room, but he would not answer. She said she heard him snoring, so she decided not to worry about the missed lunch.

Vasumati went about the house yelling. "No one in this house cares for my son. Oh, that poor boy! I know how much he's suffering."

This drama was exactly what I needed to get away from. Just then, Casper came with a leash in his mouth, nudging me to take him for a walk. I grinned and readily went out with him.

***

A week before I was due, my water broke, and I was rushed to the hospital. At first, the contractions were mild, but as the day progressed, they came faster and heavier. It felt like my body was in an incessant spasmic trance. The anesthesiologist asked me to lay with my legs across the side of the bed and bend forward so that I would be in a hunched-over position. He asked me to stay very still while he put some numbing cream on my back before he inserted the needle into my spine. I clenched my teeth when I felt a sharp sting and then a cool liquid enter my back. Later, I was taken into the labor room. I wondered where Moksh was. I had asked the nurse twice already to look for him, but she had failed to find him. I could still feel the pain of my contractions despite the epidural. Thankfully, my mother came to my rescue. She held my hand as they put me on that dreaded birthing throne. By now, all the shame of my nakedness had vanished. I wanted nothing more than to be done with this delivery, or go back to having the baby stay inside my womb. This was the middle space, an unearthly place to be.

"I see the baby's head," the doctor said, hurriedly putting on her surgical gloves.

"Ready, Nam?"

It had been almost ten hours since my contractions had begun. I was exhausted. The labor was extremely intense and had weakened me to such an extent that pushing had become nearly impossible. The epidural's effects had waned away all too quickly, and I screamed in agony as my body trembled in pain.

"Push...push...come on...push!"

"You're almost there! Come on, Nam.... Push!"

Out came a little head, followed by a small body, and my pain died all at once.

"It's a girl!" the nurse exclaimed and placed my beautiful slippery daughter on my bare chest for a minute before taking her away. The next few minutes were like scenes from a movie, the lights flickering on and off. I could see faces and objects flashing, all in slow motion. I noticed the large clock that hung on the opposite wall, almost nearing twelve thirty. The baby's flailing legs as the pediatrician held her up in the air, patting her bottom. I heard a shrill voice. Then it was all darkness.

It felt like my body had attained Nirvana. I fell into a deep slumber and woke after what felt like an eternity. I was in a different room and felt Zen-like after my profound sleep. The nurse brought in my baby, carefully wrapped in a soft white cotton cloth. I cautiously took her into my arms. She was the most beautiful baby I had ever seen. We looked at each other in amazement.

"Hi, Shloka. This is mommy. I'm so happy to finally hold you in my arms."

My little angel observed me with her wide bee-like eyes, probably wondering if it was the same familiar voice she had heard when she was comfortably floating in my belly. I gently moved her wispy bangs and kissed her tiny forehead. She had the softest skin I had ever touched. Time paused again. I was seized with an admiration for this little miracle lying in my arms. "Owah, owaahh, owahhh..." Shloka hollered all at once, her voice hitting the roof. It was feeding time.

Moksh had preferred to stay out of the operating room. I wasn't sure if he was afraid of watching me writhe in pain or if it was too traumatizing for him to witness. During the last stages of my delivery, he had hovered around the lounge area, impatiently pacing up and down. He came to see me after I woke up.

"Are you alright?"

"Yes, I'm better. Thanks."

It felt like we were strangers. I would surely never forgive him for abandoning me when I most needed him. I was in utter distress while giving birth to our daughter, and what did my husband do? He hid behind his fears! Did he feel cowardly? I didn't know, and I couldn't understand a man's perspective of this phase. I let it go, just to sustain my own sanity.

My temporary move to my parents' home didn't go as planned. Since Shloka was a tiny baby, clinically underweight, the doctor had asked us to be watchful for the first three months. This meant keeping her away not only from Casper, but also my parents' dog, Milo. Although it was a tradition in Hindu customs for the new mother and the baby to stay at her parents' home, I thought it best if we moved to our unused apartment that was halfway between Moksh's home and my parents' home. I encountered resistance from Patil initially, but he gave in eventually, for Shloka's sake. My mother had hired a nanny so that we had an extra pair of hands to take care of Shloka. The girl, Siddamma, was in her twenties. *She's too young to be holding a baby*, I thought. Obviously, my mother was convinced her choice was a good one. Finally, I began settling down with Shloka's schedule. As all mothers did, and still do, I felt like a cow, feeding every hour of the day and night, feeling delirious after spending more time being awake rather than asleep. My hormones erratic and bedraggled, I looked haggard. There were beautiful moments, too, when Shloka slept in her cradle—so divine. Sometimes smiling contentedly, occasionally breaking into giggles. We wondered what on earth she could be dreaming about.

***

Moksh came to see us every day. Although he seemed less depressed, something was still not right, and I could feel it. He made very little eye contact with me, as though he was guilty of something. Regardless, he was overwhelmed with love for Shloka. He watched her in amazement as she laid in her crib sleeping, snugly wrapped in soft layers of fleece shawl.

"Look at her—she already has a personality, sleeping with her arms above her head and her right leg always positioned over her left. She's going to be a rockstar," he said fondly.

When she was awake, he'd hold out his little finger near her hand, and Shloka would grab it triumphantly.

We had visitors most weekends. I gladly welcomed a change from routine, feeling happy to meet friends and family and get news of a world different from mine. Shloka had become everybody's darling, since she was the first grandchild on both sides of the family.

One Sunday evening, Vasumati and Patil came with a bag of toys for Shloka.

"Look at her smile! She's so beautiful," Vasumati said as she gently slipped one of the toys into the hands of Shloka, who was wide awake in her cradle. Then Vasumati looked at me and continued. "Pandit Krishna called yesterday to suggest that we name the baby with the letter D, as per her horoscope. I was thinking Disha would be nice."

Moksh quickly intervened. "I don't want to change her name. It's better she stays as Shloka. Everyone is used to calling her that."

"It's good to find a name with the letter D, keeping in mind the astrological implications. However, on a day-to-day basis, you can still call her Shloka," Vasumati said and looked toward Patil for support.

"She will be fearless, just like her grandmother, Vasumati. So she will always be called Shloka, but Pandit Ji will enter her name as Disha, to align her with the stars," Patil concluded.

I felt relieved.

Patil picked up Shloka from the cradle, looked at her affectionately, and said, "Another goddess Lakshmi has entered our home."

I wondered if this goddess would be treated as equal to a boy born in this traditional family. Would she receive the same encouragement and freedom? A grandson would have been a future heir to Patil's business, but a granddaughter would grow up in his shadow, eventually to be married off into a different home. The zeitgeist was western influenced, but that was merely the latest thin layer on the centuries-old palimpsest of the ideological Indian society. Only time could tell.

***

My tiny tot's curiosity was a notch higher than a cat's, so it wasn't an easy task to get her to fall asleep. I had been blessed by a wonderful support system. My mother took turns with me in taking care of Shloka. It had been a month since our live-in nanny, Siddamma, had assumed her role with us. She had come straight from her village and spoke only in Kannada. She did little jobs like washing the baby's clothes, changing diapers, preparing Shloka's bath, and at times rocking Shloka to sleep under the careful supervision of my mother. I was still reluctant to hand Shloka over to her for total nannying. One night, Shloka began to bawl uncontrollably.

"Did you feed her?" my mother asked, her eyes heavy with sleep.

"Yes, I did."

"I hope she's not starting to become colicky." I was extremely worried as I held Shloka on my shoulder, gently patting her back.

"Wait. I will rub some warm oil on her tummy—maybe that will make her feel better."

Saying that, my mother disappeared into the kitchen to heat a bit of olive oil. No matter how much we tried, Shloka would not calm down. Her cries woke up the nanny.

Siddamma came into the room and said in a very gentle and confident voice, "Please give her to me, madam. I will put her back to sleep."

I handed Shloka over and sat quietly pondering what had gone wrong. Was it the routine, or the food that I had eaten? All at once, the calm night that had been doused by the shrillness of Shloka's screams was overtaken by a sweet, melodious voice. Shloka gradually ceased wailing and calmly listened to the nanny, who was rocking her in her arms and singing a beautiful folk song from her village. Siddamma's long black hair that she wore tightly fastened behind her head during the day now cascaded below her shoulders, swaying to the tune. My mother glanced at me with an "I told you so" look on her face, and I couldn't agree more. After a while, we were relieved to find Shloka fast asleep.

The next day, I wanted to know all about this girl: her past, her present, and her magical voice. I saw Siddamma readying Shloka's bathtub. Her face was fresh and pure, without a mark or a blemish encroaching on her brown skin. I walked over to her. "Thank you for yesterday. You certainly have a beautiful voice. Where did you learn to sing?"

"Back in my village, we sang to make life easier—in our minds, at least."

"What brought you to the city, if you don't mind me asking?"

"There was so much poverty in my village; sometimes we would go hungry for days. The nights were the worst because we had to sleep on an empty stomach. It was tough for my mother to see us suffer, so she decided to move to the city with all five of us."

"What about your father?"

"In our region, for many years it didn't rain enough to have sufficient crops in the fields. My father had many debts, so they took away our lands, and because of this, he took his own life a few years back."

"Oh, how terrible. I'm so sorry to hear that."

Siddamma hung Shloka's towel next to the tub. Her face was stoic as she continued to narrate her story. "After my father's demise, my mother worked in the village chief's farm for a while, but she didn't earn enough to feed us and repay our debts. So, she decided to move to a nearby town, where she could work at a construction site. After that, she got a new job at a different place, and we all kept moving from one place to the other. When she had no work, we returned to our village for a while before she looked for another job."

"So you and your siblings never got to go to school?"

"We did go to the village school before my father's death. But later, my mother got so busy with work that I had to take care of my sisters and my little brother. When I turned fourteen, I worked alongside her to earn more money. Some men at the building sites were not very nice. They tried to touch me and ask for sexual favors. Because of that, my mother asked me to stay at home. I cooked and looked after the children, since I was the oldest."

I felt a sense of anger and helplessness all at the same time. How could life be this cruel to them? I lowered Shloka into the warm water of the tub Siddamma had filled. Shloka's bath toys floated all around her, and she enthusiastically attempted to grab and put them into her mouth, splashing water everywhere. A bright yellow duck in particular was her favorite. She'd watch in amazement as it waddled alongside the green frog, the purple octopus, the orange fish, and other rubber creatures. I quickly got out our video recorder to capture these moments. Siddamma watched in amazement, unfamiliar with technology. After the bath, I dressed and fed Shloka before putting her to bed.

That evening, I asked my mother how she had recruited Siddamma.

"She's from our neighbor's cousin's village. Why?" she asked.

"She's a nice girl. I'd like to keep her with us as a permanent staff—if Vasumati agrees," I said, feeling optimistic.

"Yes, she'll be of great help to you once you are back home. But honestly, I think there are too many people in that house right now. Another addition would be tough."

"That's true, but I'm not sure how else to help her."

"We'll find a way. Don't worry."

***

We moved into the post-third-month phase, where things were more settled. Shloka had finally grown into the habit of sleeping six straight hours at night. It was such a relief to be well rested before assuming mommy duties. During the day, when I wasn't reading Sidney Sheldon's *A Stranger in the Mirror*, I'd find myself listening to Siddamma's stories of her village life.

"There was only one school for the entire village. Our father never allowed us to miss a day of school. Not many children attended, until one day, the teacher announced that lunch would be served free. Since then, the school has been full!" Siddamma laughed.

"What about your friends in the village? Do you meet them when you're there?"

"Oh yes, madam, I do. They're all married and settled now, some with children too. The six of us went to school together until fifth grade, but it was all in vain—it didn't serve anything. Two of my friends, Kaveri and Jayanthi, were lucky—they got good husbands and are doing well—but the other three girls show marks on their bodies. They cannot get away from their nightmarish lives. I feel very bad for them. It's unfair, you know. The fact is, we work more than men. We tend the fields, graze the animals, milk the cows and goats, cook for the family, and care for the children. And what do we get in return? Men who treat us badly and beat us. I don't understand why, but it's like that. It's always hard for village girls, madam."

My problems were surely not of the same magnitude as theirs.

"I understand, Siddamma. You're absolutely right. Women are very capable and they deserve much better. All of that needs to change, and fast. It may not be possible right away, but soon, I hope."

My mother sat next to us, shelling garden peas for the evening meal. "What about you?" she asked. "Why didn't you get married?"

Siddamma hesitated a bit before confiding in us. She pursed her lips.

"My father passed away when I was twelve," she said. "After that, there were many men in the village whose prying eyes were on me. My mother wanted to marry me off so that I would be safe from these vultures, but I was scared. One day, I was on my way to the farm where my mother worked. I went there every noon to give her lunch. A man in his mid-thirties accosted me. I was terrified, but didn't divulge anything to my mother, for she would have forbidden me from bringing the tiffin box. I told my friends about it, and they later found out the whereabouts of this man. He was married with three kids and lived in the neighboring village. I warned him that I would tell his wife, but he continued to stalk me. My neighbor's son was always very kind to us. He offered to walk with me every day, and I felt safe around him. He was twenty-two and worked in his father's fields. Soon, we fell in love, but then I made the worst mistake of my life."

Several seconds passed before she continued.

"My stomach started to bulge after a few months, and he would not take responsibility for the child. After much persuasion from my mother, his parents said they would marry us if I delivered a boy. I went to the temple and prayed every day. My mother also made offerings to Lord Ganesha, with the little money she had. I eventually had a girl. I cried all night. How could I show my face to anyone in the village? The next day, I put the baby at the bottom of a bucket, stuffed the top with lots of clothes, and went to the river. My baby had not survived by the time I got there. I picked up her lifeless body and tossed it into the flowing water, hoping she would have a better mother in her next life."

My face went pale. Flashes of the dead baby lying on the beach came back to me. I couldn't believe it. Sadness engulfed my entire body as I felt every bit of her agony. I had pictured every scene in my mind as she narrated her story. At the same time, I understood why she had done such a thing. It all went back to women and their worth.

"My mother lied to save me from the shame. She told them it was a boy and that we lost the baby during birth, but they still didn't accept me. After a week, my mother decided we had enough of the village life and moved to a nearby town to work at a construction site. She is a very strong lady, and thanks to her, I have a second life."

Everything inside me was screaming. How was it fair that I could hold my baby and keep her safe while this poor girl could not?

"This is very common in villages. I don't want to get married, madam. I'm happy to be free without a man controlling me, beating me, or taking away what I earn for his alcohol," Siddamma concluded.

Shloka's cries pulled me from my thoughts; she was now awake from her nap and ready to be fed. I pulled myself together after that heavy conversation and hurried to tend to her needs. Siddamma's story had profoundly disturbed me, and I could not stop thinking about it. My brain pulsed as I tried to reason out this girl's life. The images of my young self holding the lifeless baby on the beach in Pondicherry resurfaced from the place I had buried them. Why? Why does it have to be this way? As adults, isn't it our duty to protect the young, nurture them, and support them without being biased about gender, color, caste, or creed?

We teach boys to be independent and assertive while we teach our girls to be dependent and submissive. We revere our boys for their high economic capabilities but consider our girls unaffordable and an economic burden. Why? Why are we still mute to these differences? One child leads a life of privilege while another is killed or silently suffers an existence filled with misery. Why are we turning a blind eye on such ghastly aspects of our society?

I shuddered thinking about how a girl as young as Siddamma had dealt with the harshness of life. How could she give life and bear to take it away? If she had decided to keep that child, would she have been an outcast, forced to live with her daughter in some wretched village that would never treat her right? The very fact that she was a woman rendered her vulnerable, and her womb had become her woe.

All of these questions did nothing to help the abject postpartum depression that crept into me. J. K. Rowling's seventh book, *Harry Potter and the Deathly Hallows*, had just been released, and I knew this was the only thing that could save me from wallowing in pity. The moment Shloka was fast asleep, I dove deeply into the book. At other times, I gave English lessons to Siddamma. She was grateful and always said that she wanted to become like me someday: a strong-minded, confident woman.

I smiled at her, but on the inside, I knew I was not the person she imagined me to be. To the world's eyes, I was a brave and independent woman who had a mind of her own, but in reality, I was far from it. I had not found the courage to walk away from a complex relationship. It hurt when my wings were clipped, so I didn't fly away. In turn, I had made peace with a life full of boundaries instead of fighting for my freedom.

***

In her fifth month, Shloka was comfortably reaching all the milestones on her growth chart. It was soon time to move back to Vasumati and Patil's home. I was dreading going back to all the drama that came with the household. But I missed Casper. Transitioning on to the next phase was emotionally challenging for both my parents and me. They had grown fond of their granddaughter and were teary-eyed when it was time for us to leave. Siddamma unfortunately had to go back to her family, as her mother needed her help, but she promised to return to work soon. I made her memorize my phone number so she could call if she ever needed help. I feared for her and prayed to the universe to keep her safe.

Moksh picked us up and drove us back home. I had been waiting to introduce Shloka to a special member of our family.

We heard Casper's barks as the car pulled into the driveway. "Bow...wow...wow...."

Shloka's eyes widened.

***

Shloka and Casper became inseparable with time. They played fetch and went out for walks numerous times a day. I had never witnessed a bond so beautiful. Casper watched over Shloka while she slept, and Shloka made sure Casper was never leashed or tied to a post. Rani and I took them to the local park every evening and watched them play ball. Vasumati and Bhavika, too, joined us at times. As for Moksh, he spent time with us on weekends in the company of our friends. Pooja and her husband, Harsh, had given birth to a handsome little boy named Dhanush. Susan and Amish wouldn't miss playing with our kids. Bhavika and Aarav adored them too. We had made other friends over the course of time. Myna and Supreet taught Shloka funny tongue twisters. Swathi and Sunder's child was much older than ours, so they gave us useful advice about parenting. Being around friends and family while Shloka was growing up felt like a blessing. Our weekends were not only entertaining but had also become my stress buster.

Moksh was different when around people. One minute, he'd proclaim his love for me and tell everyone that I'm the best mother and wife, but the next, it would be evident that he had nothing but disrespect for me. I knew there had been little improvement in our relationship. He was still angry and distant when we were alone. I had accepted my place in his life but hoped someday he would turn back into the same man who loved me very much. His problems with his father had intensified, and they wouldn't even speak to each other anymore. This had created a lot of tension at home. We finally decided to move out and live independently, which I hoped would be great for our relationship. Maybe this could bring us back together. We would have our little nest—just Moksh, Shloka, Casper, and me. This decision was met by strong opposition from Patil.

"Moksh, what are we going to do? How can we move without the support of your parents?" I asked when he was watching television one evening.

"That's not your concern," he said coldly.

"But it is my concern. I am worried." I pushed harder, trying to unlock Moksh's mind.

"I have spoken to Mom. She said she'll try to convince dad. I think it's best not to move far away. My dad might be fine if we rent an apartment next door."

There was a one-in-a-million chance that an apartment would be vacant right when we wanted it, next to Patil's house.

"I think it's quite a task to find an apartment next door in a few weeks."

"Mom said our neighbor Mishra's house will be vacant at the end of this month. It would be good to move in there."

I had mixed feelings. Not only did I feel a sense of liberation that we would be moving out, but I also felt a sense of disappointment that Moksh had not considered going back to work. If he didn't get along with Patil, he could look for jobs outside the family business. It saddened me that he still wanted to depend on his parents' finances.

***

At the beginning of the next month, we moved to our neighbor Mishra's vacant house. It had three large rooms with attached bathrooms, a compact modern kitchen, a spacious living room, and a balcony overlooking my in-laws' house. Vasumati was content that we had not moved too far away and that she wouldn't miss Shloka growing up. Patil, on the other hand, was terribly upset. He had never imagined Moksh and I would move out of his shadow.

I quickly set up the house with the help of Rani, but, to my horror, Moksh occupied a room for himself. We were supposed to come together as a couple—not live separate under one roof. It felt like I didn't matter to him anymore, like I was there only to be a part of his social needs. Our friends, too, noticed that things were getting bad between us. They tried to intervene whenever there was a problem, but his anger had only worsened. I realized that I couldn't bring him back from his abyss without him wanting to do so. Hence, I decided to dedicate all my time toward Shloka and Casper. I was so happy for some time in my new bubble that I hadn't noticed how quickly time flew past me—until one dreaded night.

CHAPTER 5
Moksh

Bangalore, India
June 2009

I showered Shloka, helped her put on her pajamas, and tucked her into bed. It was story time, so I pulled out a children's book and started to read. My two-year-old listened intently, sucking her thumb and gently caressing her blue teddy bear. After the story ended, she asked for another. I quickly made one up. Motherhood had provided me with different skill sets.

Overjoyed, she drifted into deep slumber, and I followed suit, drifting into a scene where I sat under an apple tree reading a book. A ton of ripe apples lay on the ground around me in the deserted garden. There was profound silence.

Suddenly, I felt a hand yank me out of bed and give a big blow to my forehead. Dismayed, I tried to peel my eyes open. Moksh towered over me. I wondered if I was still dreaming. He was very angry for some reason and had begun hurling abuses at me. I quickly got out of the bedroom so that the noise didn't wake Shloka. Moksh followed me, breaking a vase of flowers that was kept on a table. Casper, who slept in a corner of the living room, started trembling with fear. It was the dead of night. The world was fast asleep. I had to do something to calm him down. I tried talking, but he came close and held me by my hair.

"Stop it, Moksh. You're hurting me, please stop."

Why is he behaving like this? Has he found out that I enrolled to learn French? I worried. A lot had changed since Shloka had begun walking and eating solid food. Just hanging diapers, cleaning, and cooking wasn't giving me the mental stimulation I craved. I wanted to learn something new. German felt like the ideal choice, as I would have been able to converse with my aunt, who didn't speak an ounce of English. She was married to my father's brother, and they lived in Frankfurt. However, the German school was an hour's drive from home. I couldn't afford to be away from the house for a long time. Instead, I decided to learn French at the Alliance Française de Bangalore from the money I had saved from my baking business. It was a ten-minute drive from home. I escaped for a few hours during the afternoon when Shloka was fast asleep, while Rani and Casper watched over her. I didn't breathe a word about it to anyone, including Moksh, for fear of disapproval, similar to the course in interior designing that Patil had denied me. I would not let anyone stop me this time.

Had Moksh found out? Was he upset that I lied? I had only done this to keep my sanity. I could explain, of course. I had done nothing wrong. I struggled to free myself from Moksh's grip on my hair. The more I tried, the tighter he held me. His left hand caught my jaw. "Let go of me, or I'll call the police!" I threatened my husband in mumbled words that came out of my aching mouth.

He laughed menacingly, and his voice reverberated in the silence of the night, sending shivers down my spine. My relationship with Moksh had become extremely strained due to his issues with his father. Even moving away from his parental home had not solved this problem. He was bitter, and there was nothing I could do about it. I had become his punching bag. He had started to control me in every way. I felt frustrated, but I didn't want to quit my marriage at any cost, because that would leave Shloka broken. I didn't want her to experience separation from either of us. She loved her father, who sometimes took her for long drives and played her favorite music. How could I destroy the wonderful world she had around her?

"My life is a mess, and it's all because of you!" he yelled loudly.

What had I done that had driven him into this rage? I didn't understand. My heart beat against my chest so fast it hurt. There was a throbbing pain in my forehead, and I felt a growing lump where he had struck me. I knew I needed to leave—that was the only way Moksh could be stopped.

"Moksh, please stop. Let's talk tomorrow. Shloka will wake up," I said in a calm voice, but he wouldn't listen.

"You're not my wife, you don't even care what I go through every day. You are never there for me.... Neither are your parents."

Okay! This is not about my secret French classes, but something that has been brewing inside him. Why is he bringing up my parents?

I stayed calm. I knew whatever Moksh was accusing me or my parents of wasn't true. He spent most of his time away from home. The times he was at home, he simply locked himself in his room and watched television without wanting to be disturbed. A few months prior, I had tried to confront him with issues relating to house expenses, his work, his lifestyle, and his absence from our lives, but I was left with a twisted knee. It had taken over a month to heal. I didn't tell his parents for fear of them asking us to move back or even accusing me of provoking Moksh. I had forgiven him too quickly and focused my energy into Shloka's upbringing and learning French.

"Your parents have not even given me a penny, let alone a watch or a car."

I was shocked. How could Moksh get down to this level?

"Look at Bhavika's parents. They always gift Aarav lots of things."

I wanted to get away from this monster I had willingly married. He finally loosened his grip and let go of me.

I must call the police before he lays another finger on me, I thought.

The minute he left my sight, I grabbed my telephone and dialed the number 100.

A police officer's voice came on the other end of the line, I spoke hurriedly. "Please send someone quick," I pleaded in a low voice, so Moksh didn't hear.

It was too late. He was standing at the far end of the room.

"You called the cops on me?" His voice echoed through the living room.

My body started to shake in fear. His bloodshot eyes pierced into mine. He came closer. I prayed police would hurry.

"How dare you?" he said and grabbed me by my neck. "You want to destroy me? You want me behind bars?"

I shook my head as tears poured down my face.

"I will break every bone in your body if you ever try to humiliate me and my family."

My hands struggled to free his grip from my neck. I couldn't. Suddenly, I heard the sound of a vehicle approaching. He let go of me and went to the balcony to check. After a few minutes, there was a knock on the front door. Moksh opened it and greeted the cops.

"We got a call from this address asking for help," said the male inspector, who was neatly dressed in a khaki coloured uniform.

"It's nothing really. My wife and I were having a small argument."

The inspector looked at me. I opened my mouth to speak, but before I said anything, Moksh interrupted me.

"I really love her. Sometimes she doesn't understand me, and that's why we fight."

I wiped my tears. I didn't know what to do. To seek protection from Moksh, I would have to file a First Information Report (FIR) with the police. They would take Moksh to prison and let him out on bail, and I would have to deal with the aftereffects of his anger. Instead, I hoped they would warn him so that he would be scared and not raise his hand on me again.

"It happens in every family. You both should have patience with each other and sort out issues in a calm manner," the inspector said.

"We'll be alright, sir. Don't worry," Moksh assured him.

The inspector looked at me. I nodded. I was afraid to upset Moksh further.

"Thank you for coming and advising us," Moksh said, and the officer turned and walked back toward his car.

As soon as the patrol car was gone, Moksh looked at me and yelled.

"Get out! Leave! I don't want you in my sight."

I glanced at the window; it was still dark. How was I to take Shloka and Casper? The roads were not safe at that hour. I was certain his anger was toward me, so there was not the slightest chance he would hurt them. I left for my sister Megha's home, which was not far away. I would return in the morning to pick up Shloka and Casper, I decided.

Megha answered her phone and waited for me. As I walked through the deserted streets, my tears started to flow again. I knew I should have left long ago, at least the last time. I felt foolish to have stayed, hoping things would get better. I had tried enough. Even moving away from his parents had not worked. How could I start all over? I had nothing. I knew my mom, dad, and sister would back me up, but I didn't want to burden them. Thoughts poured in. Megha was waiting at the door with a worried look. She saw the bulge on my forehead and hugged me. She handed me some water and an ice pack to lessen the swelling and led me to the guest room.

"Get some rest. We'll talk tomorrow," she said.

Randy, their dog, ran up to me and started to lick my face. Content, he curled into a ball beside me and fell asleep. I tossed around. My thoughts kept me awake. I hoped Shloka was sleeping and hadn't heard the fight Moksh insisted on having. If she was awake, she would have cried, I convinced myself.

How could I begin a new life? Where could I start? I didn't have much experience outside of baking; could I start something on those lines? It would take me months, even years, to build up enough business to support my needs. Maybe I could work in a bakery first? But how could I balance working full time and taking care of Shloka? Baking would take a toll on me physically. I had always suffered from a sore back after long hours of standing and lifting heavy equipment. Distraught was too weak a word for the way I felt in that moment.

The sun rose, and I returned home. Rani opened the door, her face pale. I started to pack two suitcases: one for me, and another for Shloka.

"Rani, pack your clothes too," I instructed.

"Baa baa black sheep..." I heard Shloka's voice. She had woken up and started to sing, unaware of what had happened in the night.

I hurried into her room and gave her a big hug. "We're going to Big Momma's place for a few days," I told her. She jumped out of bed with excitement.

"Yippee, I'm gonna take Randy for a walk, I'm gonna take Randy for a walk!" She ran around, repeating that several times before stopping next to Casper, who lounged in his bed.

"Don't worry, Casper. I'll come back and take you for a walk. I love you very much—*muaah*. You're the best brother."

My heart felt so heavy. I had no choice but to leave Casper there, since both my sister and parents had dogs of their own. I hugged him and whispered, "I'll come back soon and get you."

My parents arrived at my sister's house. Rani kept Shloka busy as I narrated the whole episode to them. Everyone was extremely upset.

"This has happened too many times. He will never change. You can't put yourself in harm's way. Come live with us, where you and Shloka will be safe." My father had never sounded more worried.

"Yes—he is capable of hurting you again. You cannot go back," my mother added.

My parents had retired and built a beautiful home away from the hustle and bustle of the city, and living there meant living away from Shloka's school and the Alliance Française. Instead, my sister, Megha, and her husband, Nikhil, offered to keep Shloka, Rani, and me as long as it was needed. Randy, too, was happy to have us there.

Soon I started to look for a job. The readily available ones were mostly in call centers that catered to outsourced employment from foreign countries. This required me to commute and work at ghostly hours. My parents didn't see the point in a risky job like that.

"Why don't you focus on learning French? You could easily land a job as a teacher in a school. You and Shloka could go to school together and return home in the evening," my father suggested.

"Don't worry about finances; we'll support you," said Megha, and Nikhil nodded.

International schools were springing up all around town, and most had French as an optional language. I was hopeful, but knew it would take a long time before I perfected the language. But it wasn't a bad idea—I could definitely give it a try.

***

A week went by, and Moksh called. He was apologetic, but I had no time nor any sympathy for him.

"Please come home. Don't do this to me. Why did you take everything I said seriously? I love you and Shloka—I cannot live without you both. Casper, too, is waiting. Come back, at least for his sake."

My heart ached at the mention of Casper. He was caught between our crossfire.

I paused and thought long and hard. "It's too late now, Moksh. What's done is done. You cannot take back your words. Moreover, we have too many issues that cannot be sorted."

"Please, I am ready to sort it out. I'll change my lifestyle, I promise. I'll restart work. I'll spend more time with the three of you. Please...please, believe me. I have thought it through."

"Sorry, Moksh. I need to go."

Every ounce of me wanted to believe his words. I wanted our family back. Begin all over again. Moksh couldn't do without us. He needed to see one of us when he woke, whatever time that might be. He loved us, but his way of loving was complicated. There was so much hate toward me involved. He loved me as much as he hated me. I understood none of it. What could have made him change like the seasons, like the days, like time? I had given up all my dreams to fill the role of a housewife, a daughter-in-law, and a mother. What more could I do to please him?

There were plenty of people trying to advise me.

"You have to manipulate your husband."

"You're too naïve; you must learn to keep your husband in your grasp."

"Our son is a gem of a person—he needs you to care more for him."

"A wife is the only person who can keep the family together."

"Cook what he likes."

"Never answer back. Agree to whatever he says."

I had heard it all, yet nothing I did ever worked. I had felt inadequate for a long time. Now Moksh was promising to restart work, take responsibility, and be there for us. Could I believe him? Could I trust his words? I touched my forehead. The swelling had disappeared, but the pain remained. I sighed heavily and picked up Shloka's bag.

"Is my baby ready?" I asked. Rani had bathed her, fed her, and readied her for school while I was busy trying to make sense of my emotions.

"Yes, Mommy, I'm ready to go."

"You're the best baby ever."

"No, Mommy. Casper is the best."

I hugged her. "Yes, of course my love. Both of you are the best."

"Mommy, when are we going back home?"

"We'll talk about it soon, honey," I said as I helped her into her car seat. "Please put your seatbelt on." I winked to Shloka. She immediately pulled the strap toward her with her tiny little hands and tried valiantly to move the buckle near the slot. I grinned and secured the car seat properly for her. Her favorite song came on, and we both started to sing. While we drove, little raindrops splashed on the windscreen. I bent forward and peeked up at the sky. The dense, dark grey clouds were ready to burst. In minutes, the droplets increased in size. Traffic had slowed down, and the road had turned into a river.

"Oh no! It's raining cats and dogs!" I exclaimed anxiously, wondering if I would be able to get to Shloka's school on time, and then to my classes at the Alliance Française.

Shloka started to look all around, as though she was searching for something. Then she turned to me and asked in a worried voice, "Mommy, where are the cats and dogs? I don't see any."

I laughed and explained to her that it was just a phrase used to describe heavy rain. Shloka was so pure and innocent. She didn't deserve a broken family. She was still learning the ways of this life. She had a curious mind and was a fast learner.

The rain ceased, and the vehicles around me started to move again. I soon pulled over next to Shloka's school gates. We bear-hugged.

"See you in the evening, my doll. Be good and be naughty," I said.

She let out a big laugh and ran inside. I hurried to my French classes. Alliance Française had become my second home. By now, I was comfortably describing people, places, and situations in French. I had learned to talk about my likes and dislikes. French slang came easily, but I was still mixing up genders, to my teachers' horror. Nevertheless, I was progressing at a good rate.

After my lessons, on my way back to my sister's, I stopped at the school where my teachers had fueled my dreams of being the world's best chef. They were pleased to see me. I inquired with them if there were any jobs available. I was told there was a part-time job available in a *chocolaterie*. I took down all the details and called the company the next day to arrange an interview. The position was that of a head trainee for three days a week. My job would be to oversee the production process, give classroom training, put standard operating procedures in place, hire, and conduct quality control—much more than the job title suggested. The salary was meager, but it was a good start. I accepted. I was happy to begin somewhere.

***

I had lived at my sister's home for a month when Moksh appeared. He had lost weight and appeared very fragile.

"I'm ashamed," he said. "I'm sorry. I am repenting."

"Papaaaaa!" Shloka ran to him and hugged him.

"Please come back. Please. I know I was wrong in many ways. I've reflected on everything," Moksh said in a remorseful voice.

This had happened too many times and I wasn't buying into his lies anymore.

"Moksh, I'm afraid I can't. I'm happy here. I have a job and I'm doing great."

"That's wonderful, darling. I promise I won't stop you from working. In fact, I have reconciled with Dad and will be working again with him soon."

Shloka, still hugging Moksh, looked at me with tears in her eyes. "Mommy, please, let's go home. I have promised Casper a walk."

"Casper is sad," added Moksh. "He won't eat."

"I need more time to think about everything, Moksh. Please."

"Okay—but please, do what's right for our family. Our lives depend on you. You can make them or break them."

After that day, I received a call from Moksh every morning. It was true that he had made peace with Patil. He called to assure me that he was on the way to the office. He seemed to be thrilled to begin work all over again. A few weeks passed, and he came to take us back. My family remained skeptical. They were just as confused as I was, but Moksh assured them that he had turned over a new leaf and wouldn't interfere with my work. My parents weren't convinced, but they respected my decision to go with him. They let us go with a heavy heart. We drove away as my family watched and wondered if we would ever be alright.

Casper's barks were deafening as we got closer to home. He had obviously sensed us. Shloka opened the car door and ran to him. They were so happy to be reunited. I felt horrible to have separated the two. Casper ignored me the whole time I hugged him. He wouldn't accept my apologies. I had disappeared from his life all of a sudden. How could I explain it to him? How could I make him understand?

I whispered into his ear. "I'm sorry. I will never ever leave you again."

Shloka fastened Casper's leash to his collar and his tail shook in excitement.

Moksh glanced at me holding Shloka's hand. I beamed. This was wonderful. I felt a sense of satisfaction as I watched them take Casper for his evening walk.

***

The next few years, Moksh went to work religiously. The friction between him and his father remained, but he had learned to manage it. Shloka started full-time school. After a year of working at the *chocolaterie,* I quit and moved back to my role of being a housewife to keep Moksh happy and to be able to take Shloka to her golf lessons after her school. The family had expanded, with Moksh's brother, Aarav, and Bhavika welcoming twins—a boy and a girl. I became busy caring for the kids of the family. Living with Moksh was like living through uncertainty. There had been both good and bad times. It was emotionally challenging, but I wasn't giving up. Alliance Française was my only escape from everything that was happening in my life.

***

Soon, Shloka turned six. We moved closer to her school, away from Moksh's family. This time around, there was no objection from Patil. Maybe because he had accepted our life this way, or maybe because he was too busy with his two other grandchildren at home. Shloka had become independent. She took a shower on her own, ate her meals on her own, and went to bed on her own. I strongly felt the need to do something about my career, but I knew this would not go well with Moksh or his parents. Still, I made the decision to go ahead and apply for jobs. Even in my wildest dreams, I never imagined that this decision would lead me to the city of love.

CHAPTER 6
Paris

Bangalore, India
July 2013

Shloka had just left for school. I waved to her from the balcony of my kitchen as she descended the stairs, walked across the sprawling garden of the gated community, and reached the spot where a group of children waited for the school bus. After Shloka had turned six, she refused to have me wait with her and kiss her goodbye. I could see her entering the yellow bus at a distance. Content that Shloka was safely on her way, I returned to the mental turmoil I was forced to endure. As I crossed the kitchen, our new cook, Ratna, who had just entered the room, asked what the menu was for the day. I instructed her unenthusiastically.

I couldn't take it anymore. I wanted to do more in life than just manage the household. I went into a spare room in the apartment that was well isolated from the noisy kitchen. The computer blinked as I switched it on. I typed in "French-speaking jobs" on Google search, and a list appeared. Monster.com, Nakuri.com, Indeed.com...

I scanned through them. After a while, I pulled up my résumé, which I had readied the previous day, and uploaded it to the job sites.

Suddenly, I heard Moksh's voice. He was asking Ratna where I was. I quickly rushed to the kitchen. He was ready to leave for work. Moksh had kept his promise; he had been to work for his father every day since I had moved back in with him. This time, though, he had set up a separate pad away from the main office where Patil worked, so he wasn't in his father's face all the time.

I poured batter onto the nonstick pan and moved my hand in circles without lifting the ladle off the batter. After a lovely sizzle, a golden color appeared on the *dosa*. I poured some ghee over the Indian pancake and waited for a few seconds before I carefully slid a flat spatula underneath and overturned the *dosa* to let it cook on the other side. Our cook, Ratna, ladled chutney and potatoes onto a plate. I picked up the now-ready *dosa* from the pan, folded it in two, and placed it in the empty space on the plate.

"Madam, you go serve, and I'll make the next one," Ratna said, and I rushed to hand the plate to Moksh, who was now watching the news on television.

"I can't eat much—just one will do," Moksh said as he took a bite. "This chutney is terrible. Why can't you make chutney like my mother?"

I felt sad and looked away towards the fish bowl lying on the table in the corner of the living room. I took out a packet of fish food and sprinkled it over the water. Both gold fishes swam to the top and began gobbling up the tiny bits. *Why couldn't Moksh eat without a fuss?* Moksh criticized my cooking every day, sometimes even embarrassing me in front of guests. I knew I wasn't that bad a cook. Everyone else loved what I made. But over the years, I had lost the motivation to wake up energized and whip up different plates every morning. I finally convinced Moksh to hire a cook.

Having Ratna help in the kitchen allowed me to focus on something that gave more meaning to my life. Alliance Française had improved my French-speaking abilities, and I could speak a language that no one in my family, nor my friends, could speak. As soon as Moksh left for work, I went back to see if I had any replies from my postings. An IT company had written back. *That's crazy*, I thought. I wasn't an engineer, nor was I in the IT sector. There wasn't the slightest chance I would be selected. Nevertheless, I thought there was no harm in replying, so I shot off an email confirming my availability for the interview. They weren't going to write back to me, I knew. So I continued looking through other sites to see if I could find a job in a bakery or as a teacher. To my surprise, within a few hours, I received a confirmation from Alten Calsoft Labs. They had mentioned the date, place, and time of the interview.

Well, it's come my way. I must try, I thought, as Ratna brought in a tray full of little bowls filled with all the dishes she had prepared for the day.

"Can you please taste and tell me if the salt and other ingredients are fine, madam?"

I tried each of the dishes she brought. "Everything's very tasty, Ratna. Thank you."

I googled "Alten Calsoft Labs." An IT and product engineering services company founded in 1988. Offices in over thirty countries. The role was for a French-speaking engineer. I reread my résumé, just to make sure I hadn't mentioned the word engineer by mistake. The job description was that of an IT backend support for Société Générale, a well-known French bank. I was to liaise with a French team based in Paris on a day-to-day basis. Fluent French was vital for this job. *I must go for the interview to find out what this is all about. I'm going to be honest and tell them I know nothing about engineering*, I thought. Anyway, I had nothing to lose.

***

The day of the interview arrived. I dressed in an old formal dress I had put into storage. After driving for two hours in peak traffic, I arrived on time. I made my way into the lobby of a plush office and told the receptionist I was there for an interview with Mr. Shanmugam. The young lady dialed an extension on the phone.

"Good morning, sir. A candidate named Namratha is here for an interview for the French customer advocate role," she said in an appealing voice.

When she hung up the phone, she asked me to be seated. About ten minutes later, a tall man wearing circular spectacles appeared and introduced himself as Mr. Shanmugam. He gestured for me to follow him. We soon entered a large conference room, where a big television screen covered a wall and a couple of telephones sat on a large table in the center of the room. The manager dialed a number, then turned on the screen, where we saw Mr. Bernard, his French counterpart. I was convinced that this job wasn't for me and they would never hire me. I introduced myself in French and waited to hear the words, "Sorry we need someone with a tech background."

The interview lasted for an hour, and I walked out bewildered. They had offered me the job! The managers didn't seem bothered about the fact that I had no IT experience, or any formal work experience. During the interview, I asked why they were keen on my profile.

To my surprise, the manager replied, "We can train a person like you to learn the job, but it is very difficult to teach our engineers French. Especially because the job requires them to be very fluent."

But it was Bernard's next comment that truly shocked me.

"You will need to train in Paris for a month before starting work at the bank Société Générale for Alten Calsoft Labs in India."

I felt like I had just choked on something.

Oh my God, Paris! A feeling of excitement ran through my body. The picture of the Eiffel Tower in my French book flashed before my eyes. I never imagined that one day I would get a chance to see it for real. However, I was certain Moksh would never allow me to leave. I was dreaming in vain. Gathering my courage, I said, "I'll think about it and get back to you. Thank you."

I went straight back home. Casper barked when I entered the house. I hugged him and whispered the good news in his ears. He looked perplexed but licked my face. I gave him his treat, and we both went into the kitchen. I brought out the blender and put chopped plums, apples, beets, and carrots into it. The day had seemed unreal. I couldn't stop smiling. I had felt useless for a long time, but now I finally felt valued. How could I tell Moksh? He would never allow this. I looked at the clock—Shloka would be out of school in twenty minutes. I poured the freshly made juice into a bottle and packed a grilled vegetable sandwich for her to eat in the car as I drove her to her golf lessons.

"Mama, do you know what happened in my class today?" Shloka asked with excitement.

I put her school bag in the trunk of the car. "What happened, sweetie?"

"Shiv climbed up the desk and started dancing while another boy called Karan sang."

"How did the teacher let that happen?"

"It was our break time, and the principal was passing by. She called their parents, and they got into big trouble."

"Oh, that's a pity!"

Shloka was growing up so quickly it astonished me at times. She was a gifted child. She could swing her club like a pro and sing like a nightingale. I wanted to be there for her all the time. For that, I had to forget about my career. And without a job, I felt insecure. Plus, she had started to witness Moksh's anger from time to time, and I was afraid she would grow up living in fear like me. Soon we reached the golf course. Shloka drank all her juice, but left the sandwich half eaten.

"Shloka, come here and finish your sandwich!" I yelled as she opened the trunk of the car to pull out her kit.

I heard the voice of Shloka's coach. "Good evening, madam."

"Good evening, Ali."

"Madam, could you please bring Shloka here on Sunday morning at six o'clock? There is a juniors' tournament, and I feel she is quite ready to compete."

"That's great news! I'll bring her, of course."

"I will register her immediately," her coach said.

Ali took Shloka toward the range. I was elated. My little girl had practiced every day since she had turned five. Sometimes I thought I was too hard on her, pushing her after a tiring day of schoolwork to practice golf, but she had never once complained. I stood there, transfixed, watching Shloka take her stance and then swing her club. The ball soared high and landed a long distance away.

"Shot!" her coach shouted, then gave her a high five.

The thought of leaving for Paris for a month was enticing, but what about Shloka? Who would take her to golf after school? Who would pack her lunch box? I called my mother and told her about the job.

"Don't let it go, darling. I'll look after Shloka for a month, don't worry."

I felt relieved. Next thing I needed to do was to convince Moksh. I needed to find the perfect time to break the news to him. I never knew for sure how he would react.

That same evening, Moksh had invited his close friend Girish home for a drink. They were seated on the *canapé* in the balcony.

Girish's wife, Vimala, was a manager in a large multinational company, and she had recently been promoted. This was my chance. Moksh was in a light-hearted mood. I mustered up my courage and decided to break the news.

"How is Vimala's work going? I heard she received a promotion." I said purposefully.

"Yes, she's doing well at her work. That said, I'm happy as long as she doesn't neglect her home duties." Girish's voice had a tone of concern.

"What are you talking about? Vimala is certainly capable of both. You must encourage her," Moksh added.

I gritted my teeth. It was unfair. How could he blatantly lie like that? Moksh promoting the progress of women? *Well, this must be my cue.*

"Moksh, I was thinking it would be a good idea for me to work again. Shloka's all grown up now, and I have more time available."

"Why do you need to work? You have everything you need to live like a queen," Moksh said.

"It's also nice to work to understand the real world, you know. Of course, you have given me all of the comforts, and I really have no reason to work, but I'd like to try for a while. A French company has offered me a job and they would like for me to train in Paris for a month," I said in an undisturbed voice.

"Ha! What are you saying, Nam? Some crazy company is offering you a job and also sending you to Paris? You must be dreaming," Moksh said. Girish laughed, too, before he took another sip of his whisky.

I felt humiliated. Now I needed to get on that plane more than ever.

"Shloka needs you. Your priorities must be family, not some stupid job. Can you imagine Shloka and Casper without you?"

I knew Moksh's tricks very well by now. He was trying to make me feel guilty.

"I've arranged for my mother to help with Shloka, and as for Casper, the house help and the dog walker will take care of him until I return," I said sternly.

"An IT company will hire you and send you to Paris? All this without any prior work experience?" Girish said all of a sudden.

I nodded.

"This is unbelievable. It must be a scam," Girish muttered.

Moksh laughed again.

"I don't know why you want to do this. Is money so important to you?" Moksh argued.

"It's not about the money, Moksh," I said, hoping to convince him.

"Tell me, how much do you want? What are they paying you? I'll pay you the same."

"I'll try for a while. It's a tech job; it's not my forte. I doubt I'll even survive more than a month," I lied.

"I'll think about it," Moksh said, looking straight at me.

I felt horrified. Was this how it felt to be a slave? Maybe I was half slave, bound only with imaginary ropes in these modern times. I couldn't do anything without his permission. I would be tracked down if I left. My opinion didn't exist. His word was the last word. I lived in fear every day, not wanting to get on his bad side. If I did, there would be consequences. He'd go mental on me—not that he would beat me up voluntarily for no reason. The beatings would only come when I wanted to escape his piercing words and his taunting ways. He'd pour out his joy and his sorrow until the wee hours of the morning. When my body and mind felt drained and wanted to rest, then would come the climax. He'd turn on me and lash out, blaming all his troubles on me. Then came the beatings, and then his urge for sex. I was tormented both physically and mentally. However, I still felt the need to smile at my help, who came to work happily every morning, knowing that she too had a similar story. The only difference was that I was living in a bigger home, had a car to drive around, and had parties to go to. But these came at a cost: my career, my freedom, and an expectation to bear the violent behavior for the sake of family dignity.

Things started to become more tense at home. Moksh wasn't very pleased with the idea of me becoming independent again. I pressed on, deceiving him with my cheerful demeanor.

"So you've made up your mind about this job?" he asked one evening.

"Yes, Moksh. I really want to do this."

"You don't know how this world works. They'll use you and kick you out in no time."

Even though I knew this was not true, I didn't dare to disagree with Moksh.

"Yes, I know. I won't last too long there. I have no experience."

Moksh smiled. He loved it when I showed no confidence and felt proud of me when I portrayed myself as weak and vulnerable.

"Well, don't say I didn't warn you."

I looked at Moksh in disbelief.

"I'll need to start work next week." The words left my mouth instantly, my brain processing that his last phrase meant that I could take up the job.

"Just make sure your mother is not in my face and that your priority remains taking care of us, not your stupid job."

I couldn't believe it. Finally, Moksh had agreed. It felt like I was being released from a cage. My tightened nerves relaxed, and I was dancing on the inside.

The next day, I signed the job contract. The weeks after were devoted to the preparation of papers for my visa. The company travel agent had sent me a list of documents to furnish. One of them was called a "no objection letter." It had to be signed by Moksh. My heart sank. I needed him to be in a good mood again to sign these papers. I called Susan.

"There goes my new job," I wailed. "I don't think he's going to do it. I feel terrible."

"What the fuck? They need your husband's signature for you to travel?"

"Unfortunately, that's reality, since I've been a housewife and have no income."

"It's outrageous! Which century are we living in? Why doesn't a man need a woman's signature when he travels?" Susan yelled on the other end of the phone. "Be extremely nice to him the next few days. Do whatever it takes. Get him to sign, and don't give up so easily."

***

The next evening, I took the papers to Moksh. I couldn't bear the suspense—I wanted to get it over with. *I either go to Paris, or I don't.* A wicked smile came upon his face as he read the document.

"Interesting—you cannot go anywhere without my permission."

My stomach flipped. He looked at me, then picked up the pen and brought it to the place on the paper where it read, "Yours sincerely." I held my breath.

Suddenly, he put the pen down.

"I'll need to think hard about this," he said. "It's not a joke, going to Paris. You'll be on your own."

My heart sank. I'd almost had my freedom.

"No, Moksh, I'll be with the whole team," I said hastily.

"Which team? What are their names?"

My team was made up of men. Prema and I were the only women.

"Natalie, Valerie, Amelie, Sylvie, Prema, and me," I lied. I had uttered the names of all the women characters in my French textbook.

"I don't know why you want to do this. It doesn't make any sense to me," Moksh continued, trying to dissuade me. "You have the responsibility of our family. We should be your priority and not some fucking job."

"Please, Moksh. I promise, I'll forget about this job once I'm back."

"I'll think about it," he said in a stern voice, and went straight to his room. I heard him turn his door lock twice.

I felt angry that he didn't care about my feelings. I had pleaded for my freedom, but he had shown no mercy. Tears started to roll down my cheeks. I went into Shloka's room and curled up next to her. She was fast asleep, unaware what was happening in my life.

***

The next morning, I served breakfast to Moksh. Ratna was on leave, and I was in the worst mood ever. I fried *poori* carelessly and angrily dumped all the ingredients of the chutney into the mixer and ran it. As I assembled them on the plate, I noticed the *pooris* were puffy and golden in color. The chutney tasted the best I had ever made. Moksh asked for another serving. I felt angrier; he didn't deserve anything good from me. The papers were still lying on the table, waiting to be signed. I had made sure to keep a pen next to them, in case he changed his mind. After a while, Moksh left for work, and I got busy cleaning and cooking for the rest of the day. It was only when Shloka came home and I served her a snack that my eyes fell upon the scribbled signature on the document. I couldn't believe it.

"Thank you," I texted.

"I signed because I love you," Moksh texted back.

I felt happy and sad at the same time. This kind of love I didn't understand. I wanted to run away to a place he couldn't find me.

Maybe Paris would be that place. I could stay there and never return. There were complications, of course. I needed the company to hire me into the Paris team and have me on the French payroll. They would never do that, as they were outsourcing the job to India to reduce costs. Even if they did, I couldn't take Shloka and Casper with me. Moksh would never allow that. For now, I knew that my freedom would last only for a month, and I needed to make the most of it.

***

Our office was situated on the fifteenth floor of a tall building in Paris. Our manager, Mr. Bernard, who had interviewed me, welcomed me alongside another employee called Prema, who had been recruited at the same time. We had chatted on the flight to Paris, and I had discovered that she was born in Pondicherry, which had been a long-time French colony. Her grandfather had served in the French army during World War I, and thus the whole family was offered French citizenship. Prema was born in India, though, and completed all of her studies there before leaving for France to take up this job.

Mr. Bernard introduced us to the other four members of the team.

"This is Abdel. He is your team leader and will be seeing to it that you are trained on all the necessary applications."

A tall man with dark, curly hair greeted us. "*Bonjour, enchanté*!"

"*Enchanté*!" we chorused.

"I hope you had a good flight yesterday. I will assign you your desks in five minutes, and then we will start the training. Please do not hesitate if you have any questions. Er...one more thing—here are your access badges."

The day passed quickly. We absorbed a ton of information. Abdel explained everything that was expected of us in his heavy French accent, with special attention to our role as backend IT support staff.

In order for the banking application to work efficiently, there were some processes that needed to be carried out at different times of the day. "It's a step-by-step process, quite simple," he had said. And it was. We monitored the bank's servers; opened, modified, and deleted accounts for users; ran health checks on applications before bank transactions took place; executed scripts; and resolved all problems related to the applications we were handling. It all sounded complex at the beginning, but with procedures put in place and a little practice, we had mastered our job in no time. I couldn't imagine a housewife like me could manage a job like this.

***

Every day after work, I visited a new place. Musée du Louvre, Arc de Triomphe, Champs-Élysées, Sacré-Cœur, Château de Versailles, Musée d'Orsay, Montmartre, Jardin des Tuileries, Jardin du Luxembourg, Place de la Concorde, Tour Montparnasse, and many other famous places in Paris. There was never a banal day. I felt free in this city of love. My heart sang as I heard an accordion play at the corner of my street. My soul swam with joy as I cruised along the Seine. My stomach grumbled as I smelled whiffs of bread from the *boulangerie*. My senses tingled with every sip of the wine. It was magical.

I had also settled very well at work. The managers were content with my progress.

I called my mother daily and spoke to her and Shloka.

"Mama, when are you coming back?" Shloka asked in her sweetest voice.

I knew she was feeling restless without me. I could hear Casper's barks in the background too. I wanted to teleport them into this new life of mine. However, I knew this wasn't going to last long.

"Very soon, my love," I said.

I missed them. Three weeks had passed like the blink of an eye. I had seven more days of this beautiful life, then I would go back to my nightmarish life with Moksh. I knew very well that he would never, ever let me go anywhere again. I could sense over calls that he had become growingly irritable at my absence.

"The cook hasn't come today. Do I work or take care of the house?"

Another day he had complained, "I can't have you go away like this. Shloka is down with a fever. Don't you feel a little bit of responsibility toward us?"

Moksh wanted me to feel guilty for not being there and caring for Shloka, but I knew my mother would care for her in the best way. His impatience grew by the day, but there was one thing I had learned in the last few weeks of staying away from him: I was at peace. I felt no fear. No stress—other than when Moksh called. I was sure I would do much better without him in my life. But things were complicated. Our lives were entwined. Shloka and Casper needed both of us. I buried all of my dreams deep inside me and readied myself to return to India.

***

The last day in Paris, Prema and I wrapped up our work and cleaned our desks. My eyes were still heavy. As the day of my departure neared, I had begun to have nightmares. They had prevented me from sleeping for a few nights. I dreamt that Moksh was chasing me with a dagger in his hand. In another dream, he had chained me to a post, held me by my hair, and was threatening to immolate me. I couldn't function. Our meetings that day had been longer than usual. Later that evening, the team threw a leaving party for us. I felt exhausted, both emotionally and physically, as the taxi halted at my hotel. I glanced at my watch. It was midnight. I had enough time to reach the airport. Our flight was in four hours.

I pushed the main door of the hotel, which usually gave way immediately. But at this hour, it was locked. I rang the bell that was positioned on the wall on the right side of the door. There was no answer. Through the glass door, I could see the dimly lit area of the reception. I looked for Monsieur Ducousso, the evening receptionist. He always wore his round-framed spectacles on the edge of his nose. His black bow tie and suspenders couldn't be missed. For some reason, he didn't seem to be there that evening. I rang again and waited. Still no answer. As the minutes passed, I started to panic. *What if I cannot make it to the airport on time? How could I explain to Moksh? I'm such a terrible mother. Shloka and Casper must be so looking forward to having me back.* After trying for a quarter hour, I grew desperate. I banged hard on the door with my hand. Still no answer.

CHAPTER 7
The Revelation

Bangalore, India
September 2013

After I languished in my misery for another twenty minutes, the new receptionist, who had fallen asleep on the desk hurried to unlock the door. I eventually managed to get my flight on time and fly back to India.

I could smell earth as I walked through the gardens and up the stairs to my apartment. The September rains had rendered Bangalore cooler. I heard the loud barks of Casper as I rang the doorbell. Ratna's footsteps approached the door. As it gave way, Casper pounced on me in excitement. I lowered myself to him. His tongue rolled all over my face and his tail wagged furiously, showing me how much he had missed me. I felt eternally blessed to have him in my life. Ratna took the luggage to my room. I quickly showered, dressed in a Kanchipuram saree and drove to Dinesh's wedding. A mutual friend of Moksh and Aarav's was tying the knot with a girl his family had chosen.

"It's Mama, it's Mama…." I heard the high-pitched voice of Shloka as I waded through the crowded hall. Her face lit up the minute she saw me. I was filled with emotions. Bear hugs followed. I felt she had grown an inch taller in just a month.

"You've got a glow on your face," Moksh said and grinned at me.

"It must be the air in France," I told him.

But deep down, I knew it was the freedom that I had experienced that had made me happy—and thus the glow.

Susan, Pooja, Bhavika, and a few other friends came to my side to inquire about my French adventure. I recounted my work, my evenings at the museums, the monuments, the food, the wine… everything.

***

The wedding festivities came to an end after a few days. Moksh's cheerfulness disappeared as we settled into routine. I started work at Société Générale as an outsourced employee of Alten Calsoft Labs. I put into use everything I had learned in Paris. On the first day, I returned home at eight o'clock. Moksh was furious.

"What's for dinner?" he asked when he saw me, very clearly implying that my duties remained in caring for the family first.

Bless Ratna, I thought. Upon my request, she had made vegetable korma with ghee rice for dinner.

I served it onto a plate and took it to Moksh, who had comfortably settled in front of the television, watching the replay of the Formula One race.

"I can't eat this. Please make me some *chapati* and tomato *gojju*."

I went back into the kitchen to please his palate. As the onions sizzled in the pan, I added the chopped tomatoes and reminisced of my time in Paris. There, I had felt free as the wind blew through my hair. I'd confidently walked the city's streets to explore its *crêperies*, cafés, and its gourmet restaurants. The *boulangerie* was always a quick solution to my hunger.

I was now back to reality. My back hurt as I stood roasting the *chapati* on both sides. The day had been long. I folded the *chapatis* and slid them onto a plate. I ladled the tomato *gojju* on the side and took it to Moksh.

He ate one *chapati* of the three I had made, then washed his hands and came back to continue watching television.

I asked, concerned, "What happened Moksh? Is it not tasty?"

"I'm not hungry anymore."

I felt frustrated. I knew he was going to make my life hell for going away. This was just the beginning.

"I'm tired Moksh. I think I'll go to bed," I said, and left.

***

The next morning, I woke up to my alarm. I went into Shloka's room to wake her up for school. Then I went to the kitchen to make some tea to get my day started. Casper followed. As I filled the kettle with water, I noticed the empty fish bowl in the kitchen sink. Both fishes were lying dead next to it. I was horrified. Moksh had emptied the fishbowl as a warning. I couldn't believe it.

From that day on, I was more than determined to keep my job. Moksh tried to torture me in every way possible. He tapped ashes from his cigarettes on the floor. He knew that I hated a dirty house. He piled his soiled clothes on the floor instead of in the laundry bin. He forced me to stay awake in the night knowing very well I had to go to office the next day. Despite of all of Moksh's efforts to destroy my peace of mind, I persisted and soon celebrated a year at Société Générale.

That same evening, Moksh's old friend Nitesh and his wife, Meera, invited us to their home for dinner. The couple were warm and friendly even though I was meeting them for the first time. Once we settled down in their living room, I noticed how tastefully they had decorated their home. Moksh had told me that they were in the furniture business, but I had no idea how beautiful their designs looked until now. To my surprise, they served me wine. Moksh started to tell them all about my trip to Paris.

"I'm so proud of my wifey," he said, and kissed my hand.

I felt confused. Moksh was a different person when we were alone. He had tried every way of dissuading me from work. And now, he was putting me on a pedestal in front of his friends. Nitesh and Meera recounted their travels around the world.

"Let's have dinner," Meera said, and led us to a massive dining table that sat next to the kitchen. The table looked like it was carved out of a single log. Delicious aromas drifted toward us. My stomach let out a small growl. She had cooked her native specialty, *appam* and stew. It was delicious. I asked her for the recipe so I could try it at home.

***

It was almost midnight when we left. As soon as we were alone in the car, Moksh seemed to be enraged. I didn't understand what had happened between their front door and the car, but there was certainly a change in his attitude.

Moksh showed his agitation when he turned onto the highway without reducing his speed and almost crashed into the car in front of us.

"Paris...you went to Paris, you selfish bitch, and had fun. How dare you leave Shloka and me alone."

My heart sank. It was going to be another night of terror.

"Your stupid job, it's not worth anything. They throw you some silly amount of money, and you suddenly think you're worth something. You're nothing but a piece of shit!"

He was yelling at me while holding my right arm tightly and controlling the steering wheel with the other. My eyes welled and tears streamed down my cheeks.

"I will destroy your life if you continue working."

I was shouting at the top of my voice when he barely missed hitting the divider. "Stop...please stop the car, Moksh! You're going to crash!"

He slowed down, then brought the car to a halt.

"Get out, get outttttt, you fucking bitch!"

I couldn't stand to be in the car for one more minute. I nearly fell when he accelerated and sped off. I hadn't even shut the door. I simply stood there and sobbed uncontrollably, not realizing the immediate danger I was in. Momentarily, I felt safer outside than when I was with Moksh in the car. I gathered myself and looked around. It was not a very safe hour for women to be out.

I closed my eyes and whispered to the universe, "Please, help me make my way home safely." Heavy trucks passed by closely and the ground under my feet shuddered. The place was familiar. I had driven on this road many times. It would take me at least twenty-five minutes to reach home, even if I walked as fast as I could.

I needed to find something I could use as a weapon in case someone attacked me. I picked up a sharp-edged stone that laid beside a bush on the sidewalk. I held it tight in my hand and continued to walk. My tears had dried. Fear left me, and anger set in with a vengeance.

Finally, I turned toward the long lane that led to my apartment. A man in rags sat on the pavement of the street. He seemed to be inebriated and mumbling something in the dark. I slowed down and cautiously watched him from the corner of my eye. He stood up and started to walk toward me. My heart sank. I started to run as fast as I could. After a few seconds I turned to see if he was running too. He walked a few steps, then fell flat, the pavement meeting his face and body. I heard his voice.

"*Thoda paisa dena chai ke liye*, madam," he pleaded. He was asking for some money for tea in Hindi.

I turned away and ran toward the apartment at full speed. The security guard looked shocked when he opened the gates for me. I let out a sigh of relief as I walked up the stairs, slowly opened the door, and stepped in. Holding my breath, I tiptoed through the living room, which was illuminated by the moonlight pouring through the windows. Moksh's loud snores assured me that he was fast asleep.

Casper was sitting next to Shloka's empty bed. I had packed Shloka off to my mother's house knowing well that we were going to be home late that night. Casper realized that I was back and started to tap his tail on the floor with excitement.

"Shhhhh...Casper, I love you too. For now, I need you to stop making noise," I whispered into his ears and kissed him. I shut the bedroom door and settled on Shloka's bed. I was hurting badly. I wanted to pack my bags and leave with them both. To Paris, or any part of the world where I wouldn't hear the name *Moksh*. Then I imagined myself being handcuffed and taken to prison on the grounds of kidnapping. I couldn't take Shloka anywhere without Moksh's permission. He had threatened to destroy me if I left him, and I knew he would go to any length to do that. I felt bitter. I looked at the time on my phone. It was almost two in the morning. I needed to get some sleep before I went to work the next day. I had volunteered for an important task to be carried out in the office. Prema was on her annual leave, and the team in Paris was counting on me. Thoughts kept flowing, but at some point, I fell asleep.

A wet slurp woke me in the morning. It was Casper. He had his two front legs on the bed and was nudging my arm so that I could caress him. I buried all my emotions. Moksh was still asleep when I showered and left for work.

On my way, I called Susan and recounted the whole episode.

"Do you realize how dangerous that was? There's one rape every thirty minutes in India," she said, outraged, when I was finished.

"I know. It's absolutely unsafe for me to continue like this. But what can I do?"

"What is Moksh's problem? Why is he torturing you?" Her voice sounded concerned from the other end of the phone.

"It's because I'm working and I'm financially independent. He doesn't like it and fears that I won't be his slave anymore."

"That's ridiculous! I'm sure it's not that. There certainly is something else that's bothering him. You've had a lot of patience with him. He has been like this since the time you married. I don't see him changing. You've got to do something."

"Susan, I have two amazing angels who wake up every day and look up to me. I can't let them down. Shloka is doing very well at school and golf. Casper is quite used to his life with us. If I rock the boat now, their perfect world will come tumbling down. I saw what effect it had on Shloka last time. Moreover, broken families have repercussions on kids. The problem is between Moksh and me. He hates that I am working. I can't let Shloka suffer because of our problems."

"I agree, but you also have to realize that you have been lucky to survive so far. What if something happens to you tomorrow? What will Shloka and Casper do without you?"

Susan was right. Maybe I had taken my life for granted. I had lived through these episodes each time without realizing that if something awful happened to me, my parents and my children would be devastated. I decided not to speak to Moksh until I had found a workable solution.

After a few weeks of silence, I confronted him.

"I don't want you to work," Moksh said. "I get upset when you don't prioritize our family."

"But Shloka and Casper *are* my priority. Always," I protested. "Just because I work doesn't mean that I am neglecting them. I am coordinating with my mother all the time so that Shloka doesn't miss any of her classes. Apart from that, I like my job, and I feel better when I work. Shloka will grow up to be a confident girl if she grows up seeing me work."

"She doesn't need to earn anything. There is enough wealth for her and her future generations. Moreover, I don't like your mother filling in for you." Moksh's voice was filled with contempt.

I worked hard to keep my voice calm and unagitated. "Why don't you wake up early and help me get her ready for school, or come back early and be with her until I return? Why don't *you* fill in for me? She is as much your responsibility as mine."

"A woman is supposed to stay at home and take care of the family. It's a man's job to work and bring home money."

"We are not living in the stone age, Moksh," I said in a disgusted voice.

"I know," he laughed. "But sweetheart, I want to hold you in my arms when I wake up in the morning. The house is so empty without you. That's why I get upset every day. Both Shloka and Casper need you. I'll change for the better. I promise. Please do this for the family. Let's work together as a team, to make a beautiful future for Shloka."

I hated him. I was done fighting. I surrendered. All I wanted was peace of mind. I wasn't convinced, but if Moksh would stop torturing me for working, it was worth a shot. I put in my papers that week, against everyone else's wishes.

***

In a few months, I felt as bored as the furniture in my house. My financial dependency on Moksh made him feel powerful. He expected that I would be a submissive wife and bear all of his tantrums. The nights were the toughest to endure. The violent sex lasted for hours. My body became sore and bled from his bites. It was a sort of known but unspoken slavery, and I started to lash out. Eventually, I knew I had to get back to being a working woman, otherwise I was sure to lose my mind. Moksh was irked again with my retaliation.

My parents moved closer to where we lived in order to help with Shloka and Casper and also ensure our safety. Susan soon found me a job in the company where she worked. It was a French-speaking role again. To my surprise, I had succeeded in all three rounds of interviews.

***

On my first day of work, my voice trembled as I spoke to Susan at her desk and recounted every bit of what had happened the previous night. Moksh had turned violent again. Shloka had fussed about staying with her grandmother, and thankfully she didn't witness this horrific episode. Moksh picked up an argument about me working. He held me by my hair and slammed my face to the wall, but I wasn't willing to take it lying down. I grabbed the ash tray that was within grasp and banged it on Moksh's head. He howled before letting go of me. He disappeared for a few seconds before coming back with the new laptop that the company had given me to bring to work.

"*No!*" I screamed.

Before I knew it, he had broken it into two and threw it on the floor.

I felt anger raging within me. I needed to get away from Moksh. I picked up the broken pieces of the laptop, locked myself in the guest room, and bawled my eyes out.

I heard Moksh's voice just outside the room. "I'm sorry." He tried to get in, but I had latched the door securely from the inside.

"Leave me alone," I yelled.

"Open the door, sweetie," he insisted.

I kept silent. After a few seconds, I heard a loud thud on the door. Frightened, I covered my ears with my hands. It sounded like he was trying to break open the door. I needed to act quickly. After a few minutes, the place went silent. I tiptoed toward the door and peeped through the keyhole. Moksh was pacing around the living room with a dumbbell in his hand. I had to do something to stop him. It was five in the morning. I called my neighbor's phone, and to my luck, she answered. I explained my situation and asked if she could intervene. After a few minutes, I heard the doorbell ring. I also heard Moksh open the door and apologize to a male voice. *It must be my neighbor's husband*, I thought. *Bless them!*

To my luck, I heard Moksh's footsteps trail off toward his room. After an hour, I gathered courage and stepped out of the guest room. I turned to see the damage on the door. The wood had given way to form a large crater in the middle. I felt disgusted. I had accepted and learned to live with this violence without realizing the trauma it was causing me.

Susan spoke to the management and told them everything. They replaced the laptop and let me keep my job. That evening, I returned to pack all our belongings and move to my parents' house. Shloka was in her room. I spoke to her and said that we would be moving temporarily to Granny's house.

"Mama, please.... I want to stay here with Casper."

"We'll take him too."

I could see tears fill her eyes.

"I want to live here and visit Grandma. I love my room, my bed, and my toys. Please don't take me away again."

I winced. It was hard to explain to Shloka our situation. She was not even eight.

I went to see Moksh. He was sitting in the living room, deep in thought. He apologized and asked if we could go to see a counselor. Maybe it was the tears in his eyes I could not bear to see, or the fact that a move would make Shloka unstable again, or my belief in a *whole* family—it all made me want to hang on to this marriage. *I'm a fool if I believe his words again*, I said to myself. Finally, I gave in to his pleading.

From then on, we went to counseling sessions two days a week, for two entire months. Sometimes, thoughts flowed from the darkest part of my mind. My fear that this wouldn't work rolled freely in and out of my consciousness. But all the while, I could also clearly see a picture of a happy family: Shloka, Casper, Moksh, and myself smiling brightly in a frame. I had read the success stories linked with counseling. It might just be what we needed. I noticed changes in Moksh. He started helping with everyday chores. He would willingly take Casper for his walk and shop for groceries for the week. He took Shloka for her golf lessons and managed to spend time with me too. It had been the best six months of our lives together...until one night.

Moksh seemed restless after we spent an evening at Girish and Vimala's home. Susan, Pooja, and the rest of the group were there too. The kids, now a dozen of them, were all excited to be together. We had finished dinner and hung around playing cards way past midnight. Moksh had lost all hands.

Around 2:00 a.m., we said our goodbyes and left. Moksh asked me to take the wheel. I obeyed. I buckled Shloka at the back and began to drive. I was annoyed at the bird poop on the glass, so I pushed the lever that sat on the right of the steering wheel to wipe it away. The wiper blades screeched dryly on the windshield. I had forgotten to use the wash option. Moksh raged with anger.

"Stop the car, you imbecile," he screamed. "Get out!"

I brought the car to a halt. "I'm sorry, Moksh, I got that wrong. Calm down."

"Don't you dare tell me to calm down. You've only caused me misery since I married you."

Worried that this was on the verge of becoming one of the dreadful nights, I looked at Shloka through the rearview mirror to see if she was asleep. She was wide awake with a look of anxiousness on her face.

"No! Get out this instant, you bitch."

"Please, Moksh, try to understand," I pleaded in a hoarse voice.

The next thing I knew, he held my arm and started to twist it furiously.

Shloka began to howl in her seat.

"I beg you, please don't do this—not with Shloka here."

Moksh's screeching voice sent shivers down my spine. "*Get out!*

I opened the door and got out. Tears filled my eyes. I had hoped in vain that Moksh would change for the better.

"Take your daughter with you," he yelled from the lowered window, to my dismay.

I turned pale.

"Why Shloka? What has she done?" I asked and saw Shloka's frightened face through the window. She immediately unbuckled her seatbelt and jumped out of the car. We almost fell as Moksh sped away. I carried her in my arms and tried to calm her down. I could feel my inner soul dying; how could I have allowed this to happen?

Moksh had put me in vulnerable situations before. I had forgiven him. This time, not only had he put me in danger, but Shloka too. I had to do something quick.

Damn! I don't even have my telephone with me, I thought.

I had put Shloka's change of clothes bag, Moksh's laptop bag, and my handbag together into the trunk, thinking we wouldn't need it and that we'd be reaching home in no time.

"We'll make it through this. Hold onto me tightly," I said, then kissed Shloka on her forehead.

We walked a little before we found a police constable manning the street.

"What are you doing here, madam, at this hour?" he inquired with a look of shock on his face.

I explained the situation to him and asked him if he could find us a transport home. He quickly hailed an auto rickshaw for us and noted down the details of the driver. I put Shloka on my lap and held her tight. She looked at me, wanting to know if everything was alright. I was worried to death, but I smiled and said we were going to be fine. The auto rickshaw sped through the highway. Trucks lined the streets. I could see little crowds gathered around the tea vendors. As we passed them, I tightened my arms around Shloka. I prayed intensely in my mind to the universe to take us back home safely, and we reached the apartment a little before 3:00 a.m. I hugged Shloka and let out a huge sigh of relief once inside.

"We made it. I'll never let any harm come over you again, sweetheart," I said with tears rolling down my cheeks.

"Let's take Casper and go to Grandma's home. We'll be safe there," Shloka said.

"Yes, darling. We are going to do exactly that."

It was a blessing that my parents had moved a few steps away from our home. They were afraid that Moksh would hurt me again, and they were right in thinking so. He had done something unimaginable that day.

We went to the parking lot in the basement of our building, but Moksh's car wasn't there. *Where could he be at this hour after abandoning us?* I thought. I took the spare keys from security and hurried up the stairs. I opened the door and rushed to leash Casper, who had just begun to wag his tail. I went into Shloka's room to find her teddy bear that she couldn't do without, then darted toward the wardrobe to pick up our passports. I tried to open the door, but it was locked. I couldn't remember where I had put the keys. I started to perspire—I didn't have time. He would be here any minute. I started to shake both the doors furiously. Finally, they gave way. I pulled open the drawer and found our passports, and I gathered everything that was vital into a sack. I paused and took one look around me. I had spent a ton of my time here trying to keep my family together, but it was over. I would never come back here. There was nothing left for us.

"Mama, hurry up," Shloka said, standing in the living room with Casper.

Suddenly, we heard the door click open. It was Moksh. Fear gripped me. I could see Shloka's hands tremble.

He walked in and sat on the black reclining couch after shutting the door behind him. He seemed calm. Then the words came.

"I can never forgive you. You didn't give me a son!"

Moksh's confession caught me by surprise. I couldn't believe this was true, even if it was. That anger and resentment toward me finally made sense. His revelation, however shocking, finally made me understand why he treated me like he did. I never knew he felt this way. Now I understood that I was being punished because I had given birth to a girl child. How could I fathom that? There had been a certain disappointment that I had been incapable of producing a male child, and I was being tortured, time and again, by my husband for this insufficiency.

Everything came back to me—the last stains of sunset that had disappeared when I lifted the dead baby and dropped her forthwith on the shore. I ran away from her, holding my fears within, hoping it was a bad dream that I would never return to. And now, after twenty-nine years, I was experiencing the same frightful human behavior.

Shloka tugged my arm toward the door.

Moksh continued, "My father mistreats me because I don't have a son who can take his legacy forward. You are my curse. I want you to get out and never come back."

I held Shloka's hand and walked towards the door. Casper followed.

"Wait!" Moksh yelled. "You will leave. Shloka and Casper will stay with me."

Shloka started to tug at my arm more vigorously. I held her closer and slipped the bag that held our precious passports around my neck and arm so that it sat tight on my body. Slowly, I inched towards the door.

"I repeat, Shloka and Casper will stay with me."

"You monster!" I yelled as I locked eyes with him. I felt anger rise within me.

He laughed. "Your nanny duties are over. Get out, you piece of shit."

I ignored him and walked ahead with Shloka.

Moksh rushed to my side and started to twist my arm.

"I'm not leaving without them," I said aloud as my heart raced and my body trembled.

Suddenly, he grabbed my throat. "You know you're still alive because I love you."

"Let me go," I said as I tried to push him away. I couldn't stand his breath on my face. He tightened his grip on my neck with every passing second. Shloka wailed as I gasped for breath. The lights blurred, and the surroundings started to fade. Moksh finally loosened the pressure on my neck, and I fell forward. I could hear the screams of Shloka and Casper's loud barks as I regained consciousness. Moksh grabbed my hair and pushed my back against the door. I could see Shloka, tall, up to his waist, punching him with all her might. Casper was tugging at the bottom of Moksh's left trouser with his teeth. I felt too weak to defend myself. Just then, he unlocked the door and pushed me out. I coughed as I took in a few breaths. Then, gathering all my strength, I began to bang on the door. After a few seconds, the door opened and Shloka ran out, still howling with Casper close behind. Holding Shloka in one hand and Casper's leash in the other, I ran as fast as I could to the block where my parents lived. Strangely, I felt a sense of calm even though I was in the midst of a storm. I had left no stone unturned in trying to make this marriage work. I rang the bell. My father opened the door. A look of horror mixed with anger came across his face. He pulled Shloka into his arms and hugged me.

"Everything's going to be fine. I'll handle Moksh if he comes here," he said and shut the door behind us.

My father's words made me feel secure. Shloka searched my eyes for answers, but I could only smile reassuringly. We were safe, and that's all that mattered.

***

Moksh didn't show up that night, and the next day, I went to meet a lawyer.

"You must file a case of domestic violence immediately," he said. "After that, you can file for divorce, child custody, and make sure both you get financial support and your daughter gets child support."

"How long would all this take?" I asked, feeling a little overwhelmed.

The lawyer opened a big file and showed me cases of women still waiting for maintenance after two years. I couldn't believe it. How was a woman to survive with her child under these circumstances?

I consulted another lawyer.

"Do you think your husband will contest the divorce?" she asked.

"Yes, I'm more than certain he will."

"This is a long-haul battle then. I'll try my best, but you must understand that it could take up to seven years or maybe longer for the divorce to come through."

Shloka would be the center of this battle. Child custody, visiting rights, holidays...everything needs to be sorted out, I thought. I had two choices: either I could waste several years of my life fighting a legal battle, or I could work on building my career.

From the next day onward, we began our new life. My parents made sure that Shloka didn't miss school and Casper didn't miss his walks, and I went to work as I had done before. Moksh called to apologize. I never wanted to see him again. I blocked his number. He followed me and threatened that if I did not go back, he would ruin my life. I wanted to disappear at will. A magical wand or a cloak that made me invisible would have come in handy.

"You must leave this place," my sister suggested.

"Leave? Where to? Are you crazy?"

"Study further, maybe do an MBA. Or learn anything that you are passionate about. This will keep you safe and bring you better opportunities."

"You are forgetting that I have a responsibility to Shloka and Casper."

"Shloka is older now, and quite independent. Casper can surely stay without you."

"What if Moksh hurts Shloka?"

"He won't. His anger is toward you and not Shloka. He wants to make you suffer, not her. If he hurts you, he wins. If he hurts Shloka, he gets nothing."

Everything my sister said made sense.

"True. I could look at doing something in Mumbai or Delhi."

"Are you out of your mind? Moksh will still have access to you. Leave! Just go so far away that it makes it difficult for him to get to you."

"But how could I leave Shloka and Casper? What if there's an emergency?"

"We're here for you. We'll do everything in our capacity to be there for Shloka and Casper."

"I know, and I don't doubt that at all. Let's say I do decide to leave—how do I pay for everything? My finances are almost zero."

"We'll support you," said her husband, Nikhil. He had just overheard our conversation and come into the living room. "Think about it: Moksh will continue to trouble you if you stay in Bangalore. He has already threatened you. It isn't safe for you here."

It was true. I didn't feel secure in this city.

"We'll support you in every way," said Nikhil. My parents and sister nodded too.

"Think about your career; don't worry about anything else now," Megha said. "After lunch, let's sit and look up what you'd like to study and where."

"Maybe France. I always wanted to go back there."

"That's a brilliant idea! You could study an MBA while immersing yourself in the language itself."

My sister was right. Before our meal, we looked up master's programs in France. I scrolled down the list: finance, electronics, information technology, aeronautics...wine. I stopped.

"That's the one for me; I could do an MBA in wine," I said confidently. "I have studied wine all along in my hospitality and language studies."

Megha nodded in excitement.

***

During the next few weeks, I applied to schools in Bordeaux. I knew this region was world-famous for its wines. Soon I received an acceptance letter from INSEEC. The mood was mixed with both cheer and worry at home. We all wondered how Shloka would fare without me for a year or more. I explained to her that I loved her to the moon and back and that I had to leave for some time.

"I have to do this for us," I said as she hugged me and sobbed uncontrollably. I felt devastated. How could I do this to her? She was only nine years old. Her world had been torn apart. Her father had turned crazy, and now I was leaving her. My mother consoled her.

"Mama's got to do this for you. She will be back soon. Until then, let's have fun, you and I. I'll cook everything you like. I promise!"

There was something magical about Ambika and Shloka's bond. I had less to worry about when my mother was around. I trusted that my mother would care for her much more than I did. As for Casper, I didn't know how to make him understand. He sat next to my suitcase as I packed. Maybe he knew. I hoped he'd understand. My parents were still grieving the loss of their dog, Milo. Now Casper had replaced him. I asked myself time and again if it was the right thing to do. There was something within me, that inner voice, that kept asking me to surrender myself to this new path and trust the universe.

The day of leaving arrived. I had tears in my eyes when I kissed Shloka and Casper goodbye. My heart was pounding—so much was at stake. But I knew I had to do this. I closed my eyes, prayed to the universe to keep them safe, and left on my new voyage.

CHAPTER 8
Bordeaux

Bordeaux, France
February 2017

A feeling of freedom mixed with anxiousness had taken over me as the plane took off. I was leaving my family, Shloka, and Casper behind. I would be very far away from them, in a completely different part of the world. What if there was an emergency? Would they be alright without me? Was my sacrifice of staying away from them going to be worth it? I wrestled with my thoughts. I had promised them I would change our lives for the better, so there was no turning back.

I finally reached Paris and took a connecting flight to Bordeaux. As the airplane neared its destination, I peeped through the little window and saw a silver line that curved and stretched for miles. I had read about the famous Gironde estuary that divided the region into three parts. A rush of excitement zipped through my body. A new life was waiting for me down there.

After landing, I went straight to the immigration check. The line was long, but I waited patiently. When my turn came, I handed over the necessary documents. The officer looked at me to verify that I was the same woman in the photo on my passport. When he reached for the stamp, my heart skipped a beat. It was all in his hands; he could let me stay and begin a new life, or send me back to where I came from. The sound of the stamp going down on paper drowned the voices in the room.

"*Bonne journée, madame, au revoir*!" he said, handing back the documents.

I was overjoyed. I soon hailed a taxi and was on my way to my Airbnb host's home.

My room was warm and welcoming. A single bed was placed in the center, while a work desk sat in one corner of the room. A tall wardrobe stood next to the entrance, and diagonally opposite the door were windows that opened onto the street. My host, Conor, instructed me on how to close the shutters and turn on the heater. I noticed a picture of a lady that hung just above the bed. She seemed to look at me everywhere I went in the room.

"Here's the bathroom, whenever you fancy a hot shower," I heard Conor say. He was an Irishman living in Bordeaux. I had written to him from India to rent out a room. It was quite evident that he was used to foreign students frequenting his home for short Airbnb stays, since it was a stone's throw away from the wine school.

He walked from my room to the corridor that consisted of the bath and a separate toilet. I left my thoughts about the severe watchful lady and followed right behind. He walked me through the other parts of the apartment: the kitchen, the living room, his room, and a third bedroom that was soon to be occupied by another student.

"If you need anything, I'll be in the living room," he said.

He had placed a welcome note, along with the Wi-Fi code, on the bedside table. I left a message for my family in India and hit the bed straight away.

When I woke up the next day, it was still pitch dark. It felt like I had rested endlessly. *It must be a mistake*, I thought, and pulled my phone from underneath my pillow to check the time. It was almost lunchtime! The wooden shutter had blocked the sunlight completely from my room.

Energized, I jumped out of bed and pulled the shutters up to take a look outside. The blue sky was filled with flocks of birds moving toward the north. A bald tree stood next to my window. February was almost the end of winter. I knew in a few weeks I would see leaves sprout on this magnificent tree.

"Welcome to France!" I said to myself. The lady's face in the frame watched me intently. "Spooky," I muttered under my breath so she didn't hear. *A walk around the area to familiarize myself will do me some good,* I thought. *But first, I should ask Conor for a map of Bordeaux.*

I knocked on the door of the living room.

"Oh, come on in," Conor said in his cheerful voice.

He was lounging on the couch, reading a large hardback book titled *Herzog*.

"Hi there, did you sleep well?" he asked, putting the book down. "I thought I'd knock to offer you some breakfast but decided against it. I didn't want to disturb you."

"That's very kind of you, Conor. I slept very well, thank you."

"Well, that's excellent."

"I didn't quite realize what time it was, thanks to your shutters. I'm well rested."

"Oh, yeah, it's quite deceiving, isn't it?"

"Thought I'd take a walk around. Do you have a map that I could use?"

"Oh, I could show you around the city if you'd like. I need a walk anyway."

"That would be great," I said with excitement.

I dressed myself in the warmest pullover I had brought from India and slipped on my walking shoes. We were about to leave when Conor asked, "Are you sure you'll be alright in just that pink jumper? The temperature outside is about nine degrees Celsius."

I opened the door and felt the cold.

"Oh, don't worry—I'll be fine," I said.

We walked through the gardens of the community and out into the streets.

"All roads in this area are flat. Do you know why?" Conor asked.

I nodded as my teeth clattered loudly.

"Most wine merchants had their warehouses here, so when the ships came, they rolled their barrels on these very streets onto the quays, and then loaded them onto the ships that then sailed off to England."

After about ten minutes, we came to the quays that Conor had mentioned. I saw the Garonne grandly flowing across the city, just like I had seen in pictures earlier. Restaurants and cafés lined the riverside. People sauntered leisurely with their little dogs, some jogging, while a few others cycled along the water's edge. A skate park followed, where children of all ages zoomed around on wheels, practicing tricks. *This would be great for Shloka*, I thought. We strolled along and reached an area where many stalls were propped up alongside the river.

"It's the Sunday market," Conor said loudly so I could hear through all the noise.

People were selling meat, oysters, cheese, wine, and some Turkish delicacies. Conor stopped at one of the food stalls and bought some food to eat.

"You have to get one of these, Nam," he said, brandishing his purchase. "It's amazing. Five perfectly barbecued meats on a stick.

The perfect on-the-go snack for a cold day. I can feel the delicious fats and proteins insulating me already."

"Errr...no, thank you.... I'm not hungry," I said, almost wanting to throw up. I watched Conor walk the street with juices dripping down his chin as he loudly extolled the virtues of the various meats. I had long given up eating meat after my sister, Megha, had shown me the reality of the industry, but I enjoyed Conor's enthusiasm.

While we strode through the crowds, I noticed people glancing my way. I was the only one dressed in pink. I felt embarrassed. People all around me wore grey, black, and other winter colors. Where I came from, the sun shone bright all year long, and we rarely dressed according to seasons.

***

Conor finally finished raving about his meat stick and asked, "Would you like to go to a pub for a pint of beer?"

"I'd be delighted, but only if they can serve me some hot tea instead of beer. It'll warm me up."

Conor nodded at me with a perplexed look on his face. He didn't slow down though, just walked quickly toward his favorite Irish pub, The Connemara. On the way, Conor familiarized me with the various monuments around the city.

"Over there is the marvelous bridge, Pont de Pierre."

"How lovely to see it in real life," I said.

"And on the other side stands the Pont Jacques Chaban-Delmas. Both connect the left and right banks of the Garonne. If you look carefully, the stone bridge has seventeen arches that represent the number of letters in the name Napoleon Bonaparte, as it was first commissioned by him. The other bridge is a contemporary vertical-lift bridge, where the middle part is drawn up so that big ships can sail through easily."

"It would be cool to watch the bridge lift up," I said with excitement. "Where is Place de la Bourse?"

"Oh, well, that's a little ahead."

Just then, a tram passed by.

"There are three tram lines that cross the city. Lines A, B, and C. To get to my place, you'll need to take tram B. The center stop is Place des Quinconces. Every tram stop has a grey box where you can buy tickets, depending on your need. You could buy a full day ticket or just a single trip. But I don't want to confuse you. It's better I show you on the way back," Conor concluded as we reached a square.

"Voilà! Place de la Bourse. It's a classical French architectural delight of the eighteenth century."

On the other side of the street, across the square, I saw a long, elevated platform shrouded in a few meters of mist. On it were children running around in sheer excitement. I watched as tourists held their cameras still and worked to get their best shot of the city's liveliness.

"That's the Miroir d'eau—when the weather's better, you can see the reflection of the Place de la Bourse on the thin layer of water resting on the granite stone."

"Shloka would love this place," I said.

"Who's Shloka?" Conor asked, looking at me quizzically.

"She's my daughter."

"Marvellous! How old is she?"

"She's nine."

"Nam, you don't look like you have a nine-year-old daughter. Were you married off young?" Conor laughed.

"Not at all! I'll take that as a compliment Conor."

"Thank god!"

"Summers must be so much fun. Errr...what would be the temperature here around that time?" I asked, feeling hopeful.

"It ranges between twenty-five to thirty-five degrees, sort of."

"Phew! That sounds fabulous," I said as I rubbed my hands together to warm myself.

"Oh God, I should have given you a jacket."

"Don't worry, I'm fine."

We turned into an alley, and Conor pointed out the stone-sculpted face of a chubby angel on the facade of a building.

"They're called mascarons," he continued. "The city of Bordeaux is not only known for its wines, but also for its eighteenth-century architecture."

"What do they signify?" I was intrigued as I saw many faces carved on the top of doors of imposing old stone buildings while we walked by.

"'Mascaron' means a big grotesque mask—in other words, buffoonery. The Greeks and Romans used the representation of the face in the form of frightening masks to drive out evil spirits. Over time, they have just become decorative pieces of art found all around the city."

Bordeaux's architecture was marvelous indeed. I could understand why it was recognized as a UNESCO World Heritage site in 2007.

We carried on walking along the cobbled streets until we finally reached the pub. It was warm inside, just as I had hoped. We took our seats next to a window that had a perfect view of the lively street. When the waiter arrived, I said in proper French, "*Un thé pour moi, s'il vous plaît.*"

Conor ordered his beer. After the waiter had left, he inquired, "Did you live in France before? Or did you study French at school back in India?"

"I studied at the Alliance Française back in India for a while, but I still make lots of mistakes, especially with gender," I fretted.

"Oh, Nam, but your French is just fine. I can't even tell that you're a foreigner speaking this language."

We chatted for a while before taking the tram back home. Conor helped me buy a ticket and also got me used to a map. When we reached home, Conor asked if I was hungry enough to have some soup and bread.

"That would be perfect for this weather, thank you," I said, feeling grateful for his warm welcome. "But before that, I must give you some sweets and spices that I brought you from India. You can use them in your dishes. If you'd like, I could teach you some ways of cooking with them."

And just like that, our friendship had begun.

***

The following morning, I entered what was to be my school for the year. The INSEEC building had spectacular views over the Garonne, which ran through Bordeaux.

I entered a large classroom that had light pouring through the windows. Six wine glasses along with a spittoon were neatly arranged for each student on each desk. I started to feel uneasy. Would I be the worst student in class, now that I was older? My memory had often failed me. I wasn't as quick as a young mind. How would I cope with full-time studying?

A youthful, trim male teacher wearing a crisp, white shirt and khaki work trousers was making sure the overhead laser projector worked before he began his class. Suddenly, the girl on my right let out a giggle. She was dressed in a silky black, full-length, bell-bottom jumpsuit. She held out her phone to her friend sitting behind her, who burst out laughing. I looked quizzically at them. They were both gorgeous. They spoke in a different language altogether. *Sounds like Italian*, I thought.

"Hi, are you Namratha?" I heard someone ask.

I turned to my left, and there was a young man whose face I recognized.

"Yes, and you are Jake?" I asked enthusiastically, and he nodded.

A couple of months back, I had put up a post on one of the INSEEC Facebook groups looking for accommodation in Bordeaux. Jake had noticed that and contacted me, saying he was enrolled in the wine program too and was looking for a place to rent.

"Nice to finally meet you," I said.

Jake looked like he was in his twenties. He still had a youthful cheer in his face.

"Good morning, all of you," an amplified voice spoke, and the room quieted. "I'm professor Zviad. I'm from Georgia. Today, we are going to taste some wines from my country."

I had learned the basics of wines during my years as a hospitality student. It was hard finding imported wines in India at that time. Our service teacher had spoken a lot about French wines, especially the Sauternes from Bordeaux. I was twenty-one years old. Wine was a fascinating subject that I had wanted to learn more about, but as an Indian woman, I couldn't. Women in the alcohol industry were not accepted by society at that time. In 1999, Jessica Lall, a model and a celebrity barmaid was shot point-blank after refusing to serve alcohol past midnight. The accused was a son of a prominent and wealthy politician. He was acquitted due to lack of evidence and hostile witnesses. In 2006, public pressure, a strong media-led movement, and "Justice for Jessica" campaigns all over the nation lead to the eventual conviction of the man for murder, and he was sentenced to life imprisonment.

Many states had banned women from serving drinks in bars because they felt the need to protect women from the nasty behavior of drunken men. Our society tagged women who drank on par with men as indecent girls who would get drunk and have sex with strangers. Most families felt compelled to restrict their daughters from these stigmatic professions. I didn't dare to swim against the tide. By the year 2007, things had begun to change. The courts had ruled in favor of women tending bars. It was around the same time I had Shloka and began my language studies at the Alliance Française to save me from postpartum depression. There, I had learned about wine culture and how wine is such an integral part of French life. The wine bug had bit me, and I later enrolled for a course on wines, which had further fueled my passion.

I listened intently.

"Georgia has more than eight thousand years of history in winemaking. Archaeologists have discovered that wine was first created there in six thousand BC, so today, Georgia is considered the 'cradle of wine.' There, grape juice is turned into wine by burying it underground in traditional clay containers called *qvevri* to preserve constant temperature. Each earthen pot has a capacity of three hundred to three thousand liters," he said as he cautiously poured wine into our glasses.

"What you are about to taste is a dry red wine, made from a grape called Saperavi. It means 'dye' in Georgian. The grapes have thick, dark skins and fall under the rare category since their flesh is pink in color. Now, swirl the wine in your glass and smell it to ascertain the aromas. But beware! A single drop can leave a strong stain. Especially if, like me, you're wearing a white shirt!" he laughed.

I swirled the wine in my glass. Drops of it landed on the table. I felt embarrassed. I quickly pulled out a tissue and wiped the table.

"Now make a list of all the aromas you find in the nose and on the palate."

I took a deep breath, holding the glass just below my nose. It was like nothing my senses had experienced before. Then I took a sip, opened my notebook, and began to scribble in it. I couldn't think of taking notes on a laptop, but I noticed how comfortable everybody else was with their devices. They were typing with incredible speed. Maybe it was my age, I thought, shrugged, and continued to taste and write. I didn't spit out the wine. I felt I would make a fool of myself if I spit it out, so I drank every sip.

"Can anyone read out their notes?" asked the professor.

Jake put up his arm. The professor nodded.

"The wine is packed with notes of berries, both red and black, and the spice comes through powerfully. The earthiness is prominent, and there are hints of leather, licorice, chocolate, and tobacco."

The professor was impressed with Jake's answer. "Excellent!"

After a good three-hour session on Georgian wines, we broke for lunch. I continued to chat with Jake in the corridor. One of the Italian girls joined our conversation. She asked Jake where he had acquired his wine skills. He said that he came from Canada and that he was a sommelier. He was in Bordeaux to learn more about wines so he could add to his existing skills. *So that explained it*, I thought. The girl from Italy introduced herself as Isabella. She came from a winemaker's family. I wondered how it would feel to be the daughter of a winemaker.

"Have you guys found an internship? We need to start work next month," Jake asked.

In order to obtain a master's degree, our school required every student to work for five to six months in a wine company.

"Not yet," I said.

"Bordeaux is very competitive. It isn't easy finding an internship or a job, especially because we are foreigners. The earlier you start looking, the better it is," Jake explained. "Try the website Vitijob. That's where I got mine."

Jake and Isabella seemed to have everything under control, unlike me.

"Are you going to Vinitaly?" Isabella asked, changing the subject.

"No plans yet. Will you be there?" Jake asked.

I was perplexed. All these were terms I wasn't aware of. I felt like a fool.

"What's Vinitaly?" I asked impatiently.

"It's a wine fair that takes place every year in the month of April for four days in the beautiful city of Verona. It is considered the world's largest wine exhibition. Importers, distributors, international wine buyers, professionals—they all flock to this event. It's total madness. As for students, this is the best way to try great Italian wines and train our palates," Jake said. "It's in a couple of weeks, and I badly want to go."

"Bravo, Jake! You know a lot about Italy's wine scene," Isabella said.

"Will your family be showcasing Rocca Vini wines?" Jake asked.

"*Sì!*"

"We should go, too," Jake said, looking at me.

"Oh, I'm not sure. I'll think about it," I said.

"You must come visit my winery near Milan," Isabella said.

It was only this morning that I had met them, and we were already planning a trip. I couldn't believe it.

***

Jake called later that evening and persuaded me further.

"We don't need to go all four days. Just two will do. There will be walk-around tastings. Well, if we get lucky, we could do some vertical tastings too," Jake said and added, "Angelo Gaja and his daughter Gaia are going to be there."

"Who are they?"

"Oh my God, you don't know the Gaja family?"

I felt annoyed. "Of course not. I'm not a sommelier like you, nor do I have any experience in wine. It's been less than a week in the wine world for me. Now, if you'll explain, please."

"Angelo Gaja is a wine producer from the Piedmonte region, in the north of Italy. He produces the best Barbaresco and Barolo wines. He's also called the king of Barbaresco. His wines are the Italian version of Lafite. Gaia is his daughter. It will definitely be a treat to see her."

"Sounds interesting, Jake. What about tickets?"

"We could ask Isabella for more information."

"Great!"

"It's in less than a month's time. There are no hotels available in Verona. We'll have to stay in Milan and travel to and from. Flights, too, are getting more expensive by the day. We must decide quickly."

"I have an appointment at the French prefecture on the fourteenth. I cannot miss it. If I do, they'll probably deport me back to India."

"I'll make sure you're back before then, I promise, Nam."

I didn't know Jake well enough. I was hesitant, but then I gave in. I packed my bags the following week without realizing how crazy this trip would turn out to be.

CHAPTER 9
Vinitaly

Milan, Italy
April 2017

Chic and stylishly dressed, Isabella picked us up from the airport and drove us in her Audi Cabriolet to her home that was situated in an upmarket area of Milan. The lift from the underground garage took us directly to the tenth floor, which opened onto a large, tastefully decorated living room. Jake was flabbergasted.

"There's no door to this apartment, can you believe that? This is fucking amazing," he whispered into my ear.

Isabella's mother greeted us and led us to a spacious balcony that overlooked the city of Milan. The view was breathtaking. Finally, we settled down onto a comfy Hampton sofa.

"It's so good to have you both here," Isabella's mother said as she served us a glass of Prosecco.

"Thank you so much for inviting us," I said.

"Here, try our 8 Secco. It's extra dry, and made in the *méthode traditionnelle*. We produce it and bottle it in our winery. Can you smell the fruits and the blossoms?" Isabella asked as she stroked her two Birman cats that had conveniently cuddled next to her.

Jake lifted his glass for a brief moment, inspected the wine, sniffed, and said, "The streams of bubbles are fine and elegantly travel to the top. I'm getting secondary aroma notes of brioche and toast."

"Bravo, Jake," Isabella exclaimed.

"It's gorgeous," I added, as my wine appreciation lingo was quite limited.

"Where do you export these to?" Jake asked before he took another sip.

"We export most of our production to China and the United States. But we are also present in fifteen different countries."

"Here, have some," Isabella's mother said as she passed around a bowl of green olives.

"We grow these in our *masseria* in Puglia; you must visit someday. It's in the south, where the heel of the boot is," Isabella explained.

"These olives are delicious," I said.

"You will also love the olive oil we make from them. Mama has prepared pasta for lunch. And it tastes best when fresh olive oil is drizzled over it."

And so, our conversations around wine and olive oil continued until it was almost lunchtime. Just as Isabella had promised, her mother served us pasta with olive oil made in their *masseria*, and a 1969 wine made by her grandfather. I was in heaven.

Later that afternoon, Isabella took us for a tour of her winery, Rocca Vini. The aroma of wine wafted toward us when we entered the vast cellar. Gigantic vats were all arranged in a long row.

"This tank contains the varietal Negroamaro, and this one here contains Primitivo di Manduria." She pronounced the words mellifluously in her charming Italian accent.

"Can we take pictures?" Jake asked.

"*Sì, certo.* Of course. No problem."

Isabella's family owned vineyards in many regions of Italy. We walked past many steel tanks and even climbed ladders to reach the vats on the upper decks. Her winery was impressive. Every year, it produced 250,000 bottles and boasted of a state-of-the-art facility that included a bottling unit and a laboratory for testing.

"Vermentino," she said aloud, tapping a huge steel vat with her red manicured nails. "It's a white variety, grown mostly in Sardinia. In Piedmont, it's called Favorita...like you, Nam, my favorite girl," Isabella laughed and continued.

"The next tank is Malvasia."

As more varieties and new words were being thrown around, I did my best to grasp them. Some I retained, and others disappeared into thin air. Nevertheless, I was content with my induction to the of world Italian wines.

After the tour, Isabella showed us the Duomo di Milano before dropping us off at our modest hotel. Jake and I thanked her for her hospitality and checked into our respective rooms. I felt tired from the day's events and went straight to bed.

The next day, a packed train took us to Verona in just over an hour. From the Verona Porta Nuova station, we took the free shuttle bus dedicated to taking visitors to the Veronafiere convention center. When we arrived, we saw crowds of people entering the venue.

I turned to Jake. "There might be a chance we will lose each other in this crowd. In case we do, we should meet at the entrance of this café at half past six. Deal?"

Jake agreed, and off we went. The halls were large and spread across a massive area. Each room was numbered and showcased wines from different wine growing regions of Italy. We flashed our badges and entered the Tuscan area, where the stands were occupied by wineries busily pouring their wine into glasses for visitors to taste.

I followed Jake as he walked toward one of the stands and asked if we could do a tasting.

"*Prego*!" said the dapper Italian manning the stand.

"Our winery, Castello di Verrazzano, is tucked in the center of Chianti," he explained. "Our estate spreads over two hundred thirty acres, and in that we have about fifty-two hectares of vineyards at altitudes between two hundred sixty and four hundred twenty meters above sea level, in a stony soil rich in limestone. We mostly grow red grapes—Sangiovese, Merlot, Canaiolo, Cabernet Sauvignon, and Colorino—and only a small percentage of white grapes like Trebbiano Toscano, Traminer, and Malvasia del Chianti. Try our Sassello DOCG Chianti Classico Gran Selezione, which is made from one hundred percent Sangiovese from our Querciolina vineyard," he said, and poured wine into our glasses.

The happy Italian continued. "The grapes are fermented in small quantities, only fifty hectoliters, at a controlled temperature with a maximum of thirty degrees Celsius. Maceration is carried out for sixteen to eighteen days, with delicate pumping over and filling. Later, it is transferred into wooden vessels for eighteen months, followed by twelve months of aging in small barrels—seventy-five percent in Allier and twenty-five percent in Vosges. It undergoes a minimum of six months refining in bottles before hitting the shelves."

We smelled and swirled the liquid in our glasses. I noted the intense ruby red color, with garnet overtones. Jake took a sip and washed all the corners of his mouth with the wine. Then he brought his lips together and sucked in air while the wine rested in his mouth, making a funny slurping sound. He repeated this several times before spitting it out in a single stream into a spittoon that was placed next to the stand.

"Excellent! The bouquet is persistent, offering a variety of fruity notes, including cherries, blackberries, raspberries, underlined by hints of oak and vanilla," Jake said and continued impressively. "On the palate, the wine is elegant and complex, with closely woven tannins. It has a silky mouthfeel and sharp acidity. It appears to be well balanced and has quite a long finish."

"It's gorgeous," I said timidly.

We thanked the gentleman and moved on. In the middle of the hall stood a beautifully decorated stand.

"Marchesi Antinori," Jake said, then looked at me to see if the name rang a bell. "Do you have any clue about these wines?"

"Yes, I did a little bit of homework before I came," I said.

"Great! Let's taste," Jake said, and we walked in.

I had read that the Antinori estate made some of the greatest wines in Tuscany, and without doubt they were one of the biggest wine companies in Italy. Solaia and Tignanello were names that a wine professional couldn't afford to forget. Their innovations played a large part in the Super Tuscan revolution of the 1970s. Before this, using non-Tuscan grapes and blending wines wasn't allowed under the Tuscan appellation law; however, the Antinoris and a few other producers unofficially experimented by planting red grape varieties from Bordeaux in their vineyards. They knew that in order to reach international markets with their wines, they needed to sell what the world loved: French grape varieties such as Cabernet Sauvignon, Cabernet Franc, and Merlot. So they started to produce high-quality wines made from these grapes. This movement led to the Super Tuscan revolution, which in turn gave rise to Super Tuscan wines. The producers who fought gained international recognition, and eventually changes came about in Italy's wine classification.

After tasting Antinori's wines, we proceeded to taste other Super Tuscans: the Sassicaia and the Ornellaia.

"Ohhh, that was pure ecstasy," Jake said as we left hall fifteen. "Come on, let's go try wines from the Piedmont region."

I followed Jake again. On the way, we stopped to taste the wines of some smaller producers that he thought were important. I could see Jake bring out the best of his sommelier traits every time he held a glass in his hand. He was tasting and spitting artfully, while my wine ended up splattered across the spittoon.

"Jake, I'm super embarrassed. I just can't get the hang of this," I sighed.

"It's easy, Nam; bring your lips together like a fish and spit in a single stream. Here, watch me."

There was a certain elegance in the way Jake spat his wine. *Gosh, I'm not sure if I can do it*, I thought.

"Just focus and spit with confidence, Nam," Jake said as I tried again and failed badly.

Next stop were the Borolos and Barbarescos of the Piedmont region, then came Puglia and Sicily.

Soon it was six o'clock. Time had passed too quickly. We were exhausted. Our noses and palates were dead, as the alcohol in the wine had rendered them useless. We reached the station and waited for the next train to take us to Milan. Once on the train, we settled into our seats, and I took off my heeled pumps, realizing just how badly my feet hurt. As the train chugged on, I noticed a couple sitting diagonally opposite to me. The man sat upright while the woman leaned into him with her back on his chest. He was lovingly stroking her hair in one hand and holding her tight, wrapping his other hand around her. They looked so beautiful together. Oh, how I longed for that tender love, a hand to hold me and tell me everything's going to be fine. I sighed and turned to look out the window.

Just then, my phone began to ring. It was Moksh.

I felt a gush of fear take over me. Did he know I was travelling with Jake? Oh God, had he sent someone to spy on me? The sleepless nights, the abusive words, the sounds of glass shattering all came back to me. *I'm overthinking*, I said to myself. I took a deep breath and tried to calm myself down. Moksh had no way of causing me any harm. I was miles away from him. True, I had moved to France, but what choice had he left me with? I was here to build a future for Shloka and me. I needed time. For the moment, she was safe with my parents, but I was afraid that Moksh would take her away or go to court to prove that I was a bad mother and get custody.

I silenced the call and glanced at Jake. His leg was shaking uncontrollably. I bent forward and asked what was wrong.

"It's nothing. I just have this condition."

"What condition, Jake?"

"I can't control my pee. And this train has no toilets."

"Oh goodness, Jake!" I exclaimed. "Maybe you could get off at the next station and catch the next train."

"That's not possible. This is the last train for the day."

Jake was right. I didn't know how to help him. The train stopped for less than a minute in every station. There was no chance he'd make it if he got off.

"Hang in there. Only twenty minutes left," I said, feeling sorry for him.

I leaned back into my seat and closed my eyes. Memories of Moksh were still fresh in my head. I wanted to erase him entirely from my life. But I knew I couldn't as long as Shloka was in India. *What if Moksh never lets her go? What will I do?* My thoughts filled the chugging train. The instant the train hit the brakes, Jake ran toward the exit so he could be the first person to get off and rush to the men's room before it was too late for him. I let out a little giggle despite the fear of Moksh hovering in my head.

***

Morning came quickly. I woke, dressed, and knocked on Jake's door. There was no answer. I waited and knocked again. No answer. I called Jake's phone. Still no answer. I knocked hard. Finally, Jake clambered out of bed and opened the door.

He peeped from behind his black silk eye mask. "I'm running a fever and my voice is gone. I can't speak," he mumbled under his breath. I strained to hear his words. "I can't make it today, Nam."

"Oh, gosh. Take care of yourself, Jake. Do you need anything?" I asked.

"Don't worry, I have all my medications."

"Okay. See you in the evening, then," I said and walked away, feeling disappointed that I wouldn't have Jake's professional expertise that day.

The gates to the exposition were open, and when I walked toward the booths, there seemed to be a lot more visitors than the previous day. I showed my badge and started toward the exhibitors. I did a couple of tastings before I spotted Isabella. She was with Valentina, who was also studying wine at our school in Bordeaux. I knew that Jake had a big crush on Valentina. Her family, too, were wine producers in Italy. Isabella walked toward me in her long knee-high boots.

"Ciao.... Nam, where's Jake?"

I hugged her and narrated the whole story.

She let out a big laugh when I told her about Jake not waking up.

"Why would he come this far, spend a ton of money, and not attend the exposition?"

"He's sick," I said.

"Nam...you're too naive. He must have a Tinder date in Milan. I know guys like Jake very well," Isabella said, pulling her cigarette case from her bag.

"You must taste the whole range of my wines, *bella.* But before that, I need a fag," she said, gesturing toward the door that led outside.

Isabella was bold, energetic, and young. Her long golden hair fell neatly on both her shoulders, and she stylishly wore the most elaborate ensemble. We chatted as she lit her cigarette and held it securely between her fingers in one hand while her other hand moved to the rhythm of the words that came out of her mouth.

"My boyfriend, Roberto, was not letting me talk to boys in France. He was behaving like he owned me, *cazzo*...so I said to him to fuck off, *stronzo*! He doesn't deserve me," she ranted.

I sympathized with her. There were many similarities between Isabella and Valentina. I could see that Italian women came with a ton of energy and passion and were certainly not to be messed around with.

We walked back to her booth, and the tasting began.

"Try our Nero d'Avola. It comes from the far south of Sicily. It's always compared to Syrah, but that's bullshit. The taste is amazing, isn't it? You will not get this anywhere but Sicily."

I took a sip, swirled the wine in my mouth, and spat. *Not bad*, I thought, as it went in a steady stream into the spit bucket.

"This is our Nerello Mascalese," Valentina announced as she poured a fresh glass. She was proud of her wines and certainly had reason to be. After five more wines, I thanked her profoundly and left to meet other producers. The day had passed quickly. By the time my last glass was done, I had become a spitting expert.

I looked at my watch. There was a train in twenty minutes. I dashed across the hall toward the exit. My feet were tired and nearly giving up on me, but I knew if I missed that train I would have to wait for another hour. Suddenly, I stumbled and a hand caught me.

I turned to look.

"*Bella*, you have the most beautiful eyes," a handsome Italian man said.

For once, I felt unthreatened. Moksh wasn't there. There was no one judging me or accusing me of disloyalty. I felt free. It was a lovely moment.

"*Grazie*." I winked and sprinted toward the shuttle bus that was ready to take off.

I reached the station in time to catch the train to Milan. Managing to take a seat next to the window, I fell asleep immediately.

Jake was at the coffee shop of the hotel when I returned. I was surprised to find him all well.

"How was your day?" he asked.

"Well, you missed the events today. I met Gaia," I lied.

"What? No way! You met Gaia from the Gaja family?"

"*Sì*." I nodded. "And Valentina from school."

"Oh! My gorgeous Valentina... Damn, I should have come along."

"Good night, Jake," I said and went up to my room, piqued at his obvious subterfuge.

***

After breakfast the next morning, we took a taxi to the Bergamo airport so that I could get to Bordeaux in time for my appointment at the prefecture the next day. The traffic was heavy. Our flight was to take off at ten o'clock. I looked at my watch: it was 9:15 a.m. Panic set in. We rushed toward departures once the taxi dropped us off. The security check lasted ten minutes. My heart raced when I heard the last-call announcement as we ran toward the gates. A staff member stopped us. Jake began to explain to her while I stared through the glass window, into the area where the planes were parked. One of them was taking off, and I didn't have a good feeling about it.

"I'm sorry sir, you're very late. The flight is air-bound now," I heard the hostess tell Jake. My head started to spin.

How could I be so careless? We should have left the hotel earlier. What was I thinking?

"Don't worry, Nam, we can get on the next flight," Jake said, looking at my worried face.

We walked to the ticketing counter.

"All flights for the next three days are full," said the woman behind the counter.

"Please...I have an appointment tomorrow that I cannot miss."

"Sorry, madam. I cannot help you."

Jake had already begun checking for trains to Bordeaux. After a few minutes, he looked up at me and said, "Sorry, Nam. No seats left."

"Oh God, no! This cannot be happening."

"Wait, everything's not lost. There's one other option to reach Bordeaux before tomorrow. We can hire a car."

"Jake, that is the most intelligent thing you've said in the last three days."

We quickly inquired with Europcar and Avis. There were no cars available until the next day. Hertz said they only had a Mercedes nine-seater van. Jake and I looked at each other and said in a chorus, "We'll take it."

We threw our bags in and jumped into our seats. Jake took the wheel. I wasn't sure of his driving skills. I switched on the GPS and noticed that Milan to Bordeaux was almost a straight line.

"Nine hours and forty minutes!" I sighed.

"Sit back and relax, Nammers."

Jake was right; the situation was out of my control. Either I could worry about reaching Bordeaux, or enjoy the picturesque drive. After a while, we did a quick pit stop at a little shop in Turin and picked up some food to eat on our way, then headed toward

Chambéry. While we drove, bucolic settings revealed themselves all around us. As the music played in the vehicle, little Italian villages on mountain tops, scattered with charming country homes, began to emerge. Magnificent mountain ranges seemed to continue endlessly on both sides of the road.

"Namz, I'm glad we missed the flight—this has turned out better than I expected."

"To be honest, I thought I'd regret this, but you're right. Thanks, Jakey, for being the best and helping me get back in time," I said as I lowered my side of the window and held my hand out to feel the cool air.

The sun commenced a slow descent behind the distant horizon. A purple-red hazy glow followed, adorning the sky. The route was spectacular. Jake was driving at a good speed. Soon we passed Lyon, and then Clermont-Ferrand.

"So, tell me, Jake—did you meet a girl yesterday?"

"What? No, I didn't."

"Don't lie."

"Well, it wasn't like what you're thinking."

"What? So, you did?"

"No...I mean, no."

"Jerk!"

"What? Did you just call me a jerk?"

We laughed. Jake was street-smart and always strived to live life to its fullest. He had just stepped into his thirties.

"I'd give anything to have an Italian woman in my life," he had repeated several times before.

He was obsessed with the idea of "*la bella figura*"—the Italian philosophy of making everything as beautiful as it can be. Jake believed that only an Italian woman could help him achieve such effortless style and grace. Well, of course, there were many more things about him that annoyed me, but those were not of great importance.

The journey lasted about ten hours. It was just before midnight when we finally reached Bordeaux.

***

By the end of that week, I had not only attended the rendezvous at the prefecture, but I had also successfully landed an internship in an eighteenth-century castle. I couldn't have asked for a better way to begin my immersion in wine. I was to be their ambassador, which involved welcoming guests from all over the world, showing them around the château, and serving wines for them to taste. All this while living on the premises of the castle. It felt as though I was stepping into a dream.

CHAPTER 10
Chateau Siran

Médoc, France
May 2017

It was 7:25 a.m. Cold air bit into my cheeks as I hopped off the train at a small station in the Médoc. This charming French countryside was to be my home for the next five months. I felt grateful; life was offering me new experiences, I had learned about Italian wines, and now I was going to be living where the world's most famous vines are grown. I briefly paused to soak in the feeling of this new beginning as the train chugged away behind me.

It's going to be wonderful, I thought as I started to stroll along the platform with my luggage.

The sound of my boots, followed by the noise of dragging wheels, echoed through the silence. I looked around as I walked. Nobody else had got off this train stop. I recollected my train journeys in India, where empty stations didn't exist. The *chaiwalas*, who sold piping hot tea from their steel kettles, make sure of that. "*Chai... Chaaii... Garam Chaaaiii...*" they called out as they made their way through the crowds. Trains overflowed with passengers hanging out the doors. Many travelers awaiting trains on the platforms were fast asleep on sarees or blankets. It was utter chaos, but charming. My mouth watered thinking of the hot *vada bajjis* and spiced raw mangoes that were sold right at our seats. Porters, newspaper sellers, and garland twirlers all kept the station alive. I reminisced as I calmly walked toward the entrance to find a taxi.

The morning stillness felt almost dream-like. I reached the street just outside the station but found nobody there. Not a car or a truck. Not even a village dog or a cat. Just fallen leaves on the ground.

I took a deep breath and sat on a wooden bench. I pulled out my phone from my backpack and tapped on the Uber app. I waited for the information to appear on the screen. A scowl crossed my lips when the message appeared. "Sorry, no rides available."

I couldn't believe it. I rubbed my eyes and looked again. *What is it about this place?*

I stood and made my way back inside to the ticket counter with the hope of finding someone there. On the glass panel hung a printed, laminated paper that read "Fermé."

Closed? Why would they close the counter?

I glanced around to see nothing but empty seats. It all seemed very strange. I walked further in my attempt to find some kind of life. All I discovered was a ghostly place.

Maybe the staff is on strike, I thought. It happens so often in France.

It didn't take me long to find a few doors in the tiny matchbox-like station and knock on each of them. I hoped someone would answer.

"Helloooo...could somebody help me, please?" I called, then repeated in French. "*Est-ce qu'il y a quelqu'un qui peut m'aider, s'il vous plait?*"

There was only an uncomfortable silence. I peeped through a small window beside one of the doors and saw a half-eaten croissant and a finished cup of coffee on the desktop. The scene would have been perfect in a horror film. I quickly dismissed these thoughts and decided to stay focused. I had just enough time to get to the château before the start of my first day. It was only a matter of how.

I walked back to the entrance, hoping that by then at least one taxi would have arrived. The fallen leaves were still lying on the street just as they were earlier. Not even the wind had passed through.

I started to feel anxious, and it nearly paralyzed me. I glanced at my watch again; it was ten minutes to eight. It was too early to call my manager, Veronica. India was different, but in France, I knew it was considered impolite to disturb your colleagues outside of work hours.

The château was only fifteen minutes away by car. I could get there on foot, of course, but my heavy luggage would make it difficult, and I would never make it there by half past eight. Moreover, it would be awkward to be late on the first day of my job. After a few more minutes, desperation set in. I dialed Veronica's number. There was no answer.

I dragged my suitcase behind me, walking a little distance until a car passed by. I sheepishly signaled with my thumb. I was alien-looking in this part of the world. Long black tresses framed both sides of my light brown face and ran well below my breasts. My chestnut eyes scanned each and every passing vehicle, hoping with all my heart one willing driver would take pity on me and give me a ride. As car after car sped past me, I grew bolder.

I adjusted my yellow beret and straightened out my long ivory-colored woolen coat. Then I put on my red lipstick to make myself look livelier and easier to see. Soon my anxiety vanished, and I started to enjoy this chanced folly. It seemed people in this part of the world weren't accustomed to seeing strangers asking for a ride. Perplexed expressions crossed many faces as they drove by.

Thirty minutes passed, and, despite my best efforts, no one bothered to stop. Panic had set in. However, I knew I had no choice but to stride ahead in hopes of arriving at my destination in one piece, acknowledging I would be late. After I walked for a while longer, my phone rang. It was the voice I was hoping to hear.

***

In no time, Veronica picked me up and headed toward the château. When we reached the gates, I saw a beautiful castle tucked behind mature green trees. The tires crunched on gravel as she parked next to a peripheral building.

I got out, grabbed my luggage from the trunk, and followed her to a small blue-colored door. It was there that my living arrangements had been made. She unlocked the door and led me in.

"Your bedroom is upstairs," she said in a gentle voice. "I can help you carry your luggage."

I nodded, feeling grateful to have such a thoughtful manager. We carefully balanced the suitcase while making our way up the narrow wooden staircase that led into a small corridor, then into a spacious bedroom. I struggled a "thank you" as I caught my breath, and we put the luggage down.

"I'll see you at the office in fifteen minutes," Veronica said, handing me the keys to the house.

I held them and watched Veronica leave. I thought about our conversation in the car. She'd told me she spoke French, Spanish, English, and Portuguese, which was the reason she was hired by the owners of Château Siran. She was originally from Spain but moved to France when she was young. Here, she continued to study, not only French, but also English and Portuguese.

When I drew back the curtains and opened the shutters, the morning sunlight poured in. I watched Veronica enter the office building below, diagonally opposite to my window. I was glad that she was pleasant and helpful.

I turned around to get a proper view of my room. A well-made queen-size bed with fresh white linen was in the middle, adorned with motifs of vines and bunches of grapes.

I laid down on the bed and ran my hands over the sheets. It felt cozy. My eyes then fell upon the bath that was just across the room. I got up and walked across to the bathroom window. It overlooked acres of green vines that blanketed the land until it met the blue of the sky.

I must be in a dream, I thought.

These were the world-famous vineyards of Margaux. I could have stayed there all day looking at that beautiful sight.

Excited, I continued to explore my new home. The lower part of the house had a living area and a dining room, plus a kitchen with a utility area. The place was small yet contained everything needed for decent living.

I looked around for a heater. My face and hands were still numb from the early morning cold. It had been only a month since I had left the warmth of the Indian sun and traveled to France. I turned on the warmer on the lower part of the wall behind the dining table. Sitting on the chair closest to it, I rubbed my hands and patted them on my face. It felt marvelous. I was back to life.

Suddenly, my phone rang. It was the alarm. I had five more minutes before I needed to report. Just then, my stomach let out a little growl to remind me I hadn't eaten.

I reached for the brown paper bag on the table, which I had brought with me on the journey. Inside was a soft bread layered with butter, baked to golden brown with a melted chocolate filling inside it. In the Southwest region of France, it was called *chocolatine*. The rest of the country called it *pain au chocolat*. It was a war. I never understood why the French fussed about a name.

I had packed three of them before leaving Bordeaux. They smelled delightful. I bit into the treat, remembering my first time at a *boulangerie* in Bordeaux. I had embarrassed myself by asking for *pain au chocolat*.

The woman behind the counter had looked at me in disbelief. "You want *chocolatine*?" she asked in English, gauging my accent was foreign.

"*Non, je veux trois pains au chocolat, s'il vous plait.*" I preferred to insist in French.

She had laughed and said, "It's the same, *madame*. In Paris, *c'est pain au chocolat,* and in Bordeaux, *c'est chocolatine.*" Then she giggled while I paid and continued to laugh the entire time it took me to leave.

Conor, later, had an explanation.

"It is France's eternal debate," he'd said. "It's a north-south issue, and also a left-right one. It's even been discussed in parliament. It's related to the English influence in the region of Aquitaine. I believe that it was the English rulers who asked for 'chocolate in bread' at the boulangerie, and the French bakers understood it as 'chocolate in,' which later became *chocolatine*." It was a strange conclusion, but it had lasted with time.

Hope you arrived safely. Conor's message beeped on my phone, bringing me back to the present. I gobbled up the *chocolatine* like a hungry Labrador as I texted back.

Oui, *lots of adventures on the way, will tell you all about it in the evening, but thanks for checking on me.* Then, resisting the temptation to polish off another *chocolatine*, which I decided to save for the other meal of the day, I proceeded to the office.

While I walked in the morning sun, I saw the magnificent Château Siran through the clearing of the trees. I stopped and admired the elegant chartreuse architecture and the gardens surrounding it.

Château Siran is one of the wine estates of the Bordeaux region whose origins can be traced back to the eighteenth century. The charming property was owned by Jeanne-Adèle, Countess of Toulouse-Lautrec. It was later sold to Léo Barbier, a Bordeaux wine merchant, and eventually, in 1859, Fréderic Miailhe, who fell in love with Siran and devoted himself to it. Today, the estate is managed by the sixth generation of the family, Édouard Miailhe and his wife, Sévrine Miailhe.

Veronica sat at her desk, her fingers busy typing. "I'll join you in a few minutes," she said. "Meanwhile, why don't you set up your desk?" She pointed at a table opposite hers.

Next to the computer, Veronica had placed a notebook, some stationary, and a folder with reading material. The table next to mine was occupied by another trainee in his twenties.

"*Bonjour, je m'appelle Claude*," he said as he got up from his chair, walked up to me, and did the cheek-to-cheek greeting.

"*Bonjour, Claude. Je suis Namratha. Enchantée*."

"Nice to meet you too, Namratha," Claude said in franglais, as he caught my light foreign accent.

Claude then told me how he'd studied wine, too, but in a different school. Just like me, he was here to do an internship. He'd been offered the room next to mine in the house but preferred to stay in his apartment in the city so he didn't miss any parties with his friends.

"Okay, guys, let's start the tour of the château," Veronica announced.

While we walked the grounds, Veronica explained everything in detail. "The property spans over eighty-eight hectares, forty of which are under vines. The castle and woods make up the rest. Merlot,

Cabernet Sauvignon, Cabernet Franc, and Petit Verdot are the primary grape varieties grown here, and these are used in our blends. This is the basic information you need to know to begin. The rest will be explained tomorrow by Édouard himself." She nodded. "Now, to the castle."

"The château dates back to the eighteenth century. Beautiful gardens and enchanting woods surround it. Your job involves welcoming guests, telling them our history and philosophy, taking them down to the cellar, and explaining the process of winemaking. Later, you'll make sure they exit through the gift shop so they buy lots of wine. You'll see, it's not too tough." Veronica winked.

After she showed us the whole property, we returned to the office where Édouard Miailhe was waiting to greet us. With dark-brown colored eyes and a bit of grey at his temples, he made a pleasant first impression. I had met him before, when he had interviewed me on Skype. He'd offered me the job immediately, but this was my first time meeting him in person.

"*Bonjour, bienvenue dans la famille de Siran*...err, welcome to the Siran family."

I noted again his funny franglais accent.

"Have you had the grand tour?" he inquired.

Claude and I both nodded with smiles on our faces.

"I did the first briefing," Veronica said.

Édouard asked me if the house was comfortable enough for my stay.

"It's more than comfortable, thank you," I said, using my most grateful voice.

"That's marvelous! Well, tomorrow we will be staying the night here at the château. Would it suit you to join us for dinner?" he asked.

"With pleasure," I said. "But I must warn you, I'm vegetarian."

Édouard let out a little grunt. "You're missing the best part of life. Seven o'clock tomorrow, madam." He grinned and went into his office.

I returned to my desk.

What will I wear tomorrow? What will I talk about? What will I take with me?

Anxious thoughts sprang unbidden into my mind. *What if the cutlery trembles along with me? What if I choke on a vegetable? That would make quite the first impression.* I laughed in my head. As rosy as this life seemed, I realized I wasn't ready for it.

After a long pause for lunch, we continued with the training. Our jobs already had an established process, which made things easier. Claude and I were like sponges, absorbing all the information. At the end of the day, Veronica thrust a key into my hand.

"This is the key to the van." She pointed to a weathered white Renault Kangoo. "You can use it to shop at the nearest supermarket for groceries. It's quite close by. You'll need to drive out of the gates, take a right, and then the first left, cross the railway lines, then drive straight for about two kilometers, and there you will find a board that says 'Intermarché.' It's a big one, you can't miss it. They'll have everything you need."

I nodded along as Veronica explained, but then feared the directions were already fading from my head. I had never driven in a foreign country before. The day had been challenging enough, and I was certainly not up for another adventure.

I walked home, wondering if I really needed to go to the supermarket. On the table lay the last *chocolatine* that I had saved for dinner. The drive was inevitable if I were to feed myself the next day.

Mustering all my courage, I walked toward the wheeled white metal box, which was parked next to a tree. As I opened the door, I found the driver's seat on the left and not the right.

Oh God! I'll need help with this, I thought, and looked for anyone who was still around after work. All the employees had returned to the comfort of their homes.

I took a deep breath and hopped into the driver's seat. The inside of the van had a strong odor of diesel and dirt. The horrible smell was enough to make me sick. When I turned, I saw old uprooted vines and vineyard equipment in the back. I quickly lowered the windows to ventilate the interior, then started the engine. The old wagon roared. I gingerly pressed the gas pedal and moved forward.

I let out a sigh of relief. I had no doubts about my driving skills; however, what made me nervous was that I was unaware of the driving rules and regulations in France. The castle premises were large, so I drove a couple of rounds before heading out on the road.

"I did it. I did it. Yes, I did it!" I shouted as I smoothly drove in the direction of the supermarket.

Just then, Marvin Gaye's and Tammi Terrell's song "Ain't No Mountain High Enough" started to play on the radio.

Now that's perfect, I thought and hummed along.

Suddenly, a car came from the opposite direction right in my path. I swerved to the right, just in time.

"*Putain, merde, qu'est-ce que tu faissss?*" A man yelled French profanity at me.

I tried to shake it off and drove on until another car approached me in the same lane.

Holy moly! How could I forget? I'm driving on the wrong side of the road!

In India, I always drove on the left-hand side, but here it was the opposite. I chided myself and quickly moved to the correct lane.

Soon I drove past the most beautiful French vineyards. I crossed the railway lines just as Veronica had instructed. Bucolic pastures with grazing cattle and galloping horses appeared as though I were in a dream. Small, French, postcard-perfect countryside homes whizzed past before the supermarket came into sight. There, I bought a week's supply of groceries and returned to the château.

When I parked the car—still alive and with my groceries—I felt a certain sense of freedom. A vehicle at my disposal in this part of the world was a boon. It wasn't a fancy one, but that didn't matter. I could move around the region freely and visit other wine properties. Exhausted from the day's adventures, I decided to indulge in the last *chocolatine* and retire to bed.

***

An hour later, the sky had grown darker. A strange silence surrounded me. I looked out of my old wooden-framed bedroom window. The place looked deserted. I quickly changed, slipped into bed, and started to read a book to keep my mind from imagining phantoms.

After a few minutes, I noticed the stretches of total silence and then the sudden fluttering of birds. It was followed by the rustling of wind. It felt like there was so much going on outside. I knew I was alone in ninety hectares, beyond which lay a church, a cemetery, and, on the other side, a river.

I felt compelled to double check the front door and got out of bed. Once I was back up in my room, I shut the door, latched it well, and again tucked myself into bed.

"Huh!" I said, as I stared at the window opposite me. The silence wasn't helping. I needed to distract myself. I grabbed my laptop and looked for a nice song to play. Louis Armstrong's voice filled the room. I felt comforted and sang along.

I was so physically tired that I should have been asleep at the drop of a hat, but my eyes refused to shut.

Maybe I should try reading again, I thought.

After a few lines however, my mind drifted into the solitude of my surroundings.

Suddenly, I heard clattering on the rooftop. Someone or something was walking over the tiles.

It must be a bird, I thought, trying to brush my fears aside.

Then I glanced at the window and saw two glinting eyes staring back at me. I froze. I would have passed out if not for the noise on the roof.

Through the darkness, I saw a little black figure hanging upside down. It looked at me with its shiny black eyes. My heart sank to the abyss of my stomach.

It's just a bat, I convinced myself. *It means no harm at all.*

Animals and birds were familiar wonders for me, but not at this hour of the night. The racket on the roof didn't help calm my wits either.

Slowly I reached out to the woolly scarf on the nearby dresser and threw it toward the window to scare away the bat. It took off immediately. Then I banged continuously on the wall until I heard something swish past. The horrors of the night in the countryside had only begun. Dim lights in the garden turned on automatically at midnight, which didn't make me feel any better. The statues were lit with low powered spotlights, which heightened the shadows, creating an eerie glow that could scare anyone.

With every passing minute, I became increasingly restless. My first night in the castle was turning out to be a nightmare. I lay in bed, still as a stone, and asked myself a thousand times why I signed up for something like this. My unpacked suitcase stood next to the table.

I can't do this. I will excuse myself and leave first thing in the morning.

I shivered at the thought of passing another night in this house. I would have to find a different job, one certainly not in the countryside.

What if I don't? Would I have to go back to India?

My days as a housewife, cleaning and cooking, played in my mind like a movie. I shuddered thinking of the scary nights with Moksh. He would come after me and hurt me for leaving him.

There was no turning back. I had to complete this internship.

***

It was half past two in the morning. Every bit of sleep had left me. I was like a war soldier, wide awake, keeping guard. However, I knew I needed rest if I was to work efficiently the next day.

Laughter! I need laughter. Maybe that will drown the silence.

Almost automatically, I typed in *Friends* on my laptop.

Joey was saying, 'If he doesn't like you, this is all a moo point."

Rachel asked, "A moo point?"

Joey nodded. "Yeah, It's like a cow's opinion. It just doesn't matter. It's moo."

Haha! By dawn I had drifted into deep slumber with the distant sounds of laughter.

***

The morning was cruel, but, despite my lack of sleep, I quickly dressed in comfortable trousers. Claude and I were to spend the whole day in the vineyard along with Olivier, the vineyard manager, who was at the office when we arrived.

"Would you two like some coffee before we get started?" asked Olivier in a raspy voice.

"*Oui, merci*," I said.

Veronica had briefed us about Olivier and his passion for vines. As he poured the coffee, I noticed the cuts and calluses on his weather-beaten hands. After an energizing cup of Italian coffee, we left the grounds of the château and headed toward the vineyard across from the entrance.

During the day, we learned all aspects of wine growing.

"Vines need very little water to grow," Olivier said, pointing to the soil underneath the roots of the gnarled vines. "In ancient times, vines were planted outside the cities on uncultivated land. The roots were required to grow deep into the soil in order to absorb the needed nutrients. And that is what we still practice today. The vines must suffer a little in order to produce quality grapes."

He bent down and grabbed some soil in his hands. "It's all about the terroir!"

Olivier had uttered the holy word. The one that was tattooed on every wine professional's *bouche*. By now, I knew that terroir was a particular region's climate, soil, and terrain, which affected the taste of wine. I had watched videos of important people in the wine industry talking about vine cultivation and winemaking.

"Great terroir produces great wines," Paul Pontallier of Château Margaux had said in one of the interviews.

"Terroir" was by far the sexiest word I had heard from a French man's mouth. There was a certain sophistication in the way Paul said it. He had shown so much passion and dedication. France was one of the oldest wine-growing regions of the world. I now could easily understand the fuss about French wines. They were the most sought-after wines because of the French *savoir-faire* and quality it offered.

"How much did you lose to the frost?" I asked.

Olivier smiled at my curiosity question. A few days before I'd moved to Château Siran, a deadly wave of frost had devastated many vineyards across Bordeaux and other regions of France. The vintage had gotten off to a tricky start. Everyone knew what frosts during the budding season meant for winemakers: it wasn't going to be an easy year for Bordeaux wines. There were some properties that lost their entire year's crop, a few lost a bit here and there, and some none at all.

Fate can be capricious, I thought.

Olivier continued, and I listened keenly, trying to retain every bit of information he offered.

"Here at our vineyards, we were lucky this year, as very little has gone to waste," Olivier responded. "We've lost only about five percent of our vines. Frosts are dangerous for vines, especially when green shoots begin to grow from the buds. They contain water, which makes them vulnerable during frosts. The frost that struck Bordeaux and other wine regions was radiation frost, one that can occur on clear nights, where cold air flows down like water, and at the same time, the ground pushes up warm air. This creates dangerous frost pockets in low-lying areas. A few minutes of this can freeze new shoots."

I admired Olivier's knowledge and professionalism. He enjoyed sharing all the wisdom that had perhaps been passed down through generations. Or maybe it was because he tasted wine first instead of water in his infancy, or maybe it was his years as a child in the vineyards, playing and learning in the shadows of his father and grandfather. Most French vintners shared a reciprocal loyalty with their employers. *Olivier too must have become a well-seasoned man because of all these factors*, I thought.

"The previous frost that was witnessed here was in 1991, where at least fifty percent of that vintage was wiped out in one night."

I shuddered thinking what the scene would have looked like and what a big loss it must have been for the wineries.

The day had been interesting. Content, I returned home.

A message beeped on my phone. *Looking forward to seeing you at the château for dinner at 19hr.*

It was a reminder from Édouard. I searched my luggage to find something nice to wear. Thank goodness I had packed a plain black chiffon dress. It had a patch of delicate handcrafted traditional Indian gold *zardozi* embroidery that sat between my breasts. I slipped it on and looked into the mirror. It was perfect.

The eighteenth-century château stood amid a grand garden. It was simple yet charming, and typified the Chartreuse style of architecture much admired in the southwest of France. At the door, I was greeted by Édouard's wife, Sévrine, a chic lady in her mid-forties. She was dressed in a grey pencil skirt with an off-white turtleneck pullover. Her hair was elegantly knotted without a single loose strand anywhere.

As we strolled through the living room, I admired the ornately framed paintings adorning the ivory walls and the plush mahogany-red velvet upholstery that covered the furniture. Tastefully selected golden-colored silk drapes hung on either side of the window that overlooked the vineyards. A fireplace warmed the room, and exquisite antiques filled out the rest of the space.

Sévrine led me to the dinner table positioned in the center of the kitchen. When I walked in, I was shocked to see Édouard sautéing mushrooms in a pan while the children laid plates on the table. Moksh, Aarav, or Patil had never once cooked a meal. I knew that in France, household chores were equally shared by couples. But somehow, I could not imagine Édouard doing the same. Maybe because I had seen him as a person of great importance. He was the owner of a castle, after all.

"Wow, it smells wonderful in here." I watched Édouard add chopped garlic and parsley to the sizzling pan.

"Édouard's a great chef, and tonight he's working his magic!" Sévrine laughed.

I smiled and felt privileged I could take a peek into their lives. My eyes soon fell upon the exquisite crockery that had been laid on the table. Ceramic plates had figures in indigo blue of beautiful women walking in the countryside with their puffed-up robes, holding umbrellas. Other plates had men with their necks up straight, covered with strawberry frills, tall hats, and round glasses on the edge of their noses. Each plate had a story to tell.

How could I eat from them? They were gorgeous, and, from the looks of them, very expensive.

Édouard arranged the dishes on the table and waited for Sévrine to gesture toward the seating. Since arriving in France, I had learned that, at dinners, the host chooses where the guests sit, usually for ease of conversations. I was asked to occupy a chair to the left of Édouard, while Sévrine sat on his right. Ben, who was seven, sat next to his mother, and Eliot, their second oldest at twelve, sat next to me. Their middle child, nine-year-old Anabelle, who was the same age as Shloka, sat between them. Théophile their eldest was studying in a different country I was told.

"*Chérie*, you forgot the wine," Édouard said, glancing around the table.

"*Merci, mon amour*." Sévrine smiled, then fetched the decanted wine from across the room.

While Édouard's eyes followed her, I took the opportunity to look underneath the plate to determine its brand. I looked back up in time to see Édouard's eyes on me.

"Vieillard & Cie," Édouard grinned. "It's a pity they don't make these anymore."

Embarrassed, I wanted to bury my face into the plate. Instead, I smiled and tried not to look guilty of a crime. "I love their designs."

Sévrine placed the wine in the middle of the table. "Voilà, Château Siran 1995," she announced in a cheerful voice.

Édouard served the wine into exquisitely carved crystal glasses. I noticed the rim of the wine in the glass. It had tinges of brown, which was a sign of an aged wine.

"So," Sévrine started, "which part of India do you come from?"

"From down south—a city called Bangalore," I said proudly.

"Is it near Kerala?" Sévrine inquired.

"Just above that, in the state of Karnataka." I was impressed she knew the name of any Indian state. "Bangalore is considered the Silicon Valley of India. There are umpteen software companies set up there lately."

"Is it?" Édouard and Sévrine both chorused.

"We've never been there, so I cannot place it on the map, but yes, we've heard of Bangalore," Sévrine said. "Recently, our friends traveled to Rajasthan, and they just can't stop raving about it. They showed us pictures. It's magnificent! They stayed for two nights in a grand old palace overlooking a private lake. The temples, the decorated elephants, the *tuk-tuks*, the women, their costumes and their jewelry, *oh là là*...so colorful."

"India is absolutely gorgeous. In fact, it feels more like a continent than a country. There are twenty-nine states, each with different languages, cuisines, and ways of life. It's a melting pot of cultures." By now I was quite aware of the fondness the French had for my exotic country. The palace in Rajasthan, the caste system, Pondicherry, Ayurvedic massages in Kerala, yoga, pollution, population, Gandhiji—these topics made up most conversations. As for me, I loved my country, but there was still a lot to be done to protect women and their rights.

"So, do you grow wines in India?" asked Édouard as he ladled soup into the bowls.

"Yes, as a matter of fact, we do. There are two major wine growing regions. Nasik, which lies near Mumbai, and a small area in northern Bangalore. Both are quite famous. Varieties such as Cabernet Sauvignon, Merlot, Malbec, and Syrah are plentiful. In whites, Chardonnay, Sauvignon Blanc, Sémillon, and Viognier have flourished in spite of the hot climate," I explained.

"Are they any good? I'd like to try them sometime."

"The quality has been improving. I'll bring you a bottle and we can taste together. Then you can tell me whether you like Indian wine or not." I smiled, sincerely hoping he would have something good to say when he tasted it.

We wound down dinner after a delightful crumble, made from apples grown on the property, paired with another old vintage of a dessert wine from Sauternes. It was almost half past ten. I thanked my hosts for the wonderful evening and made my way back. It felt good to have neighbors. The family preferred to live in their luxurious five-bedroom apartment in the heart of the city, which was a mere thirty-minute drive. However, they stayed at the château a few days a month.

When I walked through the courtyard, dried leaves crushed on gravel beneath my feet. The crunching sound reverberated through the stillness of the night. The moonlight shimmered through the trees. I stopped midway to look up at the cloudless sky. A million stars smiled back at me. This was my new life.

"Thank you, universe," I whispered.

***

It didn't take me long to settle down at Siran. I drove the white wagon up and down the world-famous roads of the Médoc with great ease—on the proper side of the road, of course. My eyes had never witnessed a land so beautiful. A carpet of green vines blanketed both sides of the winding roads, contrasting with the blue sky.

Puffy white cotton clouds scattered across the sky, visiting each other at intervals. Magnificent castles dotted the famous Route des Châteaux, one of the most scenic roads in the Médoc. Celebrated estates such as Château Mouton Rothschild, Château Lafite, Château Beychevelle, Château Léoville Barton, Château Cos d'Estournel, and many more spread over miles. During the summer season, which lasted from April to September, tourists from all over the world came to experience the history and grandeur of the region.

Château Siran became my retreat. I embraced its solitude. As the vines cradled me safely within their arms, I finally accepted my past. My wounded soul slowly healed, and I felt alive. My fury vanished, but my painful memories remained a stark reminder of another life. A life I had left behind. A life where my daughter still remained.

CHAPTER 11
Wine

Médoc, France
June 2017

I stared at grey slated clouds that covered the skies of the Médoc from my window. It dribbled raindrops so vital for the existence of life. The swallows swiftly flew into the shelter of the trees that were scattered around the property. *Where were their young ones?* I wondered and glanced at my watch. Shloka would've been back from school by now and probably standing in front of her wardrobe struggling to decide what she was going to wear for the evening play. Casper would be out on his walk, sniffing along the trails of the well-kept garden of the community. They were safe in my parents' care. I let out a sigh of relief. It was the end of June, and so much was happening around the world, while I was living in a dream that only lacked my daughter's laughter and my furball's bark.

I trudged out of the room on my day off work. I took my umbrella and went out. The rain had picked up within minutes and now sounded like steady drum beats against the ground. I spotted the vineyard manager, Olivier, assessing the rain. He had taken shelter under the eave outside the main office. He was dressed in a raincoat with a large hood, which covered his head, and big wellingtons that were coated with soft earth.

He smiled when he saw me walking toward him.

"*Regarde, il pleut comme vache qui pisse*," he said and shrugged.

"Pardon?" I replied as I strained to listen.

"It means, it is raining like a...errr, *vache*...ah, *oui*, cow that piss. It is raining like a cow that pisses," he said, pausing to translate each word.

"Oh, yes, there's a similar expression in English. 'It's raining cats and dogs,'" I said, and let out a silly laugh.

The French certainly had bizarre idiomatic expressions for every situation. The first one I encountered was at my language class at the Alliance Française. My teacher had split the class into four groups, giving an expression to each team, then asked us to invent imaginary situations and use the expression. My group had gotten "*Pédaler dans la choucroute.*" I was shocked as to why in the world would someone ride a bike in a bowl of sauerkraut.

"Isn't water stress needed for the vines in the growing season?" I asked, tearing myself away from my thoughts. I watched Olivier's eyes wander around the rows of vines where the earth constantly swallowed the pouring rainwater.

"Some amount of rain is good for the growing vines, but if it continues this way, then there is a possibility we might lose this year's crop," he said in his distinctively charming local accent. "Excess water can have many effects. Too much rain during spring and summer months can cause grey rot and other diseases. It also affects the taste of the wine. Diluted grapes will result in the wine lacking concentration. Thick grey clouds mean a lack of sunlight, so the grapes will struggle to ripen on time for the harvest," he explained. "On the other hand, moderate rainfall is needed. Again, it depends on several factors."

I listened to him without interrupting.

"Well, to answer your question on water stress: it's always better to have a little stress at the right time. It helps to develop the grape, which produces smaller berries with higher flavor concentration. But too much may have a damaging effect on the vines. Always remember, too much of anything is bad. Water stress makes the roots of the vines delve deeper into the soil for nutrition. It is vital and this is what distinguishes wines from around the world. When you taste a good wine, you will know instinctively, as it will always take you back to the place where it was grown. For example, some regions like Burgundy and Chablis have limestone-rich soils. These soils not only drain well but also help in holding water for vines to absorb when needed. Wines made in these soils have longevity and bright, linear acidity," Olivier continued.

"When you look at cool-climate regions, like the Mosel Valley in Germany, vines grow on blue slate rocks that absorb and reflect heat, in turn ripening the grapes. The roots of the vines grow deep into the rocky subsoil, curling and wrapping themselves around slate, taking in all the minerality the soil has to offer. Likewise, gravel in the clay soil that you see here is perfect to increase drainage and helps to absorb heat and reflect it onto the grape bunches, mostly at night when the temperature is cooler. The wines turn out bolder and more alcoholic than they typically would be in this climate. That's why soil is most important in vine growing."

Olivier always encouraged me to ask questions and patiently answered each one in an elaborate manner. I sometimes felt the urge to take my imaginary wand out and transfer all his knowledge in one go. "What happens if it doesn't rain at all in a particular year?"

"Irrigation of vineyards to this day is not permitted in France. Vines have to grow naturally with minimum interference from men. It has always been the winemaking philosophy. One has to do his bit and pray to God for good weather," he said, pointing to the sky. "Warm summers and mild winters, with a little bit of rain at intervals is the best one could ask for. Unfortunately, things are getting out of hand due to climate change. Good years and bad years in wine growing are common. Because of the boom in wine commerce, every year, needless to say, has to be a good year, and that has become impossible without interference. In France, we have very restrictive winemaking regulations in place—in fact, hundreds of them.

"I cannot grow whatever type of grape I want in these vineyards. There is a strict control over the varieties one can grow in a particular appellation. Maximum levels of yield, minimum age of vines, planting densities, alcohol, wine production methods, and so on, are all specified by the governing authority, INAO. This helps guide the consumer to better understand what they're drinking, besides encouraging winemakers to adhere to quality winemaking practices, instead of focusing on quantity." He paused briefly, then said, "*Bon*! I have to go; the rains have stopped. Nam, if you have any questions, call me. Don't forget, I was in your shoes a long time back, and someone answered everything for me, so please don't hesitate."

"*Merci, Olivier, vous êtes très gentil*," I said, feeling grateful to have such a kind and encouraging teacher.

A pleasant earthy smell floated around as I strolled to the vineyards. Droplets of rain hung on the ends of the vines. The view stretched out into the horizon. A little Médoc train that traveled from the city center up to the coast whizzed through the scene, reminding me I wasn't staring at a life-size painting in a gallery. I took a deep breath. The vines were fresh and alive after the rains. Tiny white flowers with a delicate scent had unfurled at the position where grapes would begin to appear shortly. Grape vines self-pollinated, but this weather posed a risk. The clouds were low-lying and threatening. Perhaps it would clear up before any damage was done.

There was always something about the Médoc weather that changed like the moods of a capricious child.

Darkness came swiftly. Rest was most needed before I went back to work the next day. I had dinner and retired to my room upstairs. The name "Moksh" appeared on my phone. At once I felt fear seep into my body.

The phone didn't stop ringing. I was sure it was after midnight in India. I didn't dare pick up the call. I had flown more than five thousand miles to escape Moksh and start afresh. I swore never to return to that life. My phone buzzed again. This time it was a message. My body began to tremble. Moksh had this effect on me, even if I was far away. I could imagine his angry face and his bloodshot eyes glaring at me.

"Too busy?" the message read. My heart beat faster. If I avoided his calls, would he come here to get me? Would he take away Shloka for revenge? I shuddered thinking of the worst. I shook my head, took a deep breath. I couldn't let Moksh mess with my head.

I switched off my phone and looked out the window. Over the far west, the sky lit up and rumbled, causing the lights to flicker in my room. I quickly latched my bedroom door, drew the curtains over the windows, and lit a candle. Hastily, I jumped into bed and slid under the quilt. I picked up my laptop that was lying on the table next to my bed and typed in "*Friends* season ten, episode nine." With weary eyes, I watched as Joey said, "I don't like it when people take food off my plate, okay...*maharajah*." The laughter faded into another lonely night.

The next morning, the alarm next to my bed rang. I got out of bed, drew open the curtains, and peeked out my window to get a glimpse of the sky. It was clear blue. Phew! I dressed in a simple A-line full-sleeved ash grey dress, finished with a black piping that reached just below my knee, and slipped on my black pump shoes. As I passed the porch, I picked one of the smaller umbrellas that easily fit into my handbag.

"*Bonjour*!"

It was Marie-Noëlle, the *maître de chai,* or cellar master, an energetic woman in her thirties. Her tall and slender figure rushed toward the cellar, her holy place. She had been making wine for a decade and had only been hired by Édouard to work for Château Siran the previous year. When I first met her, I was absolutely overjoyed to find a woman doing a job that had always been considered a man's profession. I witnessed Marie-Noëlle dressed in a tee and cargo pants, with her hair tied up into a messy knot, rolling big oak barrels containing many liters of wine with ease.

"*Il fait beau aujourd'hui*," she commented and continued to walk without stopping.

"*On a de la chance*," I replied as I locked my front door.

A hot topic for discussion in this region was always the weather, for obvious reasons.

Once inside the office, I looked at the plan for the day. I was to receive a group of eight American women in a half hour. My first task before any visit was to prepare the tasting room with wine and glasses. It was a large room next to the office that featured a long tasting counter and wine bottles, neatly arranged in rows covering one entire wall of the room. Cards, magnets, wine accessories, and books, all for sale, made up the rest of the space. I carefully brought out three wines of different vintages and placed them on the counter. Then I arranged eight wine glasses in a row in front of the bottles. I poured a little wine from each bottle into a glass and tasted each one to check for any faults.

"Excellent," I mumbled, then checked the cash register to see if there were enough notes and coins to begin the day with. Everything was in place. I waited for the guests.

The Americans arrived. *A lovely bunch. Must be in their fifties*, I thought while I watched them chat excitedly and walk toward the tasting room. After they were a bit settled, I introduced myself.

"Good morning, everyone. Welcome to Château Siran. My name is Namratha, and I'm from India. Today, I have the pleasure of being your host. We will visit the castle, its vineyards, and gardens. Later, we will walk through the cellars and I will explain the winemaking process that is followed here, and lastly, you will all taste several incredible wines."

I proceeded with the group toward the Chartreuse-styled building. "Château Siran is one of the Bordeaux wine estates whose origins can be traced back to the eighteenth century. Through time, it came to belong to the grandparents of the famous painter, Toulouse-Lautrec. It was later sold to Léo Barbier, a Bordeaux wine merchant who recognized the potential of the wines. After many years, the management of the property was entrusted to Fréderic Miailhe, a wine broker himself who fell in love with Siran and purchased the entire shares of the property. Today, the estate is managed by the sixth generation of the family, Édouard Miailhe and his wife, Sévrine Miailhe, who take pride in making world-class wines," I explained, then waited patiently while the American women posed in front of the château.

"Smile!" I said and shot a few pictures with the cameras on their phones. After they were content, I walked them to the vineyards and continued to tell them about the different appellations and the soils and grape varieties grown in the area. Later, I took them through the cellar and explained the winemaking process.

"Harvest is always done by hand in our vineyards. The grapes are sorted on a sorting table to remove unripe, damaged, or rotten berries, then they are put into a stemmer to separate the berries from the stems, where they are subsequently passed through a crusher and lightly smashed to release the juice. The pulp and juice are then pumped into these vats." I pointed at the big wooden vats, the inox tanks, and the concrete tanks.

"Do you use all three vats for making wine?"

The lady who asked the question reminded me of Meryl Streep. "Yes, we use all three since we prefer to make interesting and complex wines." I continued. "Yeast is added into the vats and fermentation takes place under controlled conditions. Once the fermentation is complete, the contents of the vat are pressed, and the wine is racked to remove any particles. It is later placed into barrels for aging." The ladies keenly listened to everything I was saying, and I kept the visit interactive by asking questions about the wine culture in their own country. "What's America's favorite grape variety?"

"Oh, we like our Chardonnays and Cabs, they're very popular. We can find it easily, and of course, we love the taste," one of the ladies answered while the rest of them nodded in agreement.

People from all parts of the world visit Bordeaux during summer months. It was a fantastic way of learning for me. I took them to the rooftop terrace, which gave a gorgeous view of the vineyards. "You ladies are very lucky the weather has been so glorious today," I told them and watched them take more pictures to immortalize their trip to the Médoc.

One of the more curious ladies turned to me and asked, "Honey, how did you find yourself here? It's very unusual to find a young Indian woman in this part of the world."

"You're absolutely right; it was the wine calling." I laughed and winked.

The last part of the visit was the tasting. After all, everyone was here to taste the gorgeous wines. I poured about thirty milliliters into one wine glass before I explained the five steps of wine tasting. "Okay, ladies, when you are tasting wine, it's good to remember the five S's: see, swirl, sniff, sip, and savor. So, we start with step one: see. Tilt the glass to about a forty-five-degree angle and observe it under a white background. Look closely at your wine in the glass. You can estimate its age by observing its color because wines change hues over a period of time due to oxidation and chemical reactions. If it is purple in color, then it's a young wine. If it's a deep ruby color in the middle and fading into brown tinges toward the rim, then it could have some age on it. This is an important step.

"Step two: swirl. Swirling your glass of wine around in a circle helps air get into the wine. This releases aromas into the glass," I said and went on to describe the primary, secondary, and tertiary aromas. The ladies were mesmerized. At the end of the tasting, they ordered six cases of the wines to be shipped to their home country. They thanked me for the interesting visit, wished me good luck, and left.

The next visit was in fifteen minutes. I looked at the plan again. "Reservation by Arthur Dubois, visit for three guests," it read. I quickly cleared the previous tasting's glasses and placed three fresh glasses on the counter. There was enough wine in the bottles to go through with this tasting, so I didn't bother with opening new bottles. After a few minutes, a Greek-looking gentleman in an indigo blue suit with neatly polished, pointy-toed black derby shoes walked in with two other men.

"*Bonjour*, we're here for a visit," he said, wearing a nonchalant smile.

I noticed his fiery brown eyes and his skin, still young and taut, but weathered by deep sunshine. His long, greying strands had been gathered into a knot at the back of his head. "Yes, in the name of Mr. Dubois, right?"

"Yes, that's the one."

"Fantastic! Let's start the visit. First of all, welcome to Château Siran. I'm Namratha, and I have the pleasure of being your host today. In the next hour you will visit the magnificent château, its vineyards, and gardens. I will also explain..." I continued my narration. I walked them through the grounds, the vineyards, the cellar, and finally the tasting room. Unlike the earlier group, these men didn't bother taking pictures, so the visit lasted less than an hour.

I poured wine into their glasses.

"You don't look like you're from here," Arthur said with a deep voice.

He had mostly kept silent during the visit, while the other two men hadn't hesitated to interrupt me with their questions. "You're absolutely right—I'm not from here. I'm from India."

"India? That's interesting! What brought you to Bordeaux?"

"Wine!" I answered enthusiastically. "And you, Mr. Dubois?"

"Please, call me Arthur. I'm French, born in Lyon, but I've lived most of my adult life in Paris and London. Due to my wine business, I alternate between these places and Bordeaux."

"That's great, Monsieur Dubois. You have the best of all worlds," I said and continued with the tasting.

At the end of the visit, the two men bought two bottles of wine to take back with them. I packed them carefully in wooden cases to withstand the travel.

"Thank you for the wonderful visit. Here's my card. If you ever find yourself in London, do give me a call," Arthur said as he handed out his visiting card.

I thanked him and said I would surely let him know if I ever traveled that far.

The day had been long, but the sun had shone brightly for all the visitors. That evening, I lay in bed and thought about how my life had taken such a different shape. One strong decision had triggered it all. As glimpses of my journey flashed across my mind, I realized my feet hurt from the long hours of work. Nevertheless, I was more content at that moment than I ever had been. I felt peace in this place. There was an imaginary force that bound me to the vines. A strong "meant to be here" feeling had overtaken me. I really wanted to make a life here with Shloka and Casper. My job at the château was just a five-month contract, and then I would be back in school for six months. What would happen when I finished school? That was my biggest fear.

A permanent job was what I needed. It would help me to settle well, and also allow me to have Shloka and Casper with me. But I was skeptical. Often companies in France refused to hire foreigners, as it involved a ton of paperwork and money. They hired only if one was indispensable to them. India was not a wine-drinking country. I was of little use to them. I wrapped up these worrying thoughts that had kept my loneliness at bay and started redoing my résumé. After a while, my eyes started to feel droopy. I glanced at the clock. Another day would begin soon. I typed "*Friends* season ten, episode ten" on my laptop. Laughter killed the silence, and I watched until I fell asleep.

The next day was more relaxed at the château. There was an Italian couple visiting in the morning, and my colleague Claude hosted them. It was a quiet day. I had nothing much to do, so I decided to clean all the drawers of my desk. I found more stationary, which I arranged into a box. Later, I found some books on wine that

I put into a bookshelf. Then, in one of the drawers, I found pictures of the family and a small maroon pouch. Curious, I looked inside to uncover a beautiful golden brooch in the shape of a wine leaf. I took it to Édouard.

"I found this in the drawers. Thought I'd ask if you had lost it."

"No, it's nothing of great value."

"It's beautiful. I thought it was made of gold."

Édouard let out a laugh.

"It's just a regular brooch. Keep it."

"Really?"

"Yes, keep it. Keep it as a souvenir of Château Siran."

"Thank you, Édouard!" I knew he saw my excitement and heard it in my voice.

"It's nothing. Nam, I also wanted to ask if you'd be free this afternoon to take my friend Jean-Pierre—who's visiting us from South Africa—for a tour around the property."

"With pleasure. I have no visits this afternoon. What time would suit him?"

"I'll check with him and let you know soon."

As planned, that afternoon, a late-middle-aged man entered the office along with Édouard. He had neatly cut white hair and a closely-trimmed goatee of the same color. He was low in stature, but his elegant, three-piece suit gave him a certain presence.

"This is Jean-Pierre, a very dear old friend of mine," Édouard said. He turned to him and said, "Nam is a part of the Siran family. She comes from India."

"Oh, the land of the Gods. *Enchanté,* madame," Jean-Pierre said, holding out his hand to greet me.

Édouard turned to Jean-Pierre. "It's a pity I won't be able to join you, Jean-Pierre, but Nam will do a fabulous job."

"It's alright, Édouard. Nam seems like good company. Thank you for arranging the tour."

"Great, I'll see you here in an hour. Enjoy your visit," Édouard said and sprinted off.

Luckily, the rain Gods had visited Médoc only for a short time, so we were experiencing good weather for a few days. I walked Jean-Pierre around the château while he recollected spending his childhood vacations here.

"I remember playing here with Édouard and his sister as a child." He laughed. "It almost seems like yesterday. They have preserved everything the same way as before."

"Well, I didn't know Édouard had a sister. I've never seen her at the château. Does she live in Bordeaux?" I was perplexed, having never heard her name mentioned before.

"Oh, poor little Audrey died in an accident. The family took a long time to come to terms with it." Jean-Pierre shook his head with a very sad look on his face.

A shiver ran down my spine. That was the last thing I needed to hear. The nights were scary enough even without this information.

"That's Audrey, Édouard's sister," he added, pointing to a painting on the wall. "She was only a little bit older than that picture when a speeding car crashed into her."

A young girl in a pink frock with a bow on her head stood next to Édouard. *Thanks, Jean-Pierre! Now I'll never be able to sleep in peace,* I said to myself, and almost instantaneously shook off the shock that I had just endured to continue with the tour.

Édouard was waiting for us at the office.

"*Bon,* how was your visit?" he asked Jean-Pierre.

"It was wonderful, thanks to this lovely lady."

Jean-Pierre had not realized what his revelation meant for me.

"You're very kind with your words, Jean," I said.

"Well, we're all having dinner together at the château tonight. Nam, please join us if you're free."

"With pleasure. Thank you, Édouard." I turned and headed back to my desk.

***

That evening after work, I returned to my room and excitedly opened the little maroon pouch and took out the brooch. It was gorgeous indeed. It had all the indentations of a real wine leaf. I was mesmerized and thought if I ever started a company, this would be my logo. I slipped the brooch back into the pouch and carefully placed it in my bedside drawer. I dressed, then headed down the stairs. The family was in the living room along with Jean-Pierre. Chopin played in the background as Sévrine poured Pol Roger Brut Vintage 2009 into each of our glasses. It was my first glass of Pol Roger. It was ecstasy. I observed tiny bubbles floating to the top in thin streams from the bottom of my flute glass when we toasted, then took the first sip.

"I particularly love the nutty hints in this." This wine was a tapestry of rich and complex flavors, intricately woven into each other, still bursting with vivacious acidity and freshness.

"*C'est sublime*," Sévrine added.

"What's a good wine without great company?" Édouard said. We all nodded in agreement and chorused "*Santé*!" while we clinked our glasses once again.

"Jean-Pierre, it's so good to have you here. Thank you for coming and spending time with us."

"It's a pleasure to be with you all and relive our childhood days," Jean-Pierre said affectionately.

After another round of Champagne, we proceeded to dinner and took our seats as the host gestured. The table, as always, was beautifully set, but this time I didn't embarrass myself by looking under the plate. By now I had dined with the family a number of times. Édouard and Sévrine made sure to always cook vegetarian meals for me.

"Nam, I've made *courgettes farcies* for you today. I hope you like them," Sévrine said.

"Stuffed zucchini—I love them. *Merci*," I said and smiled, thankful she remembered.

Édouard served Château Siran 1993 into glasses while Sévrine served the entrée onto our plates.

"It has aged beautifully," I said after taking a sip. I always thought of wine as a piece of art in a bottle. The winemaker—the artist—blends in different grapes to make flavors come through and encases them in a bottle, as if it were the canvas. This liquid treasure that had been stored away in deep grounds for many years finally had its chance to come alive again in a cup. So divine.

Jean-Pierre and Édouard recounted their childhood memories, while also enquiring with each other about friends. Sévrine and I chatted about French cuisine as she opened another bottle of wine. Her *courgettes farcies* was delectable. She paired it with an old oak-aged wine from Napa Valley, which was a blend of Cabernet Sauvignon and Merlot. I found myself constantly comparing older vintages to younger ones, good years to bad years, winemaking techniques, farming practices, and so forth. This time, I was comparing Cabernet Sauvignon and Merlot grown in the Napa Valley and the same varieties grown in the Médoc.

"How could they taste so different?" I wondered. Just then, Édouard's voice rang out.

"Napa wines are aged in American oak. You can smell the distinct vanilla and coconut aromas imparted by them."

There was much more I needed to learn in this new world of mine. I often locked up tasting notes into one little part of my brain. And if my palate ever touched a beautiful wine, it never forgot the taste. This was an important part of being a wine student.

After a delicious dessert, paired with an exquisite wine from Hungary, I thanked the couple and wished Jean-Pierre bon voyage, since he was to leave for Cape Town the next day. I walked faster this time, not stopping to look at the sky or the stars like I always did. Tonight, I felt so uncomfortable. The darkness and the silence after Jean-Pierre's revelation that afternoon was more than I could bear. I picked up my pace and moved into a jogger's run.

When I reached my room, I secured the door from the inside, then switched on the lights. I looked at my watch; it was midnight. *I have to calm down; the whole family's next door. There is nothing to worry about.* I took a deep breath and switched on the radio. I changed and clambered into bed. However, I continued to feel frightened. I really needed to do something about this situation. My fear was overtaking my entire body. I had to get a grip and hang on.

Suddenly, I had an idea that I thought could work. "I will give you this night. If you are here, come and get me. If not, I will be afraid no more!" I nearly yelled, sitting there with the lights on, fighting my sleep so I could keep guard. I waited and waited.

The next morning, my alarm went off louder than usual, and I woke up with a fright. I had drifted into deep slumber at some point in the night. I sat up and looked around me. There was no sign of ghosts. *They must be busy*, I concluded.

***

A few weeks went by, and a long weekend followed. Since I had a few days off from work, Jake and I, along with another friend, Sofia, decided to take a short trip to San Sebastián, a coastal city in Spain. It was only a few hours away from Bordeaux. Eventually, Julie and Adrien from school decided to join in. Adrien generously offered to drive us there. It was a Saturday morning, and the sun was blazing above us as we got into the car. Little did I know that this trip would become the turning point in my life.

CHAPTER 12

The Accident

Bordeaux, France
July 2017

Adrien was in the car waiting for us. He was French, but had lived most of his adult life in China, which had tempered his Frenchness. He was kind and gentle when he spoke. We often had deep conversations about life and people. I somehow always felt as though he was looking for his proper place in this world. Sofia was a native of Colombia. Just like me, she loved animals. I had grown very fond of her since our first meeting. Julie arrived with a bag full of food. She was French. She was a free spirit, always ready for an adventure.

"Only Jake's missing," I said.

"We'll be late if we don't leave now," Adrien added.

As if on cue, Jake arrived, panting. His face glistened with sweat.

"My alarm didn't work—oh my God, such a mess today. I almost thought I wouldn't make it."

We all loved Jake. He was a true Canadian. We often bantered. He always corrected the way I pronounced "Toronto." "It's 'Torono' and not 'Toronto,'" he'd say, accentuating the nasal sound. Though annoyingly childlike at times, he was good fun to be around.

"Sofiaaaaa, that's my seat," Jake whined when he saw that Sofia had occupied the seat next to the driver.

"Oh gosh, please don't start off, Jake," I chided from the back seat.

"Jake, that seat doesn't have your name written on it," said Julie.

"Okay, okay...you can take this seat. I really don't care," Sofia said and jumped into the back.

"Thank you, Sofia, you won't regret this. I am here to unleash my DJ skills."

We all laughed. It was hard to stay mad at Jake for any length of time.

Finally, we started our journey. I could see that the route was less crowded, as I was sitting in the middle seat in the rear of the car.

It was Saturday morning, and the holiday mood had perfectly set in. In twenty minutes, we joined the autoroute, heading south. Adrien moved to the left side of the road, automatically increasing the speed in order to keep up with the rest of the vehicles. Sofia, Julie, and I looked up the itinerary on my phone to see if we had time to stop at a place for lunch.

As I straightened up, I noticed a car abruptly coming to a halt a short distance ahead directly in our path. I blinked. This couldn't be. We were in the fastest lane of the autoroute. I hastily looked at Adrien to see why he wasn't slowing down. He had gone into shock. Staring at the scene in front of him with his eyes wide and unblinking. We were traveling at a speed of 130 kilometers per hour. I had the vantage point. All at once, it dawned upon me that what was to come was inevitable. We were heading straight at the halted cars. It all happened in seconds. I lifted my hand to warn Adrien, while opening my mouth to scream. Before my voice came out, I heard the sound of the metal tearing in. Time no longer existed. I felt an infinite silence. A disappeared existence. I floated in a dark space. My body suspended for a long time in thin air with no idea who I was, or where I was.

My face was flat on the windscreen and my hands flattened on each side of my forehead. I had flown from the back of the car straight into the glass. Both my knees were resting on the gearbox when I regained consciousness. My head cracked the windscreen of the car. I peeled my eyes open and gasped for breath. Smoke filled my lungs. I coughed several times, thinking I heard some kind of commotion through the ringing in my ears. The voices seemed to be coming from afar. Time expanded while I slowly moved to the seat next to me from the gearbox, pushing aside the flattened air bag. Everything around me moved in slow motion: the smoke, the voices, the faces... Suddenly, a hand grabbed me under my arm, then another hand moved under my other arm, and I was pulled from the car. When my lungs filled with fresh air, I became fully conscious. The world felt more real as I was laid on the grass.

I heard Adrien's voice. "I can't feel my arm, I can't feel my arm..." he kept repeating. I looked in his direction with utter disbelief as he tried to move his mangled left arm, but it just hung limply by his side. I heard Sofia moaning in pain. I was terrified. Straining my neck, I turned toward the direction of her voice. She was lying on the grass. Next to her was a stranger who was working hard to console her. I saw Julie and Jake speaking to the police, who had just arrived. I was relieved to see them unhurt.

The man who had gotten me out of the car walked back to me.

"*Ça va mieux*?"

"*Oui, merci*," I said as I slowly sat up. I shut my eyes tight and hoped this was all a dream. When I dared to open my eyes, I hoped beyond belief it would all be gone. I heard sirens. I sighed. The weekend trip we had all looked forward to had turned into a nightmare.

Red fire trucks arrived with the pompiers on board. Two firefighters checked my vital signs and then put me onto a stretcher and lifted me into the back of the truck. I overheard them talking about the accident.

"The driver must have been crazy to halt his car on such a busy route."

"Apparently, he had a heated argument with his passenger and decided to stop the car, *putain*."

"Did they catch the idiot?"

"*Le connard* escaped."

"Fortunately, the first four cars avoided colliding into each other. The fifth car crashed at an alarming speed, but luckily it swerved to the left and slammed in between the metal wall of the divider and the car that had pulled up last. Luckily the passengers of that car had gotten out just in time."

"I've seen many accidents where multiple cars are involved, and it usually doesn't end very well. It's a miracle they're all alive."

Okay, so that's what happened, I thought and touched my forehead and my knees. They felt fine. I had negligible pain in my toes and my right hand, but none where I actually should have felt pain. I couldn't understand. We arrived at the hospital, and I was wheeled into the emergency room. I was scanned head to toe and checked for any injuries. Two slightly fractured toes and a ligament tear on the back of my right hand, the reports showed.

"Please, don't use your right hand," the doctor said as he fixed a brace in place over my hand. "Also, try to avoid walking as much as possible until the fractures have healed. Surprisingly, you have no concussion or cranial injuries, but please keep watch and do call me if you feel discomfort of any kind."

I thanked the doctor as he left. When I limped out of the room, I saw Isabella searching for me in the hallway. I was relieved to see her and hugged her tight.

"What did the doctor say?"

"I'm okay, just a couple of tiny fractures and a ligament tear."

"Julie called me, and I came immediately," she said.

"Did you find the others?" I inquired with mounting concern.

"*Sì, bella*, Julie and Jake are fine, but Adrien and Sofia, they are not so good. Sofia has a fractured spine and Adrien's broken his right arm, *cazzo*.... He has been taken in for surgery."

"Oh my God!" I could not stop the tears that filled my eyes. I felt helpless for Sofia and Adrien.

"They'll be fine soon, don't worry," Isabella said consolingly. "I'm so glad that you're fine. Come with me, I'll drop you home."

I decided to stay at Conor's, since I knew solitude that night would be of no help. I called, hoping he'd answer.

Conor was quite concerned after listening to what had happened. He had cleaned my old room and spread fresh sheets on the bed just before I arrived. The moment I entered he reached out, pulled me to him, and gave me a tight hug.

"I'm so glad you're alright, my friend."

I smiled wearily. He led me to my room and settled me down. Isabella left after promising to come back the next day to check on me.

"Rest well. I'll bring you some soup later." Conor pulled down the wooden shutters and went out of the room, closing the door behind him.

I tried to fall asleep, but the accident and the events of the morning kept playing in my head. It felt as though someone had taken me out of the car just in time and placed me back after the accident. I tried to recollect where I had been during that time. I had felt as light as a feather, floating somewhere in the darkness. I still couldn't believe I survived that terrible crash. *What if I hadn't? Shloka would have been devastated. Moksh would have finally been happy to have gotten rid of me without blood on his hands.* I thanked the universe for keeping me alive. My thoughts went deeper. *There must be a reason why I survived this crash. Maybe my life has a greater purpose. Perhaps I am still here to fulfill an important job for God. But what is it?* I kept asking myself.

After a while, I heard a knock on the door.

"Come in," I said in a frail voice, and Conor entered with a big tray and placed it on the side table.

"Here you go—a nice hot veggie soup, cheese toasties, and a *cannelé* for dessert," he announced.

"Thank you, Conor. You are such a darling."

"Oh, it's nothing. I'm worried about you. Are you feeling any better?"

"Yes, I am. Thanks."

"Great. I'll get you a bottle of water so that you don't have to get out of bed."

I ate dinner, took my medication, and put my head down on the pillow. I wondered if my thoughts would keep me awake, or if my dreams would save me from the trauma that I had endured.

***

The next morning, I woke only when the sun peered through the little openings of the wooden shutter. I was limping and immobile in my right hand, but I did feel revived. I walked to the living room and found Conor there.

"Hey! Good afternoon, buddy. How are you today?" he said in a cheerful voice.

"I'm feeling much better, Conor. Thank you."

"I checked on you a couple of times in the night and was relieved to see you sleeping like a baby. Would you like tea or coffee? Or lunch straight away? I've made penne in *arrabbiata* sauce and a nice lettuce and tomato salad dressed with vinaigrette."

"Sounds yum, Conor. I'll jump straight to lunch."

"That makes sense. We can have tea at teatime of course," he said with a grin.

"Can I help you with anything?" I asked as I attempted to get up from my chair to follow him.

"No, no, please, let me. You rest," he insisted and disappeared into the kitchen.

Conor's Irish roots were very strong. Eight years of living in France hadn't made him one bit French. He was always a happy soul. There wasn't a day he didn't read a book or forget to drink a glass of wine. He collected my post, held my extra luggage in his storage, and even let me stay at his apartment every time I visited the city. I was grateful to have a friend like him.

***

I rested another day in Bordeaux and then returned to Château Siran. Édouard and Sévrine were concerned, too, and asked me to rest until I was well. But I protested and went back to work. I needed to keep my mind occupied so I wouldn't think about the accident. I took desk jobs that didn't require walking and moving around. I was determined not to let anything bring down my morale, yet I found myself feeling distraught. I began to read articles and books on wine when I had extra time at the office. Write-ups on wine investments caught my attention.

One title read, "Fine Wine as an Alternative Investment during Equity Market Downturns," by Elie I. Bouri. Another one read, "Investing in the finer things in life: Wine," by Mike Colagrossi. I had also heard about En Primeur, an event that took place every year in Bordeaux. I knew it was a way of investing in wines too, just like futures. Here, they were talking about trading bottles of wine. Investors seemed to store their bottles in bonded warehouses and watch their investments grow. These wines each carried passports that helped a new buyer trace it back to its origin. How could people invest in wine? Wine is wine. *It's to share and drink*, I thought.

My sister's husband, Nikhil, was an investment advisor. I called him and discussed it at length. He was very encouraging and asked me to further research it. He also helped me understand investments in order to understand the world of wine investments. It took me several weeks before I got my head around it. There was so much more to wine than one could see on the surface. The UK was a hub for fine wine investments. Numerous firms were located in London, where wines were traded and wine funds were created. Wines came under the category of alternative investments called SWAG—silver, wine, art, and gold—and these investments had superseded some traditional asset tools and had proven that investments could be unconventional. It was even tax free. I read on. Fine wine had been giving great returns on investments. A bottle of Carruades de Lafite appreciated by 3,000 to 4,000 percent in five years, which meant a jump from £140 to a phenomenal £4,500 a case.

After learning this, I was gobsmacked. It was a different world altogether. These investors were mostly people who used their excess money to invest for the pleasure of having a Romanée-Conti or a Lafite in their collection. Intrigued, I followed the news and insights of Liv-ex, a global marketplace for the wine trade. It gave me regular updates on which wine was trending and which ones to look forward to in the future. Nikhil said we could offer these investments to potential clients in India and Indians across the world.

This was a new concept, but I needed to know more before we dove into it. After a few more days of researching, I rounded up two companies in London who were performing very well and fixed meetings with both.

It was around the same time that Arthur Dubois returned. He brought a different client this time for the tour. My injuries were completely healed, and I could walk about easily. I greeted the men.

"It's lovely to see you again, Nam," Arthur said in his gravelly voice.

That's a bit odd—he remembers my name, I thought.

"The pleasure is all mine, Mr. Dubois." I used my most courteous voice. "If you're ready, gentlemen, we can begin our tour," I said, and continued while they nodded. "I'm Namratha, and I have the pleasure of being your guide today..."

I did the usual tour of the château, the vineyards, the cellar, and then we went to the tasting room.

"So, will you be visiting London anytime?" Arthur asked.

The question took me aback.

"Well, yes. Quite soon, in fact." I wondered if he was just making conversation, or if he could read minds. "I've planned meetings with wine investing companies to explore opportunities in offering alternative investments to clients in India."

"Then you must surely meet my pal, Richard. He's big into wine investments. I could introduce you to him when you are in London. Give me a call before you leave Bordeaux, and I'll arrange that."

"That would be wonderful. Thank you, Mr. Dubois."

"Please, call me Arthur. I insist."

"Yes, Arthur."

I was not in the habit of calling clients by their first names and hoped it would be acceptable if they insisted. The wine business kept expanding for me, and I totally enjoyed the learning process.

I needed to find a name for my company. Every evening, I came back from work with all the names I had thought of during the day. Wine Escapade, Wine Indulgence, Wineology, Vin et La Vie, Bacchus Wines, Dionysus Wines.... Most names were already taken. It was the end of the week when I actually succeeded.

"It's an equation, Wine Equation," I muttered. "Wine Equation!" I looked all over the net, checking to see if the domain was available. It was. I felt euphoric. I registered the name and looked up tickets to London. I needed to take the Bordeaux-Paris train and then the Eurostar from there. *Maybe I could make a pitstop that night at my friend's place before I take the Eurostar the next day*, I thought. Both Swathi and Vivek were from the same city as me in India. Vivek had come to France many years ago for work. He had settled well and eventually moved his family here. Susan had introduced us on a call before I arrived in France. We met, and we hit it off immediately. Their six-year-old son, Sparsh, reminded of Shloka. He always looked forward to playing Monopoly with me. Visiting them was like going back to Bangalore. We chatted in our mother tongue, Kannada, and they always cooked delicious South Indian meals.

In a few days, it was time to leave.

***

I got off the Bordeaux-Paris train and waddled across the platform with a medium-sized suitcase in one hand and a kitbag that contained gifts and wine in the other. A laptop bag hung across my shoulder, which I kept close to me since I knew Paris was notorious for theft. I bought tickets to Maisons-Laffitte and slowly proceeded toward the platform. I was always amazed at how complex yet efficient the metro system was in connecting all parts of Paris, beyond which the Réseau Express Régional was the most convenient way of getting to the suburbs.

People all around me were hurrying to catch the train. I had just missed getting on the quarter-past-eight train, so I waited and got into the next one that chugged in fifteen minutes later. I noticed that this train was less crowded. I didn't bother climbing up to the upper deck or going down to the lower deck. Instead, I stood holding the long bar that was rather close to the entrance in order to disembark easily with my luggage.

This time tomorrow, I will be in London. A surge of excitement ran through my body. It was a new me, being a businesswoman. I had never imagined myself this way. I had shopped to change my attire and look more businesslike. In the store, I'd walked past all the dresses that I usually purchased and went straight to the section where blazers and trousers were displayed. I bought three suits, each a different color, for my trip. The hairdresser had given me a layered cut and then done a balayage. When she handed me the mirror, I could hardly recognize myself. A laptop bag now took the place of my handbag. My professional diary contained details of all my meetings. I was all set for the urban jungle.

"Nanterre Préfecture," a voice announced. I had three more stops to go.

I glanced at my phone to check the time when a hand grabbed it from behind and jumped off the train just before the doors slammed shut behind me. I couldn't believe it. Someone had stolen my phone. London would be a disaster.

This isn't real. I must be dreaming, I thought when I saw the thief take to his heels through the window. It took me a few minutes to come to terms with what had happened.

The train stopped at the next station. I got off and hurriedly looked for a policeman. I couldn't find one. I looked around for a staff member who could help me. There were none. My contacts and precious photos, all gone. I dragged my luggage behind me, feeling furious. All of a sudden, I heard a noise then felt the suitcase scrape the ground. One of the wheels flew off my suitcase! This can't be happening. I tried in vain to fix the wheel. This was all too much to handle in a single day. I walked out of the station, balancing my suitcase on one wheel.

"Taxi!" I screamed at the top of my lungs when I saw a black car with a taxi sign on top passing slowly across the street. The driver halted immediately. He must have never encountered anyone hailing a taxi with the same vigor as I did that evening.

My friends were waiting for me with decanted wine and fancy glasses set on the table. They were quite worried since they hadn't been able to reach me for the last hour. My voice trembled while I recounted the events that had unfolded that evening.

"Oh my God!" they chorused.

"It's alright, sweetie, you're safe now," Swathi said in a sympathetic voice.

"I need to go to the *poste de police* and lodge a complaint."

"We can report it, but it's a long process and there's a very slim chance of getting your phone back. I've seen many cases like this. The first thing you need to do is erase all data on your phone," said Vivek.

"Nam aunty," Sparsh came running down the stairs to give me a hug. "Come, let's play."

My stress disappeared and I laughed. Sparsh reminded me of Shloka. She was always full of energy.

"Give me twenty minutes; I need to take care of something before, sweetheart."

"Sparsh, get to bed now, please; aunty will play with you in the morning," Swathi demanded.

"Mommy, that's not fair! I want to play with Aunty...."

"Sparsh, get to bed now, please. I'll come in five minutes and read you a story," Vivek added.

"Dada, please read 'Ali Baba and the Forty Thieves' to Sparsh. It's his favorite story," Swathi said cleverly as she hugged him.

After kissing me good night, Sparsh picked up his teddy and went upstairs to his room, followed by his father.

Swathi and I spent the next twenty minutes erasing data on my phone from the computer.

"God bless technology," I mumbled.

It was quite evident that I would never get my phone back. I was disheartened.

"Don't worry, you will always find a way to deal with tough situations. London will be great. You'll see," Swathi said, trying to lift my spirits up. She was right.

***

The next day, the Eurostar whizzed through the dark tunnel and finally came out into the bright southern countryside of England. I looked at my watch—it was almost time for a cup of tea in the land of the Queen.

CHAPTER 13
The Queen's Land

London, UK
August 2017

The air was nippy that evening when I stepped off the train at St. Pancras station. I bought an Oyster card at the travel desk and proceeded toward the underground. People were hurrying in all directions. The vibe was very fast-paced, vibrant, and energetic. The northern line took me to Waterloo first, then I changed to the southern railways, which took me to Surbiton, as per the instructions of my cousin who was hosting my stay in London. At the station, I hopped into the famous London black cab. I had seen these cabs with their characteristic silhouette and the yellow roof sign only in movies. So quintessentially British.

The scenery from the cab was amazing. There were brick houses with white windows and chimney tops along the tree-and-grass-lined street. These beautiful homes were so different from the ones in Bordeaux where houses were built with stones. London was exactly as I had imagined—an urban jungle.

In less than five minutes, the driver halted in a parking space of an apartment block.

"That'll be six pounds please, love," he said in a cockney accent.

I handed over a ten-pound note, charmed as I was by his mellifluous voice, despite the high fare.

"Will you be wanting the shrapnel, ma'am?" he asked, rattling some coins.

"Shrapnel?"

"The change, darling—do you want it?"

"Errr, well, you can keep it as your tip," I said, feeling embarrassed that I could not understand his accent even if it was the same language I spoke.

"Cheers! Have a fabulous day," the driver said, then sped off.

***

The next day I quickly got dressed in a formal blue suit and hurried to my meeting in Mayfair, central London. I had noted all the directions on a scribble pad after having looked up the map on my laptop. I hopped on the southern railways, then onto the tube, and soon reached Robert's office. Mayfair was the most expensive piece of real estate in London. There was just something magical about this place, and as I walked in my blue pumps, I felt confidence oozing out of me just like the aromas of fine wine from a glass.

I extended my newly printed card. A shiny golden wine leaf glittered on a black background. It was the brooch that Édouard had given me. I had placed it over a black background and taken a picture. It was perfect as my company's logo.

"So, as we had discussed, Robert, I'm here today to see possible ways of collaborating with your company to offer fine wine in the form of investments and wine funds to my clients," I said in a business-like tone.

"It would certainly be a pleasure to partner with your company."

We talked about storage and liquidity of the wines and agent fees, and then, after I said I was leaving on Friday, he invited me for dinner the following evening.

That went bloody well! I decided as I walked toward my next destination.

London's best wine store, Hedonism Wines, was just a few streets away. For some reason, it reminded me of Hansel and Gretel's candy home. The place had the most exquisite range of fine wines and spirits on display from across the world. I walked around in amazement, exploring every part of the store that was decorated in pale wood and patinated bronze, amplifying the amber and caramel hues of the room. At the center of the store lay a wooden case with a long conical wine bottle. "Block 42 Kalimna 2004," it read at the bottom. I glared at the price unblinkingly. *Holy moly, I could buy an apartment for the same price.*

I swallowed and pinched myself to feel my existence in this ridiculously expensive world, then I walked down the stairs that led to the bottom of the store. I looked above and noticed the hand-blown, inverted sommelier glasses tipped with LEDs at the base of their stems, suspended from the top to give an impression of a grand chandelier. A glazed cabinet caught my attention. It displayed neatly arranged bottles with shades of liquid gold. All vintages of Château d'Yquem appeared to glow from within.

I wished I had a billionaire's wallet. Every part of this store was designed to speak of luxury. I gaped at rare bottles, the Mathusalems of Cristal Roederer and Krug, costing thousands of pounds. I couldn't believe my eyes. I entered an alcove where colored hands jutted from the wall delicately holding bottles of Sine Qua Non. The shop's owner, Evgeny Chichvarkin, had a whole dedicated space for his favorite wine.

After a good two hours of ogling, I headed to the London Wine Festival, in the heart of Westminster. I knew I would meet more people from London's wine industry, and it would be a great opportunity to network. I walked to Bond Street underground station to take the Jubilee line to Westminster. While I sat in the Tube, I noticed two women dressed in Victorian-era ball gowns, wearing charming evening headdresses of ribbon, lace, and feathers, sitting opposite me. From their chatter, I understood that they were going to a tea party. *Oh gosh, I shouldn't eavesdrop*, I thought. However, I couldn't help myself.

"George was out on the lash again last night, and his girlfriend called to check if he was at mine."

"Why would she call you?"

"Coz she thinks we're having an affair. Silly cow!"

"That's insane! Are you?" asked her friend while she straightened up her stocking.

"Of course I am," said the lady, breaking out into loud, braying laughter.

I was intrigued. Their conversation was entertaining. The Tube was also filled with charming, James Bondish-type men dressed in neatly tailored suits, probably heading back to work from lunch. Everyone else didn't seem to bother too much about the ornately-dressed women. *Maybe it's a common sight*, I concluded.

"Westminster," the disembodied voice announced, and I hopped off the Tube into the hubbub.

The festival was well underway in the magnificent grand hall of One Great George Street. I made my way into the hall on the upper floor. It was filled with oenophiles holding glasses and walking around tasting some of the three-hundred-plus wines on display. I went from one table to another tasting the Rieslings, Cabernets, Merlots, and Syrahs. Finally, I landed at the English sparkling counter.

An elderly-looking, dapper gentleman who was tasting wine next to me held out his glass and said, "Neat and crisp, ain't it?"

I nodded, and he held out his hand and introduced himself. "Henry. Nice to meet you."

As I took another sip from my flute glass, Henry began to brag about his connection with Eric Heerema of the Nyetimber vineyards. It was one of the most famous sparkling wines that the UK produced. Later, he asked me what I was doing in London. I gave him my business card and explained.

"Well, that's very interesting. I'll keep this in mind for the future," Henry said and slipped the card into his wallet. "Are you going to be at the auction tomorrow?"

"Auction?"

"The one at Pall Mall."

"I'm sorry, but I'm not aware of it," I confessed.

"There's an auction there at eleven o'clock tomorrow. If you fancy going, here's my card. Just tell them you are attending on my behalf."

I was thrilled. It had been a fantastic day already, but I decided I could take more surprises. *I must do some sightseeing*, I thought, and proceeded toward the Bridge. Soon, I found a river cruiser that was serendipitously ready to set sail. I hopped into the waiting vessel. The Thames river cruise offered breathtaking views of London from the water. As the boat surged along the river, the guide spoke about London's historical links to each of the iconic monuments on the scenic route from Westminster to Greenwich. The Houses of Parliament, Westminster Palace, the Shard, the National Theatre, the Globe Theatre, the London Eye, Big Ben, Tower Bridge, St Paul's Cathedral... London was mesmerizing.

Next, I stopped at the Shard, a ninety-five-story, glass-clad skyscraper. I had to experience this wonder, so I decided to have a glass of wine there. I pressed level thirty-one in the lift, which took me to the bar. I sat facing the floor-to-ceiling glass window that offered a 360-degree view of London. A young member of staff handed me the menu and asked what I would like to have. I scanned the wine list and ordered a glass of Barolo.

"Good choice, madam," the sommelier said in a pleasant voice.

I grinned. The wine list was long and spanned at least sixteen countries. I took a sip of the wine, and it felt marvelous. The wine from Borolo was almost like a woman—elegant and delicate on the outside, yet so powerful on the inside. The world seemed to pause while I sniffed the roses and cherries and tasted licorice, leather, and chocolate. *What a lovely end to a fantastic day*, I thought as I gazed at the glittering skyline.

The day had been exhilarating. I returned and recounted the events to my cousin, Ragini, who was still awake watching television. She was excited for me. Later, I headed off to my room and began writing a post for social media about an outrageously expensive wine bottle I had witnessed that day at Hedonism Wines. "Block 42 Kalimna 2004: A Hedonistic Indulgence," I titled the article. "London's outrageously decadent wine store, Hedonism Wines, in Mayfair, has this extraordinary wine by Penfolds on sale, and it costs a whopping £120,000 for 750 ml..." I wrote.

***

The next day, I called Arthur before leaving home.

A deep voice answered. "Hello?"

"Hi, Arthur. It's Nam."

"Welcome to London, madam."

"Thank you, Arthur. I was wondering if you could introduce me to your friend Richard, who is in wine investments."

"Yes, certainly. We could meet for lunch tomorrow at the Dorchester hotel. I'll check with him and see if he's free."

After a short catch-up, I hung up and peeked out the window. Cold air stung into my skin. *I must dress warmly*, I decided. Just then, there was a knock on my bedroom door. It was Ragini.

"Morning, Nam. I've made *puri* and *aloo palya* for breakfast. Why don't you have some before you leave."

"Oh God, Ragini, that sounds heavenly."

"Do you have time? Your hair needs a bit of ironing. You can't go out looking all frizzy."

It was incredible how Ragini thought of everything even before I could. After a scrumptious breakfast and the straightening of my long tresses, I slipped on a navy blue, full-sleeved, midi pencil dress with boots and a warm coat, then headed out. The Tube took me to Vauxhall, and from there I took another line which stopped at Green Park. I walked down St. James Street. It was a busy world. Books and movies had given me a fair idea about London's eccentric life, but to be here and witness the folly was something else. There were things that astonished me in the Queen's kingdom. I wondered why on earth they would use two faucets instead of one, when one could leave you with blisters and the other could freeze you? How could one love to eat Marmite, a foul-smelling, bizarre salty paste that looks like something you'd use to polish a shoe?

Thoughts left me when I entered the underground hall at Pall Mall, a private gentleman's club. It was meant for an oenophile with deep pockets. I was guided to a seat, served a glass of Champagne, and given a booklet that contained the list of wines that were being auctioned that day. About thirty members had gathered in a brightly lit room. At the front, a tall man wearing a checked grey suit with a matching tie and an indigo blue pocket square stood behind a lectern with a wooden hammer in his hand. He chanted in a monotonous tone into a mic attached to his left collar.

"Lot number one hundred twenty-three, we're opening this at twenty-four hundred sterling pounds...twenty-six hundred...twenty-eight hundred...four thousand...the bid is at four thousand, going once, going twice." My head was spinning— £4,000 for three bottles of wine? Some people were on telephones discussing in mumbled voices, while others judiciously lifted their hands to bid.

"Four thousand it is, four thousand pounds!"

A lady sitting next to me in a pink sheath dress raised her arm. She seemed to be conversing with someone over the telephone.

"At four thousand pounds, sold!"

"Yesss!" she uttered under her breath in triumph.

I turned to look at this woman, who had just bid against all the men in the room, and our eyes caught each other's. I could see her flawless face with a touch of rouge on the cheeks framed with blonde straight-across bangs. Her pastel-colored lips stretched into a smile when she saw me. I grinned and wondered what this lady's life could be like. I heard hushed chatter ripple across the room, but it soon went silent when the next lot was announced.

"We're starting here with lot number one hundred twenty-four. Five vintages from the Château Mouton Rothschild series, ten thousand pounds to start with, ten thousand pounds, twelve thousand... twelve thousand it is, looking for fifteen thousand pounds, at fifteen thousand...looking for fifteen thousand, eighteen thousand is bid, eighteen thousand is the bid here in the room—twenty thousand pounds, and it is sold!"

I clasped my mouth and whispered, "Oh my God."

After about an hour of witnessing the madness, I decided to leave. I was baffled. How could there be so much difference between the world I once lived in and the world I was witnessing?

I wasn't an abused housewife anymore, but a businesswoman wearing a suit and sitting amongst oenophiles who were bidding for thousands of pounds for a bottle of wine. I shook my head in disbelief and proceeded to grab a cold sandwich in a Pret A Manger store, where they served freshly prepared food on the go. I quickly had a bite and headed off to my next meeting in Hammersmith.

Later that day, I went to Claridge's to meet with Robert from the wine investment company for dinner, as planned. The day had been thrilling and tiring in equal measure, especially while trying to make my way to places without the help of Google Maps. Upon reaching Claridge's, I headed straight to the powder room and freshened up before finding Robert, who was comfortably ensconced in the on-site restaurant, The Foyer & Reading Room.

The evening unfolded pleasantly in his company. We chatted business while surrounded by shimmering walls of the original art deco mirrors and music drifting from the grand piano in the background. Robert was a charming man in his sixties. There was a certain chivalry about him. He was also a shrewd businessman. After all, he was here making sure I would work with his company to offer wine investments to India, which was still an untapped market in the wine sector.

"Champagne for the lady, please," Robert said to the waiter who had come to ask what we would like to order. "Actually, make it two." We savored our drinks for a while, then ordered our main course. Mine was a wild mushroom and truffle risotto paired with a lovely rouge from Crozes-Hermitage. Robert, on the other hand, ordered Claridge's chicken pie that he thought went very well with Gevrey-Chambertin. For dessert, we ordered a refreshing Sauterne with a strawberry cheesecake.

The wines kept flowing, and I tried my best to drink enough water at intervals. Being a wine professional and saying no to wine when served was impolite. The evening was splendid. I thanked Robert and headed back home.

***

The next morning's rays of sunshine were cruel enough to get me vacillating between rising and snuggling deeper into the duvet for a while. It was my last day in London. I met Arthur Dubois for lunch. He was early, waiting at the entrance of the Dorchester hotel.

"*Bonjour, madame.* I'm very pleased to see you again," he said and continued in his heightened, franglais accent. "Unfortunately, Richard could not make it today, but he has assured me he will get in touch with you soon."

I felt disappointed as I walked inside with him. The restaurant was quite busy. Most tables were occupied, but we were guided to a table with a reserved badge placed on it.

After we settled and ordered our wines, I looked at Arthur. "So, how's your business going?"

"It's going well, but I'd like to do a lot better. Since I have multiple businesses, it's difficult to find the time to do everything."

"You must certainly have enough staff to help you."

"I am my own boss, and I have no staff." He paused and continued. "I mean, I work alone, but collaborate with different partners from time to time."

"I know you are in the wine business, but what exactly do you do?"

"Namratha, you ask too many questions," Arthur laughed.

"Er...I'm just a bit intrigued, as you often come to Château Siran with your clients. But it's fine with me if you don't want to answer."

"I deal in fine wines—very fine wines."

"Sounds like a dream job. What's the best wine you have in storage?"

"You really want to know? You won't believe me."

"I'm listening."

"So you want to know all my secrets. I can't tell you, but I can show you if you come to Paris."

There was something mysterious about Arthur. Why would he ask me to go to Paris? *Seems creepy*, I thought.

"I will show you the world's best cellar, filled with the world's best wines. It's highly confidential. There are more than twenty thousand bottles of collection wines, which are auction-worthy. I own half of the cellar, and my partner owns the rest," Arthur continued, not realizing I was making my own judgments about him.

"Fascinating," I said, before taking a sip of the Meursault I had just ordered.

"I'll take you there."

Maybe he is some kind of psychopath luring me into a room to shut me there forever, or sell me as a slave to some sheik in Saudi Arabia. I laughed in my head. *But what if this secret cellar really exists? Would it be worth going there?*

"If you can manage to sell a few, I can give you a commission of ten percent on profit made from the sale of each bottle. What do you think, Namratha? Are you up to it?" Arthur's words interrupted my increasingly paranoid thoughts.

"Yes!" I said, jumping instinctively at the opportunity. If this man sitting in front of me was telling the truth, then this would be a great source of revenue.

"I'll be in Paris next week; I will let you know the exact time and date soon."

"Sure," I said, feeling overly motivated.

"Now, no more business talks. Tell me more about you," Arthur said, then took a bite of the milk-fed lamb from the Pyrénées, which was accompanied by carrots and wild garlic.

I felt sick. A baby lamb growing happily in the Pyrénées, taken from its mother and slaughtered. *How delicious could that be?* I wondered.

"Mmmm...this meat is so tender," Arthur said. "What urged you to make this drastic change? Changing countries is not a joke. You would be lying if you said it's because of the wines."

Arthur had sensed it, and now he wanted to know the truth, maybe because we were getting involved in selling his wines. He needed to make sure who he was dealing with. *I need to be sincere for him to trust me completely*, I thought. But not about the lamb. I laughed to myself before giving him a brief history. In between sentences, I would take bites of my cauliflower coated with *comté* cheese and sprinkled with black truffle and sip a glass of Barbera d'Alba.

"My respect for you has increased tenfold, Namratha. You're a very special woman. I will make sure that I do everything in my capacity to help you succeed."

"Thank you, Arthur. You are very kind."

Did he feel compelled to help me genuinely? Or did he perceive my past as a weakness? Only time would tell. Either way, I couldn't wait to uncover his secret cellar.

A few days after I returned from London, I received a text from Arthur Dubois on my new phone mentioning the date, time, and place to meet. As much as I wanted to believe in everything he said, I also knew I had to see it in person to believe it.

I took the TGV to Paris and waited at the given place for Arthur. He arrived in a 2008 Peugeot hatchback and picked me up.

After about twenty minutes, Arthur drove through a large, white gate and parked in the corner of the premises. A tall, hefty man with an older-looking face came to greet us. I saw no sophistication in this man and wondered how he was in the fine wine business.

"*Ça va,* my friend?" he asked as they hugged each other and did the *bises*.

"*Oui....ça va*. I can't complain in this nice, beautiful sunny weather."

"I agree!"

Arthur gestured toward me and said, "This is Namratha. She's a princess from India."

"Oh, not really," I said and blushed.

"Namratha, this is Fabrice."

"*Bonjour*, nice to meet you," he said and smiled. I noticed his golden incisors that glinted in the afternoon light.

"Nice to meet you too."

"Arthur, take her down to the cellar. I'll join you there after securing the gates."

Oh gosh, why does he need to secure the gates? This isn't right. I slid my hand into my handbag and rechecked the existence of my pepper spray. We walked through the front door into the office of the building.

"Namratha, you can leave your handbag here," Arthur said.

My heart sank. How could I believe someone blindly and walk into a place like this all alone? Or was I overthinking? I did as he requested and put my handbag containing the pepper spray on the table and followed Arthur. Now, all I could do was run as fast as I could if I sensed any danger. At the end of the corridor was a door, beyond which a staircase led us to the underground cellar. I heard footsteps behind me. *It must be Fabrice,* I thought. I looked at my nails; they were quite long. I could definitely do some damage if they tried anything.

We descended into the cellar in total darkness. My heartbeat quickened. I could hear its sound in my ears. The stairs seemed never-ending. Suddenly, there was a click and the lights came on.

CHAPTER 14

The Secret Collection

Paris, France
August 2017

The room was stocked with wines from floor to ceiling. I took note of the vintages. Some of the finest and rarest wines were stacked in rows with tags attached on their necks so as to easily identify each one.

"Voilà, madame," Arthur said, his voice echoing in the dimly lit cellar.

"Excellent collection, Arthur." I cleared my voice. I stared at a large wall filled with an array of vintages from Château Lafite. I noticed that each bottle was neatly wrapped in cling film to preserve the label. My eyes flew to the top shelf of the Lafite collection. "Château Lafite 1888," read the tag. It was the oldest bottle in the collection. I wondered how it would taste. Would it be the billionaire's vinegar? It was a collector's item, of course. The bottle would be of high value, even if it was vinegar by now. There were only two bottles in the whole world I knew and one of them rested right in front of me. I felt tremendous relief. There was none of the danger I had imagined.

"May I?" I still stared at the bottle as if it were unreal, without turning to look at Arthur or Fabrice.

"Sure, just be careful," Fabrice said, after a quick anxious glance at Arthur.

My fear had left me by now, and I confidently lifted my agile body onto my toes to carefully lower the bottle. It was a moment I would never forget.

Arthur broke from his discussion with Fabrice and said, "Unbelievable, isn't it?"

"How much is it priced at?" I asked.

"It's priceless, Namratha."

"This is a collector's dream," Fabrice said, pointing to the shelf filled with all years of Lafite from 1888 to 2012.

I lifted the bottle toward the light. There was no cloudiness or any other wine faults. The wine still looked alive.

"So are you looking at auctioning this?"

"Yes," Fabrice said.

"Namratha, if you can find auction houses or individuals interested in these wines, as promised, I will give you a commission of ten percent on each bottle sold," Arthur said.

"I'll surely work on it," I replied, but I worried how I would be able to reach out to these people.

"It's a deal," Arthur said while I carefully placed the bottle back onto the shelf.

"Come take a look at the rest," Fabrice said.

We walked to the adjacent room that was filled with Yquem. Bottles containing shades of golden to brown liquid glowed in the room. Another room dedicated to Burgundy sat opposite. It was packed with wines from Armand Rousseau, Chambertin-Clos de Bèze, Bâtard-Montrachet, Charmes-Chambertin, Joseph Drouhin Montrachet, Domaine des Héritiers, Louis Jadot, Corton-Charlemagne, and many others. My eyes were feasting.

A third room in the corner had rare vintage and non-vintage Champagnes from some of the best producers. This was pure treasure.

A year before, there had been a grand theft in central Paris. Thieves had stolen 300 bottles of fine wines worth €250,000 after making their way through the maze of underground tunnels housing the catacombs and drilling a hole in the wall, before breaking into the treasure trove of wines in a private cellar. I wondered why this place had no cameras, nor any security guards—or maybe they had placed them discreetly.

"You can do it, Namratha. You have everything here; it's your playground. I'll send you the whole list by email soon," Arthur said.

Arthur had tried to motivate me, but he didn't have to. I was very motivated.

"Won't the client want to see the wine for real before buying? How could we arrange that?"

"You cannot take any bottles from this cellar unless it's paid for by the client, so if anyone is interested, I can send them the pictures. Later, they can visit this cellar to see the wines physically stored. If you let me know the date and time, I will coordinate that with you."

"Sure, but I still don't understand why you prefer that I work on selling these wines. You have treasure here. Anybody would want to buy these."

"You're absolutely right. This is treasure, but sold at the right price to the right client. That involves a lot of work."

Fabrice broke his silence. "Arthur and I both have various businesses and can't dedicate time to one alone. Moreover, hiring a person just for this will cost a lot of money and training them is another problem. That's why we work with agents. They get paid when the job is done."

"How would the client know these are not fake?" I asked.

"Each bottle has a bill and can be traced back to its origin. I will give you all details about the wine once you tell me which bottles they are interested in."

"We have other agents working on the wines. Whoever sells them first will be given the commission," Arthur said.

"Understood!" I said, worried in case, after all my efforts, somebody else sold the bottles before me, it would be an utter waste of my time and energy.

***

I returned to Bordeaux that evening. Conor welcomed me to stay the night since it was too late to return to Margaux. I told him all about Arthur and his secret cellar.

"It sounds too good to be true, but maybe I'm just overly cautious, like one of those hobbits," Conor said while serving me dinner on the tray he had named Fergie.

"I'm not sure how this is going to work," I said, feeling worried. "I've never done this sort of thing before. I'll give it a try and see."

That night, I read every article I could find online about fine wine auctions. The famous documentary *Sour Grapes* surfaced in one of my searches. I fretted, but Arthur's words came back to me. He had everything to prove the provenance of the wines in that cellar. *I need time to think clearly about this*, I thought.

***

I sat up in bed early the next morning. It was Shloka's sports day; she was competing in the 100-meter race. I wanted to wish her good luck before she went to school. I had never imagined that I would miss her birthday, her golf tournaments, parent-teacher meetings, and other important days. I was working hard to construct a beautiful future for her and had to make some sacrifices for that. I picked up my phone and rang my mother.

"Good luck, baby." The tone of my voice was filled with enthusiasm, but despair roiled around inside me. I missed her. I missed her terribly.

"Thank you, Mama," her chirpy voice said. "When are you coming back?"

"A few more months, baby," I lied.

Before I moved to Bordeaux, she had handed me a note saying, "Study well, Mama." Then she locked herself in the bathroom and cried. She didn't want me to see her tears. I promised her I'd be back soon, but it had been more than five months now. I had broken my promise.

"You always keep saying that every time I ask you."

I felt guilty. I had to work out a way to bring her to me.

"I know I keep telling you that. But I need a little more time to make things right for us, sweetheart. Trust me."

I wanted to cry, but I didn't dare show her weakness of any kind. I was her mother, the person she looked up to.

"Love you so much. Can't believe I'm missing your Sports Day."

"Love you too, Mama. I miss you so much, and Casper misses you too."

"We'll be together soon," I said, feeling more determined than ever to be with her.

My eyes welled. I wanted to kiss her childish cheeks. I wanted to tell her those tales she would innocently listen to before falling asleep.

"Have you packed your apple and plum juice? It will give you lots of energy."

"Yes, Grandma did. My school bus is here. I have to go. I'll call you in the evening."

"Okay, sweetheart. Have a lovely day, and remember, I miss you tons!"

I hung up before she heard me crying. At least she couldn't see the tears that ran down my cheeks.

***

I took the train to Château Siran. Life had changed so much since I had arrived in France. I never imagined back then that I would be housed on the premises of an eighteenth-century château in the middle of the French countryside, or travel to Italy and miss my return flight. Nor did I ever dream that I would be involved in an accident that nearly cost me my life, or travel to London to speak about wine investments, or discover a secret underground cellar in Paris, all in five months.

"Macau," a voice announced the train stop in the Medoc, and I scrambled to get my belongings and waited for the train to come to a halt.

Unlike my first time here, I knew that the station master was alive. He sometimes took breaks between the arrival of two trains. I walked out and didn't look for a taxi, since I knew now that taxis didn't exist in the countryside. I also didn't bother to hitchhike, because I knew nobody would stop. This time, I only had a little bag. I had left most of my luggage at Conor's. I had two more weeks of my internship at Château Siran to finish before restarting school in October. I couldn't wait to meet all my friends again. Just then, a car that had sped past me stopped.

A familiar face peered out the driver's window and asked if I needed a lift. I chuckled and hopped in. It was Olivier, the vineyard manager of Château Siran. He was getting ready for the harvest. The year had been tough on Olivier. Frosts in the beginning of the growing season, a scorching summer, then excess rain in the first half of September had caused him to worry about the threat of rot and dilution of the grapes. He and Édouard often went into the vineyards with a refractometer to test the grapes for their ripeness. They had also sent them to a laboratory to determine pH and titratable acid levels. The tension was high, and he had his team of pickers on standby for the harvest, which was to take place soon. As for me, it would be my first harvest ever. I knew we weren't going to pick grapes under the blue sky in pretty baskets, nor stomp them in large vats with bare feet, like in the movies. A harvest was far from that; it was real work. Tough work.

***

The following Wednesday, Olivier and Édouard finally decided to begin the harvest. I finished all of my tasting duties and went to the vineyard. Tractors laden with bins were stationed next to the rows of vines. I walked toward the group of pickers who had gathered next to it. I saw Olivier instructing the team. I walked faster.

When I was closer, I heard him say, "*Attention les doigts*!" which meant "Careful with your fingers!"

Claude, my colleague, joined me. We looked at each other with a feeling of excitement. Like me, this was his first harvest. We each grabbed grape shears along with a shallow bucket that had a handle. The plan was to pick the parcels of Merlot that had attained the desired sugar level. This variety had thin skin and ripened much earlier than the other varieties. I hunkered down at the beginning of a row of vines to access the grape clusters.

The shears were sharp, and I easily cut my first bunch and ran my fingers through the velvety skin before placing them in the bucket. I had watched these babies grow, and now they were going to be made into one of the best wines. Someone in some part of the world would be drinking this wine in the future. I didn't know when or where. All I knew was that this wine was being made to share and to inspire enjoyable moments with family and friends, and that was the beauty of its life. After I had taken control of my emotions, I moved on to the next bunch, and then the next, then the next with increasing speed, developing a rhythm. I understood why Olivier had been warning us about our fingers when I nearly cut my thumb.

When my first bucket was almost full, a tall, muscular man carrying a large and deep basket strapped to his back stopped next to me so I could empty my bucket into his *hotte de vendangeur*—his harvester's hood. He wasn't cutting the grape bunches. Instead, he walked around so that everyone could empty their buckets in his *hotte*. Then he would return to the tractors, empty his heavy load of harvest, then return to collect more. I moved on to the next row, then the next, and soon it was lunchtime. The canteen was abuzz with stories from past harvests. We sat around a big wooden table and ate from our lunch boxes as we listened to how one picker tumbled over while trying to empty his basket, and how another man chopped off one of his fingers when he harvested absent-mindedly.

After a hearty meal, Claude and I headed to the cellar. We were curious to learn how the grapes that we had harvested were being turned into wine. The moment we entered, a strong aroma of earth and berries greeted us. The room was large enough to house twelve vats that held more than 120 hectoliters, which was equivalent to a little more than 3,000 gallons of wine. We walked over the wet floor, which was cleaned from time to time to maintain hygiene during the process. We jumped across the long, wide orange pipes that ran across the floor into the vat, transporting the crushed grapes from the machines.

Marie-Noëlle stood next to a vat wearing her wellingtons, and as usual, her hair was tied up out of the way. The noise from the machines made it hard to hear what she was trying to tell us, so she gestured for us to join the sorting team. The cellar had an opening where a long rotating sorting table was placed. Four seasonal workers quickly sifted through the harvested grapes as they arrived. At the end of the table was a destemming and crushing machine, into which the grapes rolled automatically after being sorted. Claude handed me a pair of gloves that he pulled out from a box kept nearby.

We started scanning each bunch as they arrived, pulling out dried leaves, rotten berries, and other unwanted material. After a couple of hours, Marie-Noëlle called us to handle the pipes that transported the crushed grapes along with the liquid, which in wine language is called "must." I climbed up a ladder and walked onto the metal platform from which I could access the top of the vat. Claude hoisted the pipe. I grabbed it and secured it at the opening of the vat. The must gushed forcefully into the hollow steel tank. Once it was full, I carefully moved the pipe to the next vat. After all the harvested grapes were in the vats, we called it a day.

We washed our boots and walked out of the cellar, which was much calmer now that the machines were turned off.

Claude inquired in a concerned voice, "Did you find a place to stay?"

I grimaced and shook my head. My family was sending me enough money to sustain my expenses until I finished studying. But it was another challenge to find an apartment in Bordeaux. The city, I had been told, had grown beyond everyone's imagination. The former mayor had restored and beautified it. Many families had relocated over the years, and property prices had shot up. The region had also gained popularity as a tourist and student destination. Renting a place here, especially if non-French, was a painful task. I had been searching for a long time with no success. Sofia, too, had been looking for an apartment. Since we got along really well, we decided to share one together. She had taken a while to recover from the accident that had nearly killed us. Thankfully, she was now back on her feet. Our school started in mid-October, so we had just enough time to settle down if we found an apartment. The clock was ticking, and I had to do something.

***

The next day, Sofia called with good news.

"Hi, Nam. *Ça va*?" It was refreshing to hear her voice. "I've finally found an apartment; it's in the city center. I'll be visiting the place tomorrow. I'll try to send you a video, and you can tell me if you like it."

"I can't thank you enough, Sofia. Don't know what I would have done without you."

"Oh, it's nothing, really. Moreover, we have Conor. I'm sure he would never leave us on the streets," she said, and we laughed.

It was true. Conor had been a darling—he always watched our backs. We were eternally grateful to have him in our lives. I was relieved that we had made some headway with the apartment. I looked at the clock to see that it was almost dinner time. The day had been long. I threw myself on the bed, wanting to rest my tired body for a little before I went down to cook dinner. My eyes shut for a few minutes. Without realizing it, I drifted into my dreams.

***

The next morning, Arthur called before I left for work to tell me that he had sent an email with the list of wines available in the cellar. As excited as I was, I didn't know how and where to begin. I slipped on my shoes and walked out of the house with my thoughts. It was another day of visits. I soon got to work.

***

On my last day at the château, Édouard and Sévrine invited me for dinner with their friends from the US. A long table was placed on the terrace that gave a 360-degree view of the vineyard. White plates and silver cutlery were neatly set for eight. The family brought out dishes from the kitchen and placed them around the table. I had freshened up after the long day and came for dinner dressed in a rose-colored midi dress and matching shoes. I had thrown away my inhibitions about wearing colors in France and just stuck to my style. When I walked toward the terrace, I saw Sévrine.

"Nam, you're looking beautiful!"

"Thank you, Sévrine, and so are you. How can I help?" I asked.

"Maybe you can pour wine into the glasses. Could you ask Édouard for the wines, please?"

After I had poured the 2009 Château Siran into everyone's glasses and we had all taken our seats, Édouard toasted, "*Santé*. Here's to another great year of friendship."

A loud, cheerful "*Santé*!" rang all around the table.

"Nam, the vegetarian dishes are for you." Édouard, who was sitting opposite, pointed at a vegetable gratin and a salad that were conveniently placed in front of me.

"Thank you, Édouard."

Sévrine and Édouard had always somehow managed to remember that I was a vegetarian.

"So, you are leaving tomorrow?" asked Sévrine, who sat next to me.

"Yes. I'm so sad."

"We'll miss you here."

"I'm going to miss you all too, but I'm happy that I'm taking so many memories with me."

"You are always welcome to come visit us at Siran, you know that," she said, and smiled warmly.

"Thank you, you are very kind. Château Siran will always be close to my heart, thanks to you and Édouard."

As the sun set over the vineyards, Édouard poured more wine and replenished the breadbasket. Soon, the chatting turned into laughter, then into singing old French songs. Château Siran had been an unforgettable experience for me that had brought about an immense amount of change. I had healed—I was strong again. I understood now that in life everything happened for a reason, and every day was a new day, a new lesson.

Now I was more certain than ever about the way forward. Looking around me, I saw joyful faces and remembered the beautiful moments from last five months. We were all united with one common bond: wine. The wines wouldn't be anything without these people, nor would these people be the same without these wines. After dinner, I thanked the family and walked toward my little house. I looked up at the sky, which had turned a deep Prussian blue, littered across with stars. I closed my eyes and thanked the universe. I would surely miss everything here: my room, where I conquered my fears; the view of the vineyards when I showered every morning; the little van that I drove up and down the Médoc; the office; my colleagues; the family; the château. I would miss everything and everyone. Heavy in my heart, I left for the city the next day, along with Claude.

More adventures were awaiting me. I was far from imagining that I'd cross paths with Bordeaux's very own Godfather, who would so gracefully integrate me into the city's life.

CHAPTER 15
Monsieur Alain

Bordeaux, France
October 2017

Sofia waited for me in the new apartment. She helped me unpack and put my things in place as soon as I arrived. The apartment had a living area, bath, toilet, and a kitchenette, along with an open space on the mezzanine where the bed was placed. Even though it was very tiny for the two of us, I was happy that we had a place to live until we completed school. Just then, there was a knock on the door.

"It must be Alain," Sofia said, then opened the door.

"*Bonjour, mesdemoiselles,*" the grey-haired man who stood in the doorway cheerfully declared.

"Nam, this is Monsieur Alain. Alain, this is Nam," Sofia said.

Monsieur Alain looked like a well-preserved man in his early seventies, who possessed an air of raffish sophistication.

"Would you both like to join me for the event in my other apartment?"

Sofia and I looked at each other. I saw a silent "yes" in her eyes.

"It would be a pleasure," I said.

"It will begin at six o'clock. I will come to pick you up. Be ready," our landlord said, and left.

"Seems like a fancy person. Where did you find him?" I asked Sofia, who was now zapping through the channels on the television.

"Ufff, it's a long story. My friend Caro's friend, Venessa, lived here a long time back, so when I was searching for flats, Caro suggested I get in touch with her. When I did, she said that another friend of hers was just moving out from here, and then I contacted *her* friend and she gave me Alain's telephone number. I called, and he readily accepted."

"*Oh la la*, that is a long story. But thank you so much, Sofia; I really appreciate all the effort you've put in finding us this apartment."

"You can thank me more, because the guy you just met was the previous mayor's advisor."

"No wonder he's fancy," I said, then laughed.

To our surprise, Monsieur Alain turned out to be someone of importance in the political sphere. There wasn't a person he didn't know in the city.

"Let's get ready. The event starts in an hour. What are you going to wear?" Sofia asked as she opened the ancient wooden wardrobe where she had neatly hung her clothes.

"Maybe my navy blue evening dress," I said.

We quickly got ready, and as promised, Monsieur Alain arrived on time to pick us up. We walked down a few streets, then entered an eighteenth-century stone building. A hubbub of laughter met us as we climbed the stairs that led to an apartment on the first floor. He lived in two flats, both of which housed grand pianos in the living room. When we entered, I noted the spacious high ceilings and baroque-style walls. The event was about to begin. We hurried and took our seats on a beige antique French *canapé* that sat near the window. At the far end of the room, a beautiful voice began to sing from the old record player. A lady wearing a gypsy red off-the-shoulder laced cancan dress, holding an umbrella, moved gracefully to the center of the living room. Her doll-like face shimmered in the bright lights that focused solely on her. Her smile was very enchanting, and her eyes, laden with dark kohl, were mysterious.

I delicately held a glass of Champagne. The drink had been served to us just as we had entered the room. As the peppy old French song played, the dancer made her way to a man who was sitting next to us and handed him her umbrella. Then she slowly bent and kissed him on his cheek. The man, who was dressed in a charcoal-colored checked suit looked embarrassed, and nervously glanced over at a woman who stood next to a lamp at the far end of the room. She smiled at him, and he seemed to relax.

The dancer then sensuously moved around the room, taking off a layer of her dress. Sofia and I looked at each other in utter disbelief. She continued to strip, layer by layer, while moving her body to the tune. Her pouty red lips synced with the song that played on the disc. Toward the end, there was nothing left but two red embroidered stars that covered the peaks of her breasts and a thong. Claps rang through the room as the song ended. The dancer stood with a beaming smile, bowing from time to time.

Sofia turned to me with a flabbergasted look and said, "Oh my God. What was that?"

There was a stark difference between my life in India and my life here in France. Even though I was shocked, for a moment I felt privileged to have witnessed the extremes of these cultures.

We generously applauded while the dancer blew kisses and walked away. A waiter with an hors d'oeuvres platter made his way through the numerous guests. As I lifted my hand to pick up one of the delicacies, I noticed that there was nothing I could put into my mouth. The platter consisted of caviar, foie gras cubes, and bacon slivers on bread. I shook my head in dismay.

"Madame, they are sourced from the best producers in France," the waiter added. My stomach squirmed. I couldn't fathom how anyone could forcefully pour fatty corn mash down a duck's throat in order to slaughter it for its liver. How could anyone cause so much suffering to an animal and place it on the most gorgeous-looking platter?

Sofia quickly said, "We're vegetarian."

The waiter looked astonished.

"Cheese...okay for you?" he asked.

We nodded. In about five minutes he had brought out a plate filled with cheese canapés. Monsieur Alain joined us.

"Wasn't that performance fantastic?" he said as he clinked his glass with ours.

A long microphone was being placed in the center of the room.

"It's Madeleine. She's going to sing now. Listen to her—she is sixty-one and her voice is sublime," he said and settled into a chair next to us.

A woman walked into the room wearing a white one-shouldered maxi dress that gracefully trailed behind her. To complement her dress, she had fixed a white-feathered jewel onto the right side of her hair. Madeleine still looked like she could give all the women in the room a run for their money. She was a dear friend of Monsieur Alain from his yesteryears. An opera singer by profession, she ran regular singing classes for adults and children from her grand apartment in Paris. Today, she was here, singing an aria at Monsieur Alain's request. Her beautiful voice came through the microphone as we were served another round of drinks.

"Oh my God, a voice like that at the age of sixty-one. She's really gifted," Sofia whispered into my ear.

Madeleine sang for what seemed like an eternity. The whole room roared and cheered when she ended the song. The next performance was to start in ten minutes.

"Come with me," Alain said.

We walked around the room with him. He stopped often to introduce us to his friends. Alain was a charming man, even in his early seventies. He had a debonair style. He wore a v-necked sweater over his shirt and rolled an Indian silk scarf around his neck, which he tucked into the sweater. A blue blazer and matching trousers gave him the classy French look. Alain had studied political science in his younger days and had later joined the cabinet of the mayor, Jacques Chaban-Delmas, in Bordeaux as an advisor.

"This is Sofia from Colombia and Namratha from India, new additions to my family." A warm smile spread across his face as he introduced us.

"*Enchanté*," we said as his friends shook hands with us.

"Where in India?" one of them asked.

"From the south, a city called Bangalore."

"I visited India with my wife when I was younger. It is such a beautiful country. It was our best trip ever," he said with a sense of satisfaction.

"Where in India did you travel?" I asked.

"Rajasthan, Udaipur.... Ahhh, the palaces are magnificent. We also visited the Taj Mahal and traveled to Kerala in the south. Every place we visited was so diverse—the people and their smiles, the food, the culture, the traditions. It was all so different."

"That's the true beauty of India," I said with a feeling of pride.

The room went silent when a young man started to play one of Chopin's Nocturnes on the piano. I felt transported to a beautiful garden in a far-off place, in another world. I shut my eyes and sat lucidly, dreaming of a land so peaceful and divine, where all things seemed to exist in perfect harmony. I walked among the flowers as the music played. When the pianist concluded, I was drawn back to this earth, this reality, this moment, this room that I was in, and the people who surrounded me. We broke into a loud applause. It was glorious. After a little more socializing, Sofia and I decided it was time to head back.

"It was such a wonderful evening," I said to Sofia while we walked to our apartment with music still ringing in our head.

"*Mon Dieu*, this is just our first day at Alain's place," Sofia exclaimed.

I laughed.

"Tomorrow is school. Jake, Isabella, Julie, and Adrien—all of them will be back," I said, feeling a sense of excitement.

***

The next morning, Sofia and I entered the INSEEC building. It was once again to be our school for the next six months. We wandered around, looking for our classroom. I noticed familiar faces in the corridor.

"*Ciao, mie bellezze*," loud voice cried. It was Isabella.

"How was your internship in Saint-Émilion?" I asked.

"*Fantastico*! It was surely a different experience from that of my family's," she said. "What about you girls?"

We shared stories and soon settled into our seats. Jake came to us.

"Hey, you guys! What do you think of my tattoo?"

He pulled up his sleeve to show a bunch of grapes tattooed on his arm.

"Wow," we all chorused.

"When and where did you get that done?" I asked.

"I've been wanting one for a while, so I saved up my internship money and got it done by the tattoo artist near my block."

“Bravo, Jake. Next time, ask him to tattoo the face of your Italian girlfriend,” Isabella joked, and we all laughed. Jake hadn’t yet succeeded in finding an Italian girlfriend.

“I’m going to be the most romantic guy on this planet with my Italian woman.”

“Did it hurt?” Julie asked him.

“A little, in fact. But I’m highly tolerant to pain.”

We all talked about our internships before the teacher arrived. Jake had worked for a wine shop in Bordeaux and was very happy with his employer. Julie had worked for a wine travel company and had done fabulously well for herself. Isabella had worked for a château in the beautiful region of Saint-Émilion instead of returning to her family vineyards in Italy.

She wanted to experience French winemaking, and the internship had been a great learning opportunity for her. Sofia hadn’t been able to complete the six months because of her accident, so she had taken more time from school to finish her internship. It felt good to have them all back in my life. As the girls suggested increasingly ridiculous new tattoos for Jake, many of which he seriously considered, I felt both removed from and entirely present in the scene. The laughter, the smiles—I had missed them all.

***

I walked home with Sofia that afternoon, as we had classes only for half a day. My phone rang as we walked leisurely on the quays. It was Arthur.

“I’m coming to Bordeaux soon, and I’d like to meet you,” he said.

“Sounds great. Let me know the date and time.”

When I ended the call, Sofia laughed and asked, “Who is this new person in your life?”

“He’s nobody, really.”

"Huh...I thought you would give me some exciting news."

"Sorry to disappoint you; it's just business," I laughed.

Just then, the phone rang again. My face went pale.

"Hi, Nam. Happy birthday."

"Thank you, Moksh," I said in an unexcited voice.

"Hope your first day of school after break went well."

How did he know this information? How could he track me? Maybe it was Shloka. She and my parents were the only people who knew this. Shloka must have told him innocently.

"Yes, it's good to be back to school."

"Who are you with?" he asked brusquely. I was taken aback by the harshness in his voice.

The last thing I wanted to do was to deal with Moksh on my birthday.

"I'm with my friend."

"Boyfriend?"

"Moksh, stop. I'm with Sofia."

"Oh, no boyfriends around?"

My heart started to race and I began to shake.

"Sorry, I have to go," I said as I worked hard to regain control of myself.

I was relieved by how very far away from Moksh I was, and that I was able to silence his voice with the click of a button.

Sofia had sensed the tension in my voice. She asked if everything was alright. I nodded, and she gave me a very sympathetic look.

"Let's forget about Moksh. Tell me about Shloka and Casper. How are they?"

"They're holding on to hope," I said, feeling down. "I need to have them with me as soon as possible."

"I'm sure you'll figure out a way. You're a tiger mama."

"Thanks, Sofia."

"What about finding love again?"

"I have other priorities."

"Nam, just because you have a child doesn't mean you stop living your life."

"I'm not even divorced."

"Doesn't Moksh want a divorce?" she asked as we turned into our lane.

"No. He will never give me one; he has made that very clear."

"Why can't he let you live in peace?"

"It's because he doesn't like to lose. He's going to make me suffer for leaving him."

"So what are you going to do?"

"I have only one way forward. To make a life here in Bordeaux and put all my strength in bringing Shloka and Casper here."

"A job is what you need," Sofia concluded.

We heard a piano playing on the upper floor as we entered our building. It was coming from Monsieur Alain's home. We climbed the flight of stairs to reach our apartment. In a few minutes, there was a knock at the door. It was Monsieur Alain. He had come to invite us for dinner at his home that evening.

"Come eat with us. My music students and my friends from the town hall are dining with me tonight. It would be marvelous if you both could come too. It would also be good for you to connect with them."

Sofia and I looked at each other and smiled.

"Is it okay if we join in half an hour?" Sofia asked.

"Of course. We'll wait for you in the apartment."

Soon we got ready and went upstairs to Monsieur Alain's apartment. It turned out to be another lovely musical evening. His students played classical music, and we were served wines. During dinner, he and his friends discussed French politics with us. Sofia and I were relatively new to France, but we could have short conversations about president Macron and ex-presidents François Hollande and Nicolas Sarkozy. Then we heard names like Alain Juppé, Marine Le Pen, Anne Hidalgo, Rachida Dati, the scandalous Jacques Chirac, and François Mitterrand. We were in the midst of a classic French dinnertime debate. As we were served dessert, the conversation moved toward India and Mahatma Gandhi. Later, the evening ended with more music and wine.

I was so grateful that I was having such rich experiences of French life. I lay in bed that night and reflected on how my life was taking shape. I had never imagined that someone like Monsieur Alain would be our landlord. I felt that everything was happening for a reason. I looked at the time—it was midnight. Just then, my phone beeped. I looked at the email notification. My heart skipped a beat.

CHAPTER 16
Germany

Bordeaux, France
December 2017

It was an email from Baccharis auction house. I quickly wrenched open my laptop to read the email more clearly. The auction house had responded to the mail I had sent regarding Arthur's wines. They wanted to visit the cellar. A shiver of excitement ran through my veins. I called Arthur the next day.

"Arthur...it's me again. Sorry to disturb you, but last night I received a response from Baccharis. They would like to visit the cellar."

"That's great, Nam. See, I told you! You are magical. You make things happen."

"Thank you. They are asking for our availability."

"Please tell them we can show them the cellar in the second week of November, as I'll be in Paris then."

"Sure!"

"You're doing well, Nam. Go, go, go, get the world. You can do it."

It felt great to have Arthur believe in me and motivate me, but I still wasn't sure how to secure this deal. I had no experience in this kind of job. I put the phone down and began to work on my response to Baccharis.

***

A few days passed before I received a message from Arthur: *I'm in Bordeaux. Would you be free to meet this evening at half past six at Café des Arts?*

I texted back saying that I'd be there and continued to listen to the German teacher explain the difference between Qualitätswein or Prädikatswein. We had six glasses of Riesling wine placed in front of us. They were presented in increasing levels of ripeness: Kabinett, Spätlese, Auslese, Beerenauslese, Eiswein, and Trockenbeerenauslese. My love for these wines was evident. My nose fluttered with excitement when I sniffed the glass. The floral notes were tantalizing. The wines had a refreshing acidity and a minerality so alluring that they made my mouth water. The Garden of Eden had come alive. *If I had many lives, I would sip on Riesling every morning*, I thought.

That evening, I waited for Arthur at the French café. Edith Piaf was playing in the background.

I heard Arthur's voice as he approached. "All the sunshine of India has come to Bordeaux. *Bonsoir madame, ravi de te revoir*," he said as he shook my hand.

"Good to see you too, Arthur," I said. "So what brought you to Bordeaux again?"

"I moved here to be with my son."

"Moved? For good?" I asked, startled.

"Yes, I think it's better I'm closer to him."

I nodded as I sipped on the Earl Grey tea served to me.

"You've done an excellent job on Baccharis. You need to accompany their representative, Laura, to the cellar in Paris next week."

I coughed.

"I thought it was *you* who would be giving a tour of the cellar to Laura."

"I won't be able to make it. I have a court hearing which I cannot miss."

"I don't know what to say to her, Arthur."

"You'll figure it out. I've let Fabrice know. He will open the gates and let you both in."

"Okay, so let's say next week I take Laura from Baccharis to the cellar, and let's say she's convinced and would like to acquire a certain number of bottles. What happens next?"

"We will open a bottle of vintage Pol Roger and celebrate."

"Huh...well, I mean in the real world, is there a process you follow?"

"You ask too many questions, Namratha." Arthur smirked. "We have to provide an inventory list, like we did. After that, they send a member of their staff for inspection—that's Laura, who is coming next week. Then they will send us an estimate. Once we agree on the prices and the payment comes through, we will then pack and ship the wines to their temperature-controlled warehouse."

"Just to have some clarity, when would I receive the commission? And can we make a contract for the same?" I questioned.

"You will receive your commission thirty days after the payment is made. There is no written contract, only my word," he said, brushing his hair behind his ear. "You have to believe me completely, Namratha."

I had no way of testing Arthur's trustworthiness. *If I want to work on selling these wines, I have to keep my calm and bear with his absurd ways,* I thought.

"Remember: there are other agents trying to sell these wines as we speak, so the early bird catches the worm."

***

The week after, I accompanied Laura to the cellar. As promised, Fabrice let us in. I took her down the stairs and to the room where the most exquisite bottles were kept. As she observed each label, I tried to read signs of excitement on her face, but in vain. She was good at her game. Her poker face didn't reveal anything. Before leaving, she examined a few bottles, then exchanged cards with Fabrice and said that she would get in touch with us if there was any interest. I reported back to Arthur, who seemed content with my job.

***

After that day, I eagerly waited for Laura to get back to me. In the evenings, Sofia and I attended the lavish soirées at Monsieur Alain's, as it helped us network with the locals and gave us a sense of belonging in the new city. I also focused on my classes at school. Our exams were nearing. I couldn't afford to fail my MBA. Simultaneously, I searched for jobs on different sites. Arthur's wines were a shot in the dark, and business would take time. I needed a solid job that would give me financial security and allow me to move Shloka and Casper to be with me.

***

The first week of December had flown past me. That weekend, Sofia and I met Conor for a glass of wine at his apartment.

"What are you doing for Christmas, Nam?" Conor asked.

"I'm not sure yet," I said in a dull voice.

December was around the corner. Everyone was going back to be with their families. I couldn't. I was afraid that Moksh would stop me from flying back. I couldn't let him jeopardize my career again. My exams were in a few months. It was vital that I finish my master's. With that certificate, I could apply for an extension of my visa, which would give me enough time to look for a job or set up a company.

"You can come with me to Ireland and celebrate the Irish way," Conor said.

"You are also welcome to fly with me to Colombia," Sofia added.

"Awww...that's very kind of you both. I'm afraid I'd need a visa to go to both your countries."

"Huh! But Ireland is not so far. If I had political powers, there wouldn't exist any borders, so no one would have to deal with that visa shit."

"I wish," Sofia and I chorused.

We spent a lovely evening at Conor's before Sofia and I walked home. It was almost eight o'clock. I noticed the holiday cheer had already set in the city. Luminous Christmas trees had been placed around the streets and squares of Bordeaux. It would have been so wonderful to have Shloka, Casper, my parents, Megha, and Nikhil celebrate Christmas here with me. They had been there for me every step of the way, motivating me, supporting me, and cheering for me every day. *Someday we will all celebrate Christmas in Bordeaux*, I thought as I walked next to Sofia, who was busy chatting about her dog in Colombia. I was nodding but hardly heard a word she'd said. Suddenly, my phone rang. It was Uncle Arun. I excused myself and answered the call.

"Hallo, Nam. *Wie gehst du*?"

"*Sehr gut*, thank you. And you?"

Uncle Arun was my father's youngest brother. Four decades ago, he had fallen in love with Aunty Helga, who was from Germany, and moved to Frankfurt. She was the first foreigner to become a part of our family. Whenever they visited us in India, they always brought a big box of gifts to distribute to all the children in the family. If they couldn't travel for whatever reason, they sent the toys by post. Now that I was older, my gifts were wine, euros, and unlimited pampering.

"Do you have any plans for Christmas?"

"Nothing as of now," I said.

"Aunty Helga and I thought we would invite you to come and spend Christmas with us. We could also visit some wineries here if they are open. Would you like that?"

"That would be lovely, thank you."

"*Wunderbar*!" Uncle Arun said with a perfect German accent.

"I will look up the tickets tomorrow and let you know."

"*Sehr Gut*!"

I put the phone back into my bag and told Sofia the good news.

"Oh, thank God—I was feeling terrible that you had nowhere to go on Christmas Day. I was going to ask Monsieur Alain if he was throwing a party. You surely wouldn't be alone with him and his fancy friends."

"Awww, Sofia. You're so thoughtful. I'm so lucky to have a friend like you," I said and hugged her.

***

Uncle Arun had picked me up at the airport, and now we were in his warm home clinking our glasses together. It was a Riesling Kabinett from the Mosel region. "*Prost*!"

"Did your internship go well?" Uncle Arun asked.

"Yes. In fact, it was a wonderful experience."

"Nam, you are very brave. Cheers on completing your internship." We clinked again.

"Did you find an *arbeit*?" Aunty asked, her Germanic practicality coming to the fore.

"No, unfortunately I haven't found a job yet. I have sent out my résumé, but nothing yet. I've also started working on setting up a company to offer wine services. And I'm trying to sell some rare wines." I took a sip of wine and continued. "I visited London in October to look for a wine investment company with whom I could collaborate to offer alternative investments. London's where all the wine trade happens. It's tax free, you see," I explained, and Uncle Arun translated into German so that Aunty Helga could understand. They listened intently while I told them about Liv-ex and the world of investment wines.

Uncle Arun looked concerned. "All of that is fine, but you need to find a job. Business will take a long time to establish. With all the responsibilities you have, it's better to have a stable salary."

"You're right. I've been applying for jobs, but nothing has come through yet," I said, feeling disappointed.

"Keep trying. Don't give up," Uncle Arun said. "Have you thought about your divorce?"

"Uh…it's complicated. Moksh will not give me a divorce easily. I need to fight it out in the Indian court."

"Do you have a lawyer?"

I took a deep breath and explained. "Yes, an advocate called Vidya will be handling my case. She says it will be difficult if the divorce is not mutually consented to. And it could take up to seven years or more to settle everything. I was disheartened, believe me. But I am thinking of starting the process soon."

"I thought laws would have changed by now," Uncle Arun said with a look of disbelief. "Would you be travelling to India to sign the divorce?"

"No, I will give someone I trust my power of attorney so they can sign on my behalf."

"*Gut*! It's not safe for you to fight the case yourself in India."

Uncle Arun was right. There was no telling how long the divorce would take to settle. If I went back to fight in court, then Moksh would not let me live in peace. I was certain of that. He was also capable of harming me. I couldn't take a chance.

"How is Shloka doing without you?" Uncle Arun asked in a concerned voice.

"She's growing more restless by the day. I can sense it in my calls with her. She keeps asking when I'll be back. My mother has left no stone unturned in taking care of her. Despite that, Shloka feels my absence deeply. She cries herself to sleep every day. My mother finds fresh tear stains on the pillow every morning." My voice choked, but I continued. "I intend on moving her to France as soon as I'm a bit more stable."

"I'm sorry to hear. But would Moksh allow that?"

The situation was complex. I knew that without earning enough, I would not be able to afford a stable life in France for Shloka. There was another challenge, though. If I did succeed with a job and eventually make a life here, I would still have to deal with Moksh, who would probably not let Shloka leave India. The odds were stacked against me. Uncle Arun noticed me deep in thought and reached out to pat my hand.

"Things look difficult at the moment, but I'm sure there is a bright light at the end of the tunnel," Uncle Arun said, trying to sound positive.

Later that night, I went to bed praying for a miracle.

***

The next day, I left a message for Arthur, asking how he was doing and if there were any developments with the sale before we headed off to visit the regions of Rheingau and Mosel. Both regions were famous for their wines. Our first stop was Kloster Eberbach.

This abbey was a former Cistercian monastery dating back to 1136. It was situated in Eltville, in the region of Rheingau. To my left, I saw two tall church-like white buildings that were attached to a series of other buildings. A tall tower sat in the midst, where their roofs met. Constructed in a typical German style of architecture, the ash grey slates sloped from either side of the roofs, while a red color painted the half-timbered construction and the framed windows. As we walked toward the entrance of the Vinothek, Uncle Arun told me they had converted the abbey into a hotel. I noticed the Prädikatswein symbol: a black eagle with a cluster of grapes in the center. There were two classifications in German wines: Qualitätswein and Prädikatswein. The basic level of wines, mostly inexpensive, made it into the list of Qualitätswein, whereas the top level came under the Prädikatswein.

A man in his late forties welcomed us and asked what we'd like to taste. He handed us a menu that described the different wines they produced. Eberbach Abbey was very successful economically because of profits from the cultivation of vineyards and the production of wine, the man explained in German while Uncle Arun translated into English for me. As he spoke, I imagined monks harvesting the grapes in their long white gowns and bringing them into the abbey to crush and make wine.

"Wine has a special status in Christianity. Jesus's first miracle was turning water into wine at the wedding at Cana. He also gave wine the highest honor of representing his precious blood during the last supper and asked his followers to use wine in remembrance of his death until he returned," our host explained as he unconsciously swirled the wine in his glass from time to time, without drinking it.

Here in this abbey, I wondered how many bottles were guzzled by the monks themselves. Which one was their favorite? The *kloster* now produced a large range of wines. They were delicious.

"Originally, the term 'Kabinett' meant a wine of high quality, and it was usually set aside inside a cabinet to be sold at a later stage," our host continued. "It was treated a bit like reserve wines. Well, it was here, in this monastery, that the term originated. The Cistercian monks had set aside the best wines to be stored in a special cellar below the monastery. Many years later, it came to be known as the Cabinet cellar, and so the word 'Kabinett.'"

I was fascinated. I looked at Uncle Arun, who was now going through the brochures. "We produce two and a half million bottles a year, and seventy-five percent of it is Riesling," our host explained as he poured more wine into our glasses. The aromas and flavors were tantalizing. We also tasted Chardonnay, Pinot Blanc, Pinot Gris, Pinot Noir, and Dornfelder. All these wines were grown on three hundred hectares of vineyards spread across the Rheingau.

"Have you watched the movie *The Name of the Rose*?" our host asked.

We nodded.

"It was shot here in this abbey. It stars Sean Connery as the Franciscan friar William of Baskerville."

After the tasting, we took a quick tour of the abbey. We strolled across a large courtyard to a room where the ancient wine presses were still kept. As we walked under the low stone vaulted ceiling, I noticed dates—1494 and 1668—carved into the presses.

"In the fifteenth century, the monks had a seventy-thousand-liter wine barrel made, which was lost during the Thirty Years' War," explained our host.

In the next hour, we learned that the monks copied books. There was no other way of duplicating them, other than by hand, since there were no printing presses at that time. This was a way of keeping themselves occupied, apart from making wine. In 1631, the beautiful library had been looted by the Swedish army, who unfortunately lost all the books, artifacts, and wine when their ships sank.

The history of Kloster Eberbach was captivating. Even though we were tempted to stay longer, we thanked our host and left for another vineyard, which was waiting for us in the region of Mosel.

While we walked to the car, I checked my phone to see if Arthur had replied to the message I had sent that morning. There was nothing. *He must be busy*, I thought.

We made a quick stop for lunch on the way to the winery. I was about to dig into a plate of fresh tomato and olive salad when my phone rang. It was Shloka. She was sobbing.

"Mama...Papa's being nasty to me."

"Why, darling?" I asked as my heart raced. "Please don't cry. Do you want to tell me what happened?"

"He saw me speaking to Rohan and Sunil on the street while he was passing by in his car."

"And what happened?"

"He got upset and he ordered me to get inside his car. I refused and ran back home."

"Did he follow you home?"

"No, he called on Grandma's phone and started to yell at me for speaking to boys. I explained to him that they are my friends, but he wouldn't listen."

"Oh my baby, don't let that bother you. He might just be a little paranoid."

"He threatened that he would take me, keep me with him, and never let me be with you."

"Oh! He can't do that. I'll talk to him and make him understand."

"I told him to his face that I hated him," Shloka said vehemently.

I feared this day would come. Shloka was vulnerable. I knew Moksh would try to control her. And if she retaliated against his dominating nature, she would bear the brunt.

"Please, Mama, can you take me from here? I want to be with you."

"I'll try asking, sweetheart."

After a few minutes of calming Shloka down, I hung up the phone and explained everything to Uncle Arun.

"You have to be with Shloka. She needs you."

I felt guilty for leaving her back in India. Uncle Arun was right; she needed me. *Should I just forget about everything and return to India? We wouldn't be safe living in the same city as Moksh, but we could move to Mumbai or Delhi or Chennai.* Then, almost immediately, fear took over me. What if Moksh showed up there? He would have visiting rights as a father. He would continue to trouble us. France, on the other hand, was far away. It would not be easy for him to get there. Plus, he couldn't mess with us in this part of the world. He didn't know the language, and he hated French food. He couldn't be a king there, so there was little chance he'd hang around for long.

"How did you find the Weingut Heymann-Lowenstein in Mosel?" Uncle Arun asked, bringing me back from my thoughts.

"Oh, it is a well-known winery in the region. They have quite a unique way of making wine. I called them to check if they were still open for tours before Christmas. They were extremely kind and told me they will do it exclusively for us."

"*Gut*!" Uncle Arun said while he typed the address into the GPS device that was attached to the windscreen of his car.

As we reached the winery, I noticed a large cube made of charred wood in front of an old building. The shell around the wood was enshrouded with calligraphy made of stainless steel. It contained the text of the poem "Ode to Wine" written by the Chilean Nobel Prize winner Pablo Neruda. It looked quite modern. Reinhard Löwenstein received us and took us to his vineyard.

"Mosel is Germany's oldest wine-growing region," he said when we got out of the car. I caught my breath. The view was spectacular. The steep terraced vineyards along with the River Rhine flowing at the foothills was postcard perfect. He led us toward the vines that grew on the sixty-degree vertical slopes. My head started to spin. I grabbed the nearest post. It was nothing like I had imagined.

"How do you harvest grapes at this height?" I inquired, feeling dizzy. "I cannot imagine standing on these slate-laden steep hills, let alone harvesting the grapes."

Reinhard chuckled and said, "We've had accidents, but very rarely. Most of our workers are used to this kind of manual harvesting."

"It takes a lot of courage to harvest in these conditions," Uncle Arun added.

"Pardon me for asking, but this is a lot of work. What about the returns? Is it worth the pain?" I asked bluntly.

"We produce wine because we have passion for it. Yes, it is a difficult job, but in the end, we feel it's worth the effort when the world appreciates and drinks our wines."

I understood the craziness. I read about Reinhard's thought-provoking philosophies that he put into practice since creating his estate in 1980. Coming from a family making wines since the fourteenth and fifteenth centuries, his passion for wines was quiet, but obvious. Uncle Arun and I nodded in acknowledgement. A big boat sailed by while we spoke. I pulled out my camera and held it behind the vines. The shot was perfect. It captured the grey sky along with the steepness of the vineyards and the river. Uncle Arun and Reinhard started a conversation. I went over to the place where the vineyards were carved to make way for terraces. I could see the roots of the vines running deep into the blue slate. It looked like they were arranged one on top of another. I ran my hands over them. My mind went back to Shloka. She was growing up with a lot of insecurities. Her foundation itself was shaky. I felt afraid that these incidents would have an adverse effect in her life.

Eventually, Reinhard and Uncle Arun joined me.

"Vineyards in Mosel largely depend on the slate to capture the heat of the sunlight during the day, and transfer it onto the soil after the sun disappears. The river also plays a vital role in trapping the heat and reflecting it on the vines." Reinhard went on to explain the soils and subsoils. "The vineyard itself consists of seven different slates. About four hundred million years ago, the collision of the old continents compressed the silt, which washed up in the South Seas. Slate was created. The years of continental drift lifted and shifted the slate from the depths of the earth. Today, we are growing our vines on the same slate." Uncle Albert and I listened intently. "These vines transfer the character of the stony soil to the glass, so that you can taste the prehistoric sea."

"That's incredible," I said as I took another glance at the landscape.

"Let's go back down, and I'll walk you through our cellars."

Reinhard drove us back to the winery and took us straight to the cellar. Faint music played in the distance. It grew louder as we walked through the room. This, Reinhard explained, was for the wines.

"The wines are alive," he said. "It has been proven that music improves the quality of life. Why not the quality of wine, then?"

We listened intently. "The Apollonian forces unfold energetic effects through the sound of the panpipe. You'll tell me what you think when you taste the wines," he smiled.

By now I was yearning for a sip of this nectar. An array of wines was placed on our table in the tasting room. The wines had a refreshing acidity and a minerality so alluring that it made all sides of my mouth water.

We bought a case of wine to take back for Aunt Helga. We thanked Reinhard immensely for giving us a wonderful tasting and drove straight back to Frankfurt.

***

The next day, I helped Aunty Helga and Uncle Arun decorate the tree that they had removed from storage and placed in the living room. Christmas was in five days. As I arranged the gifts underneath it, I remembered how excited Shloka had been every time she woke up and discovered the gifts Santa had left under the tree. This year, I sent little gifts by post. It certainly would not fill in for my absence. Nevertheless, it would bring everyone cheer, I thought. My mother had placed Shloka's and Casper's presents under the Christmas tree and sent me a picture. Shloka was ten years old now and certainly knew that Santa didn't exist.

Aunty Helga handed me the star to place on top of the tree. As I stretched my arms to reach the top, I heard my phone ring. *It must be Arthur*, I thought, and hurriedly pulled the phone out of the pocket of my jeans. A feeling of shock came over my face. I stared at it as it buzzed continuously.

CHAPTER 17

The Mountains

Frankfurt, Germany
December 2017

It was Patil, Moksh's father. I hesitated, then picked the phone up.

"How are you, Nam?"

It had been almost a year since I had heard from Patil. I had informed him that I was leaving for a short time to France over a call a day before I took my flight. He had been terribly upset.

"Please consider getting back with Moksh. He still loves you. I spoke to him last evening. He is ready to forget the past and accept you back into his life."

I was silent. Patil didn't understand that I didn't need his son's acceptance nor that I could never go back to that life again. My mind was set.

"Come back for Shloka's sake. She feels abandoned. Don't do this to her."

I didn't answer. I knew Patil wanted me to succumb to my own guilt as a mother. If I did go back to that life, I knew that once she was older, Shloka probably would be married off to another large family whose ethics and values rested in convenient business deals. I couldn't let that happen. I was constructing this life for Shloka, for her to be free.

"What will people think of us? We are living in a judgmental society, and we should not give them a chance to gossip about our family," Patil continued. "You are the goddess Lakshmi of this house. Please come back," Patil said, and I listened quietly as he tried his best to convince me.

I could hear my mother-in-law Vasumati's voice raging in the background. "Goddess? What about me, then? Am I the devil of this house?"

"Vasumati, please stop! What are you saying?" Patil tried to take hold of the situation.

"My son is kindhearted; he doesn't deserve this. Nam is taking advantage of his love for her and she will pay for making him suffer," she said to Patil.

"I'm trying to patch them up and you are doing just the opposite," Patil pushed back.

"Do what you want; my son and Shloka are all I care about. I don't see tears in their eyes." I could hear Vasumati's voice trail off along with her footsteps.

"Nam, please think about everything I said. You are the only one who can save this family. I'll book your tickets if you tell me what date you want to return. Don't worry about anything—I'll transfer some funds to your bank account as soon as you are back."

I wanted to tell Patil that I didn't want to come back. But I looked at the Christmas tree in front of me and took a deep breath. I wasn't going to reveal anything or even react. Shloka was still in Bangalore. I couldn't afford to get on the wrong side of anyone in Moksh's family for fear of them not letting her come to me.

"Take care, Nam. God bless you," I heard Patil say, ending the one-sided conversation.

***

A new year began, and I returned to Bordeaux. I waited for a week before calling Arthur. He seemed a little agitated.

"Is everything okay?" I asked, concerned. "Have you or Fabrice heard back from Laura?"

"No. In fact, I forgot to tell you that the lot in the cellar is sold already."

I felt sick to my stomach listening to those words. I had spent a ton of my time and energy working on selling those wines, and all of a sudden, they were gone.

Why had life been so cruel to me? I was trying my best to succeed. I had sent out more than one thousand résumés and still hadn't landed a job. I should never have believed in my stupid plans. What was I thinking? I should have stayed back in Bangalore. Put up a fight. Instead, I had left with stars in my eyes. Why had I chosen this path when so much was at stake? I felt cheated. It was as if time had been stolen away from me. I couldn't believe how harsh this world was. I grieved, as if someone was dead. I lost my appetite and my willingness to speak to anyone. Sofia and Conor were terribly worried for me. My mind swam at the bottom of the abyss. Not a single ray of light...until after a month, my phone rang.

"Hi, can I speak to Namratha from Wine Equation, please?" a plummy voice spoke on the other end.

"It's Namratha here. What can I do for you?"

"Hello, I am Jack Baker, a friend of Henry Abbott. He said you might be the one to contact for fine wine investments."

"Yes, I advise on fine wine investments," I said, trying to feign confidence while struggling to recollect if I had ever met a man named Henry.

"I have been thinking of diversifying my assets, and I happened to discuss this with Henry at a dinner. He told me you were working on managing portfolios."

It came back to me. I chided myself. How could I forget Henry? I had met him at the wine tasting in London. Thanks to him, I witnessed the wine auction and went into a tizzy.

"That's right, I do help manage portfolios. I'll be very glad to walk you through the process. Investing in fine wine is quite simple. I will send you a form that will ask you for your preferred region of interest, such as Bordeaux or Burgundy, your risk appetite, and so forth...."

I spent half an hour explaining the process and timelines to Jack. Toward the end of our call, I told him that I would be happy to meet him and explain in person, if need be.

After I hung up, I called Nikhil, my sister's husband, who was an investment advisor. He was thrilled to hear the news.

"You must meet him. It's always important to know your client. Don't worry about the finances; we are here to support you. Just remember, this is the foundation you are laying. Whatever you do now will go a long way."

Blood didn't define Nikhil's relationship with me, yet he was by my side, mentoring and guiding me. My mother and father had come together to care for Shloka and Casper in my absence. My sister had motivated me to be strong and fearless. I knew with their support I could achieve anything.

***

In mid-February, I flew to Switzerland. I took a flight to Geneva and from there a train to Lausanne. I called Nicolas, my Airbnb host. He directed me to his apartment. It was only a five-minute walk from the train station. It was uphill. I dragged my little suitcase behind me as I walked. I reached the apartment and rang the buzzer, trying to catch my breath. The door sprung open. I got into the lift and pressed the button to the fourth floor.

A tall man in his mid-thirties was waiting at the door. He offered to take my coat and my luggage and place it in a room that he had tidied for me. Then he walked me through his apartment, explaining where all the necessities were. A whole wall in the living room was made of glass, which gave a spectacular view of Lake Geneva and the mountains across it.

"Which mountains are they?" I asked, feeling awed by their magnificence.

"They are the French Alps. Aren't they beautiful? I'm going to miss this view. I quit my job last week. I'm moving to Berlin to work in a bank. My girlfriend, Karen, will continue living here. I've stayed all my life in Lausanne, and now I feel like I could use a break," he laughed.

Nicolas was a stranger to me, yet I felt at ease speaking with him.

"Do you have anything planned this evening?"

"Nothing really. I need to sleep early. My meeting is at nine a.m. tomorrow, so I'm just going to grab something to eat at a nearby restaurant. Why do you ask?"

"Would you like to have dinner here instead? Karen and I are cooking Italian tonight. We could have an early dinner, and you wouldn't need to go out in the cold."

"That sounds lovely, thank you," I replied, feeling grateful for such a warm welcome.

We chatted a little while before I told him that I was here to meet some clients who were interested in investing in wines.

"I never knew people invested in wines," he said, astonished. "I do collect wine, but it's only a few bottles. I've never held any of them for more than five years."

"You see, it's quite simple. Investment-grade wines come from the most renowned winemakers in the world. The value of the wine depends on a number of factors, such as the brand, its history, vintage, quality, availability, and critics' scores. Finite quantities of fine wines are produced every year. These bottles improve with age. Every bottle consumed means there is one less in the world. They become more desirable," I lectured.

He took me down to his cellar to show me his collection.

"Please, pick a bottle of wine that you'd like to drink tonight."

"That's very generous of you, I really shouldn't."

"You're my guest. Please, I insist."

I chose a bottle of Barolo to go with the penne and truffle sauce that Nicolas was cooking.

"If I could, I would savor a glass of Barolo every evening by the fireplace. That is, if I had many lives," I said as I fondly looked at the label.

"Sorry to let you down, but I'm such a novice. What's so special about this wine?" asked Nicolas, perplexed.

"It's the king of wines and the wine of kings. It's delicate, yet powerful. It is deceptively simple yet harbors great depth and complexity. It's structured and firm, yet elegant and classy. It comes from the Piedmont region of Italy and is noted for its rich, intense cherry, rose, leather, and spice aromas. The wines are full-bodied with pronounced tannins and acidity. And it marries perfectly with truffles."

"Nam, you make the wine sound delicious."

"I assure you it is," I chuckled while we walked back up the stairs.

***

The following day, my meeting with Jack Baker went very well. He was happy to have met me and showed some positive signs toward investing in fine wines. I went back to the apartment feeling excited.

There was no sign of Nicolas or Karen. Maybe they were still asleep, or maybe they were away. A photograph of them caught my eye. They looked happy as they smiled into the camera and the sun set behind them. It was wonderful to see how they lived as a couple. Nicolas wanted to move to Berlin, as he wanted a break from this city, and Karen completely supported his decision. Whereas Moksh had put me through hell just because I wanted to work.

Bless them, I thought as I made a hot, steaming cup of tea for myself and went out onto the balcony. It was a marvelous day. The sun shone brightly despite it being cold. Clouds floated in thin air, slowly moving in and out of my view of the gigantic mountains.

A message beeped on my phone. *How are you darling?*

A second message appeared. *Miss you.*

I could feel my heart turn stone cold. I took a sip of my tea. Despite everything, I still felt calm. I had a clear vision of my future with Shloka and Casper, and nothing, or no one, could stop me. I glanced at the mountains in front of me. *They have stood tall over centuries, over eons*, I thought. They withstood seasons, always sheltering life. There was so much to learn from them. I wondered if I stood on top of one of them and wished for Shloka, would they bring her to me? Just then, Nicolas came in.

"Tea is a good idea. I'll make some for myself too," he said, and dashed into the kitchen.

As he sat down next to me with his cup, I asked him if there was a mountain close by that I could hike to.

"Most mountain routes are closed during winter, but there is one that I think might be open. It's not too far away from here. It's my favorite place when I need to do some reflection," he said as he brought out a map, unfolded it, and pointed out the route to me. "I will need to drive you there though, if you wouldn't mind."

"No, I can't have that; you already have done so much for me."

"It's nothing, really. I'm not working this week. Moreover, it would be a good detox for me."

We laughed. In the next hour, I packed all the essentials for our journey while Nicolas made some sandwiches to eat en route. Soon, we were on our way. We drove through the Valaisan vineyards and up the mountains into a mesmerizing landscape. I gazed dreamily out my window. The sun's rays reflected off the surface of a lake as we passed by. I could see clearly that Nicolas enjoyed driving, zig-zagging through the meadows and forests. As he said, it didn't take us long to reach our destination. We parked the car and headed off to the top on foot. The higher we climbed, the heavier I began to breathe in the higher altitude. Soon, we came upon an open space.

"Voilà!" said Nicolas. He gestured toward the stupendous view.

The bright blue sky was like a canvas where an artist had painted the dazzling snow-capped mountains, the turquoise-blue lake, the soaring coniferous trees, and the little wooden cabins that sat amidst the slopes. I had seen the beauty of Switzerland in many Bollywood movies while I was growing up. Yash Chopra, one of the biggest filmmakers in Bollywood, was famous for producing big-budget films. He filmed the majority of his movies in Switzerland, most of which invariably became blockbusters. In *Dilwale Dulhania Le Jayenge*, he had beautifully captured the charming mountains, the colorful flowers, the lakes, the cows with their hanging bells, and a number of the iconic sights of Switzerland.

"This is amazing," I exclaimed, steadying myself.

"I'm glad you like it. It's my secret place."

"Thank you for bringing me here." I truly was grateful.

"You're most welcome. And now it's time to make your wishes."

I turned away from Nicolas, took a deep breath, and said a silent prayer.

"When the sun comes up and brightens the land, let there be no hate, only love, and when the moon comes up as darkness falls, let there be peace. I seek to hold my baby close to me, for that is what I wish. Please lead her to me and I will, in all my strength, work to preserve thee."

I had asked for peace in this world and to reunite with Shloka, two wishes that were close to my heart. For the last wish, I wanted nothing more than to be successful in my business. Through this I knew I could change the lives of other women, just like I had done for myself. I closed my eyes and wished a third wish.

It was a beautiful moment. So peaceful and divine.

"There was no better place than up here to make my wishes," I said as I walked back toward Nicolas.

"Well, I'm not going to ask you what you wished for, but I know it must have been super important."

I smiled and nodded.

***

The sun had begun to set when I entered my apartment in Bordeaux the next day. My trip to Switzerland had been magical. *I will never forget it*, I thought. Sofia wasn't around. My stomach began to hurt with hunger. I gobbled up a banana and soon fell asleep.

The next morning, a phone call woke me. It was a UK number I did not recognize.

"Hi, this is Sanjay. Can I speak to Namratha, please?"

I cleared my throat and said, "Yes, it's Namratha speaking."

"Hi, Namratha. I got your number from your friend Surekha. She mentioned that you are in the wine business," he continued. "I was looking to create a private label of a wine for my hotel."

"I could certainly help you with that," I said.

I jotted down his requirements. Finally, everything was falling in place.

Sofia returned from her morning run.

"Nam, I'm so glad to see you back in your cheerful mood. How was your trip?"

I recounted my Swiss adventure to her.

"That sounds like it was fun."

"Yes, it was. What are you doing for lunch today?" I asked, wondering if she had any plans with the boy from her workplace that she had just started dating.

"Oh, I forgot to tell you. Monsieur Alain is hosting some friends from America and would love our company."

"It's going to be another crazy day," I chuckled.

***

Sanjay wrote to me, and I started to work on his private label. He had put his complete trust in me, and I was not going to let him down. I checked for the availability of the brand names of his preference. Next, I found suppliers for the wine, bottles, capsules, and corks. I sketched designs for the brand and looked for a graphic designer to convert it into digital form. I was learning something new every day.

***

In the coming months, I visited Vinexpo, one of the most eagerly awaited expositions in the wine sector. Every year, thousands of importers, buyers, and oenophiles flocked to Bordeaux to meet wine producers and taste their wines. Vinitaly, which I had visited with Jake the year before, was the Italian version of Vinexpo. It had been an eventful trip. Isabella's hospitality, Jake pretending to be sick, my embarrassment as I spat all around the spittoon, a flight that took off without us, our scenic drive back to Bordeaux...fond memories flooded back. I missed Jake terribly.

After finishing school, Jake had found a job and moved to Italy in search of his future Italian *amore.* Isabella, too, had gone back to work for her family's winery.

I held my pass and walked the red carpet, which was laid out on a long bridge over a lake that led to a big convention center. The floor was packed. I went from one stand to another, tasting wines and spitting in the most professional manner.

Suddenly, I noticed a board that said "Label design and print." I was searching for the right graphic designer to convert my label sketches into digital form for Sanjay. I was intrigued. I walked over and inquired about it after introducing myself to the lady at the stand.

"I'm displaying the board for a friend, Bernadette, a graphic artist. She has designed this beautiful label for my wine," said the lady, pointing to a wine bottle that had a lovely illustration of a vine leaf on it.

"It is beautiful indeed. If you don't mind, could I have her details, please?"

"Voilà," she said, then handed over a card. "She lives close to our vineyards, in Blaye. Come by and you could visit my winery too."

"That's great! Thank you so much, Corinne," I said, reading out her name from her visiting card. "Is it possible to taste your wines?"

"*Bien sûr*," she said, and poured the wines into glasses, one after the other, for me to try.

***

A few months later, I visited Blaye. Corinne was an attractive, wise-looking woman in her fifties, with a shock of white hair. She walked me through the vineyards, explaining the growing season.

"It's like pregnancy. The buds slowly turn into flowers, and then into grapes. The harvest is like giving birth. The doctors, nurses, all of them need to get ready for the delivery, and the equipment, too, needs to be cleaned and sterilized." We laughed. I felt at ease with Corinne. She was spontaneous. Later, she took me to the cellar and patiently described the process of making wine.

"Can you teach me winemaking?" I asked with ardor. I had been yearning to learn more ever since I had witnessed it at Château Siran.

"*Avec plaisir*!" she said enthusiastically.

***

Days passed like the wink of an eye. It had been almost eight months since I had passed my exams, and now I had a different dilemma. The status of my visa had changed from a student to temporary residence permit. The word "temporary" made me nervous. I knew I had a year to prove that I would be useful to the economy of France. My sister, Megha, and her husband, Nikhil, came to my rescue again. They gave me enough confidence to go ahead and launch my business. I already had a name and logo ready, but I needed a proper business plan. I scribbled on paper all of the wine services I could offer. Then I discussed it with Megha and Nikhil to make sure I was on the right path. I found a template online and started to elaborate on each service. Then came the forecast for the next four years.

At last, I was done. I had a clear picture of how my business would look in the near future. I felt proud. In the beginning of

February, I submitted the plan to the French authorities, along with all the other required documents, and waited.

If there was something that life taught me during that time, it was patience. Four months passed, and I was asked to resubmit all the documents. I did, hoping the result would be positive. Another two months passed, and I had no news. I meditated. Two more months passed without any information. My anxiousness heightened. The future of my business—and the future of Shloka, Casper, and myself—was in the hands of the French authorities. By the ninth month, I had given up hope. I readied myself mentally to move back to India. Then, one afternoon, I received a letter asking me to present myself at the prefecture. This was the day of judgment. Would France let me stay, or would it lose me forever?

CHAPTER 18
Solicantus

Bordeaux, France
November 2019

The golden seal of Marianne, a symbol of the republic of France, glittered on a card that was just thrust into my hand by the lady behind the counter. I stared at it in disbelief. The date of expiry: 2023. *I've got four more years to prove my mettle in this country*, I thought, feeling jubilant.

When I was back home, I called Megha and Nikhil to give them the good news.

"Thank you for standing by me," I said gratefully.

I shuddered to think what my life would have looked like if it weren't for them and my parents. A sea of emotions flooded over me when I spoke to Shloka. I wasn't sure if she even realized what this day meant for us. With the universe by our side, I felt even more determined to succeed.

***

That evening, I celebrated with Conor and Sofia.

"That's fantastic, Nam. I'm so happy for you," Conor said as he served the delicious *gratin dauphinois* that he had just pulled out of the oven.

"How was the harvest?" Sofia asked.

"It went very well. I learned a lot. Corinne is a very patient woman," I said, feeling blessed.

"What about that label you were creating for your client?" Conor asked.

"I'm working on the last bit of that project," I said.

"Will you be creating your own brand too?" Conor asked, to my surprise.

"No, I've never thought of that."

"That's a pity; I thought you were creating your own wine."

Conor had a point. I had gathered enough experience to create a brand of my own, and it wouldn't hurt to explore the idea. *But first, I must speak to Corinne*, I thought. Maybe she wouldn't agree to such a thing.

I called Corinne the next day.

"*C'est une excellente idée*," she said enthusiastically.

A frisson of excitement ran across my body. Soon I started to imagine what my brand would look like. What would I call it? I sketched designs that came to my mind on paper. Unsatisfied, I tore them apart.

***

It was around my birthday that Uncle Arun and Aunt Helga sent me a letter with some euros as a gift. I decided to take a break and visit Bruges. The city was showcasing the paintings of one of my favorite artists, Salvador Dalí. *Maybe he could inspire me*, I thought. His mind was so complex, and his vision larger than life. As I walked through the museum, I noticed that he used implied lines in some of his paintings. I loved the idea. While I stood there admiring his works, I knew exactly what I wanted my label to look like. I went back to my hotel and quickly sketched my design on paper. It felt perfect. I could imagine it on the bottle.

***

Soon I returned to Bordeaux and continued to do an extensive study on the influence of color in consumer behavior. I read that red represented good luck, while gold stood for richness; black meant power and elegance, and grey, on the other hand, depicted intellectuality and wisdom. I sketched a golden curve that depicted the journey of wine in a vat. Then I colored the inside bottom of the curve with profound shades of red to represent the process of fermentation, and the top of the curve I painted plain red that showed the must turned into a clear, glowing wine at the end of its cycle.

The label was finally complete. I was content. What would I name it? I asked myself every day. My mind had no rest. I couldn't eat; I couldn't sleep. All I could think about were names for my wine. I had succeeded with a beautiful and elegant design, and now all I needed was a name to justify the same. *What is wine?* I questioned myself. *Melody! It's the melody of the terroir...melody of the soil.* The answers came spontaneously. Then I looked for meanings in Latin. "*Soli*" meant "soil" and "*cantus*" meant "melody." I quickly put the two together and called it "Solicantus." I secured the copyrights and sent the labels for printing. My heart skipped a beat when I received an express delivery after three weeks. I opened the carton to find rolls of my design brilliantly printed on paper. At last, my brand had come alive. However, I knew that without Shloka, all efforts were vain. I was constructing a strong future for us, but Moksh held the key. He had the power to make everything come crashing down. That night I lay awake wondering how to convince him.

I called my lawyer the next morning.

"We've discussed this. It is impossible to take your daughter away without Moksh's consent," Vidya said. "You both need to settle things legally; only then you can take her to France."

"But that could take years," I said, hoping she had a different solution.

"The judge usually orders both the parents to be in the same city for ease of visitation. He would also never uproot a child and move her to a different school in a different city, let alone a different country," she said. "Your case might be considered only if you prove that your company was extremely successful, and it is imperative for you to be in France."

My business was in its nascent stages; there was no way the judge would consider my situation or Shloka's wishes even if Moksh had put us in harm's way.

"To begin with, we could file a case of domestic violence and get a restraining order. Simultaneously, we can file for child custody..." Vidya continued, but her voice faded as my mind started to race for solutions. I knew that Shloka was only safe for the moment. My father and mother did their best to protect her, but they couldn't stop Moksh from taking her. After all, he was her father. I felt anxious every time I imagined her sitting in the car and Moksh driving in a rage, like the day he had almost crashed into a tow truck. Shloka had begun to complain that she felt insecure around Moksh. She had started to speak her mind fearlessly, sometimes questioning Moksh's actions. This irked him, and he became upset that his once-docile girl had turned her voice against him. He began to abuse her verbally whenever she retaliated. This left her afraid and helpless. I knew I needed to do something soon.

I called Moksh and tried to persuade him to let Shloka move to Bordeaux.

"It is better if Shloka comes to live with me. I have found a very good school for her."

"No, she is better off here in Bangalore," he said sternly.

"She needs me, Moksh. She is twelve now but will be entering a delicate age next year. My parents have done enough. It's time they were relieved of their responsibilities."

"If they cannot take care of her, please ask them to send her to me. I will hire a nanny for her."

I grit my teeth. "Shloka wants to be with me, not with a nanny. Please agree, for her sake," I begged.

"Why don't you come back instead and live here? If you do care about Shloka, you will book the next flight to Bangalore."

"She will have a good life here, Moksh," I said, trying to keep myself calm.

"You're a selfish bitch," he suddenly roared, and even half a world away my heart contracted in fear.

"Please, Moksh, try to understand," I continued relentlessly.

"You will never have Shloka with you."

The line went dead.

I called back in vain.

Then I called my mother.

"Moksh's never going to let her go," I cried.

"Try again...keep trying until he agrees. Don't give up."

My mother loved Shloka unconditionally. She fed her the most nutritious food and cared for her tirelessly whenever she fell ill. If she came here to live with me, it would leave a void in her life. However, she still knew Shloka needed me and was ready to make that sacrifice.

My father came on the line.

"Don't worry about anything. Shloka is fine with us. Please focus on your work," he said.

***

I couldn't sleep that night. *How can I convince Moksh? How can I make him do the right thing for Shloka? I should stop this craziness of becoming an entrepreneur in France. Moksh will never let Shloka go. I should pack up and leave for India.*

I got out of bed and began to dump my clothes into my suitcase. Tears rolled down my cheeks. The abuse, the torture, the dead fishes, the broken laptop—it all came back to me. I fell to the floor and started to cry aloud. I didn't know how Shloka and I could escape Moksh.

After what felt like an eternity of crying, my eyes dried up. I looked at the time. It was almost three in the morning. Sofia wasn't home yet. *Maybe she had decided to stay with her boyfriend*, I thought.

I made myself a hot cup of tea and sat sipping it. All of a sudden, it came to me: I was doing everything wrong. In reality, Moksh was using Shloka to cause me pain. I had to change my strategy. Maybe I should tell him that Shloka would just visit me for a short time instead of begging him to let her go for good. *I must tell, not ask or beg*, I reminded myself.

***

The next day, I called Moksh. I was surprised that he picked up my call on the first ring.

"Yes, sweetie, tell me," he said.

Sweetie? I felt puzzled. Was he sarcastic, or was he really in a good mood? There was no telling with Moksh. I didn't beat around the bush and went straight to the point.

"Shloka will be visiting me for a couple of weeks during her summer holidays," I said in a firm voice.

"That is not necessary; you should come see her instead."

"I'm not asking you to send her for good. I'm only telling you that she will be with me for two weeks in May."

I could hear people conversing and laughing in the background. *He must be at the golf club*, I thought.

"Let me think about it."

"I've already got all the papers ready," I lied. "You have my word; I'll send her back in two weeks."

Suddenly I heard music on Moksh's end of the telephone. Then, someone called his name. It looked like he was at an event or a party, which one I couldn't say.

"Okay. I'm agreeing only for two weeks," he relented.

Oh my God! He just agreed, I thought. My heart jumped with joy, but I tried to contain my excitement.

"I'll send you all the papers to verify," I said in an unwavering voice.

***

Soon I flew to India to bring Shloka back with me. My parents, Megha, and Nikhil were thrilled to see me. Casper didn't leave my side. Age had caught up with him; he was now thirteen years old and had developed arthritis like most Labradors. I wasn't sure how he would survive the move to France, in a cage, in the hold of a plane. I went to see his doctor.

"He's too fragile," he said. "Moving a pet to a different country is a stressful process, both for the pet and the owner. Casper is old. It's risky. I cannot assure you that he will survive the journey."

I was torn. As those words seeped into me, I felt sadness engulf every inch of me. How could I leave him? We had come this far together.

My mother convinced me. "Maybe when the time comes for the real move, he will be better and can be flown across. You never know with pets," she continued. "Now, you have to focus on taking Shloka for two weeks."

In the following days, we took our flight. Moksh had signed the "no objection letter," and we passed through the immigration check without a problem. I shuddered to think what would have happened if I didn't have that piece of paper.

***

The taxi dropped us in front of my apartment.

"Welcome home, sweetheart," I said, feeling overwhelmed with a mix of joy and relief.

As we entered the little studio, Shloka suddenly asked, "Why's your apartment so small?"

I felt a lump in my throat. How could I tell her this was my life in France? Renting needed luck and was an expensive affair.

"Where's my room?" she continued.

"We'll stay together in this apartment for now. When you move for good, I'll find a bigger place, and you'll have your own room."

"Yayyy!" she said with excitement.

"Now, shower and get ready. I'll take you out for pancakes, and then in the evening we are going for my graduation ceremony," I said and smiled.

I was thrilled to have Shloka witness my special day. Even though I had taken a leap of faith in moving here, studying, and starting a new life, it was Shloka who had hung on without creating a fuss. I knew I could not have achieved all this without her cooperation.

The evening was exhilarating. As they placed the black hat above my head, I felt proud of myself. I wished that, along with Shloka, my whole family could have been there to witness that moment.

***

Two weeks flew quickly by. I showed Shloka the city, its parks, its river, and its golf clubs, among other things. She even met Sofia, Conor, and Monsieur Alain. I felt greedy. I wanted more time with her. I couldn't let her go. Heavy in my heart, I put her on a plane back to India after promising that I would try to have her here before her next academic year began.

***

I was at Corinne's vineyard when I received a call from my mother, Ambika.

"What's the matter?" I asked, sensing tension in her voice.

"It's Shloka; she's crying."

"Why?" I asked, feeling anxious.

Something unpleasant must have happened for Shloka to weep. She wasn't one to break down so easily. My mind raced for a few seconds before my mother caught her breath and began to explain.

"She was in an accident," she said as her voice shivered.

"What? How? Where?" I screamed into the phone.

"She's not hurt, but she's a little shaken."

"Could you please put her on the line, Mom?" I asked, trying to calm myself.

Shloka's voice came on the other end.

"I don't want to stay here. I want to be with you," she sobbed.

"Yes, sweetheart...soon," I said and probed further. "Do you want to tell me what happened?"

"I didn't want to come back with Papa. He was very drunk and not in a state to drive back from the party. I begged him, but he wouldn't listen."

I was afraid this day would come. I continued to listen as anger grew inside me.

"He was driving very rash and crashed into a wall. I thought I was going to die today," she recollected as her voice trembled.

"Oh my God, I'm so sorry you went through this. You're home and you're safe now."

"Please do something, Mama. He's going to want me to spend time with him again. If I refuse, he'll come here. I don't want to see him, please." I could sense panic in her voice.

"You rest, darling. I'll call the lawyer and see what we can do."

Vidya answered the phone. "I'm sorry to hear this, Namratha. This is a case of child negligence. We need to file for a restraining order immediately."

"So, if I go ahead with that, could I claim full custody of my daughter?"

"If we prove it in court, yes. We need to show that Moksh has a history of violence. It could turn ugly, but it can be done. You've got to hold on."

"Will the court allow Shloka to move to France?" I asked, wondering if this incident would change anything.

"We discussed this earlier. Usually, the courts will not uproot the child. It's the parents who will need to work around the needs of the children."

"We can't stay in the same city as Moksh. This will happen again. It could be worse," I said, feeling helpless.

"I understand. But the police will handle him."

"I'm not certain about that. I called the police on one of the occasions when Moksh had raised his hand to me. It wasn't of any help," I continued, feeling exasperated. "The constable advised Moksh against violence, then he turned to me and asked me to be more patient with my husband."

"I'll push for more stringent action. You shouldn't worry."

I wasn't convinced. There was no solution. It was obvious that any legal action I took could risk Shloka being caught in a battle that could take years to settle. I had two choices. Both needed sacrifices. I could listen to my attorney, take the legal route, move back to India, prove Moksh's violence in court, secure Shloka's custody, and judiciously fight the case. Or I could take a chance and convince Moksh in a nice way and bring Shloka here. Once she was here safe, I could quickly make a short trip to India, then file for divorce and child custody. He had allowed her to visit me for two weeks. I had some hope. Now, I needed a plan to persuade him to move her for good. It was worth a last shot.

***

It was January 2020 already, and I focused all my energy on registering my limited liability merchant company, Wine Equation, in France. As every foreigner, I felt overwhelmed with the paperwork. My accountant became my savior.

Then, I started to work with Corinne to see my vision become a reality. She had agreed to produce the wines for me and bottle them since I didn't have my own vineyards. I gave her a hand during harvest, de-leafing, blending, and at other times when she needed me or when I wanted to learn a particular step in the process.

I watched as my labels rolled on the labelling machine, slapping the wine bottles with the beautiful golden swirl. Holding one in my hand, I stared at it. It looked gorgeous. Monsieur Alain bought a few cases of wine to encourage my entrepreneurial debut. He was my lucky charm. I called importers in different countries. Some were interested and requested to try the wines. I sent them samples and followed up with calls. I had been so busy selling wines that I had forgotten to eat a proper meal. The word began to spread.

Meanwhile, I had started to speak to Moksh more regularly. I asked how he was doing, what he ate, whether his game went well, all the small talk that I could do. Then, one day, I told him that I was deluged with work and it would be better that Shloka stayed with him. He was surprised.

"What do you mean?" he asked. "You don't want her to be with you anymore?"

"It could get complicated having Shloka with me. My workload has increased, and I don't think I'll have time for her," I said, hoping he'd buy my lies.

"What kind of a mother are you?" he asked, spitefully.

"I understand how you feel, but I'm helpless. My parents too are old now and can't handle the responsibility of Shloka. Maybe you should think of hiring that nanny you were taking about."

There was a long silence before Moksh spoke.

"All you care about is your work. What a shame!"

"I can't take care of our daughter from here, and you didn't let her come to me when I pleaded. Now my priorities have changed, so technically, I can't do much."

"Priorities? You speak about priorities?" he said. I could feel his temper rising in his voice. "You are a black mark on motherhood. Anybody else would have given up everything to care for their child. But all you can think about is your work."

"I can't move back, Moksh. I've just started a company. I'm not going to abandon my dreams," I said, sensing that my reverse psychology technique was having the desired effect. "Moreover, Shloka has you in Bangalore. She is equally your responsibility."

"You know what? You're a piece of shit who doesn't deserve a child. I'll let your daughter know that you've abandoned her," he yelled as my heart pounded.

My plan was working. I had already spoken to Shloka and told her my strategy. My girl was smart. She fully understood how this could just be our chance. She began to call Moksh and persuade him to let her come to me. Later, I called and pressured him to keep Shloka instead of burdening my parents or sending her to me. I knew Moksh was afraid of responsibility. That's why we had failed as a family.

"If you and your parents don't wish to care for Shloka, she can live with my parents or my brother's family," he said, one day, feeling frustrated.

"This is your solution?" I asked, feeling dismayed. "Shloka would bring the house down."

"She won't have a say in this," Moksh continued.

"So you will force her to do something against her wishes?"

"Yes, if I have to. It's all because you don't want her with you. I'm left with no choice other than to ask my family to care for her."

My heart skipped a beat. These were the words I was waiting to hear. There was nothing else in the world that I wanted more than for her to be with me. I contained my enthusiasm and continued to sound serious.

"I'll see what I can do. Even if she comes here, I'm not sure how she will adjust to this life."

Finally, Moksh was on the verge of letting Shloka go. My strategy worked. Every cell in my body was celebrating.

I called my parents immediately and broke the news. They were overjoyed.

"Be careful. He hasn't signed the papers yet," my father warned.

"I'll wait until tomorrow before sending them to him. I don't want him to think I'm desperate."

Shloka was in the midst of her exams. I couldn't move her before she was done with them. However, I felt this compulsion to fly her to Bordeaux before Moksh changed his mind. I held my breath. It was the middle of March. *A few more weeks*, I thought.

***

In the next few days, I gathered all documents in the checklist for the visa. Shloka's flight needed to be reserved. The fact that she'd be flying solo made me nervous. She had flown back alone when she visited me last time and thankfully had not encountered any problems. It was I who sat biting my nails all night wondering if she was all right. I searched for accompanied service for minors on Air France. After an hour of trying, I decided it was best to visit their office the next day to seek help with the booking.

That same afternoon, I received a call from an importer in Belgium.

"We tasted your wines and thought that it would be a great fit for our portfolio," Laura explained. "Can I order a pallet to begin with?"

I felt like I had won a Formula One race. I imagined myself popping a Champagne bottle and spraying it all around. At last, my brand was validated and accepted in the market. I called Corinne and gave her the good news. She was jubilant.

"Thank you for believing in me," I told her, in my most grateful voice.

Corinne had given me a string of hope to hold on to. She had put her trust in me. With her support and my family's, I felt like I could fearlessly make a life with Shloka in France.

***

Conor called just after I had finished my dinner that evening.

"Nam, you need to turn on the news," he said, in an impatient voice.

"Why, is the world ending?" I giggled and pressed the button on my remote.

My laughter faded and I dropped my phone. *No, no, no...this cannot be happening*, I thought. The next second, my mind went numb.

CHAPTER 19

Freedom

Bordeaux, France
March 2020

Tears poured down my face as I watched President Macron announce the closure of borders. Why was the world scheming against us? Moksh had almost agreed. It was a matter of a few weeks and Shloka would be with me. Why today? Why now?

Macron's voice sounded on every news channel.

"From tomorrow afternoon, the frontiers at the entry into the European Union and the Schengen area will close. Concretely, all travel between European and non-European union countries will be suspended for thirty days...."

I hurriedly pulled out my laptop and typed in "French visa."

An article read, "France suspends issuance of all types of visas."

Heaviness filled my heart. I looked at the black file lying on my desk. It had all documents to be submitted for the visa except Moksh's "no objection letter" and Shloka's air tickets. I sighed. Why was everything so challenging in my life?

I dialed Monsieur Alain's number, hoping he'd offer a solution.

"You must call the Indian embassy in Paris first thing tomorrow morning and explain your situation," he advised. "Did Moksh sign the papers?"

"Not yet!"

"Get him to sign immediately and ask your daughter to be ready to leave. I'll try to see if anyone in my network can help."

I looked at the time. It was half past one in India. *It's too late to call*, I thought.

The next morning, I telephoned Moksh to ask if he had signed the papers.

"The borders are closed, aren't they?"

"Errr...yes, but I'm f-f-figuring that out with the embassy," I stuttered.

It was too late; Moksh had sensed the panic in my voice.

"I'll sign once they begin issuing visas," he said bluntly.

Almost immediately, I called the embassy in the hope that they'd agree.

"I'm sorry, madam. Only nationals holding a French passport are being allowed back into France."

"Can't you make an exception? My husband has finally agreed for my daughter to move here. I've been waiting four years to have her with me. Please do something!"

"I understand, madam, but we have orders that we need to conform to."

***

Monsieur Alain spoke to me that evening.

"It's not only France, but it's the whole European Union who have decided to stop foreigners from entering the area. At the moment it seems impossible. Let's wait for the next announcement."

Nevertheless, I wasn't giving up. I started to write emails every day to the French and the Indian authorities trying to sensitize them to my situation. I even called the minister of foreign affairs in Paris. My call was held and transferred several times before the secretary came online and tried her best to help me. Somehow, it seemed like nobody could come to my aid. A virus had taken the world hostage. A strict lockdown was put in place. Masks became mandatory. Schools, offices, restaurants, hotels, and all public places were ordered to close. People were asked to stay indoors and work from home while children attended online classes. A filled attestation was obligatory if one needed to venture out, without which, a fine of €135 was to be coughed up.

The first time I went to the supermarket, I was shocked. I had never seen Bordeaux this way. The city was usually bustling with tourists. But, all of a sudden, the streets looked like the aftermath of an apocalypse. I rushed back home, feeling frustrated.

Like everyone else, I turned on the television every day hoping for some positive news. Instead, I watched country after country fall prey to this invisible monster. People were dying in masses, mostly the weak and vulnerable. Little did I know this was just the beginning of a lengthy ordeal. I called Shloka daily to make sure she didn't lose hope. She kept busy with her friends and avoided her father. Moksh finally got fed up of her excuses. To ward off his loneliness during the lockdown, he moved to his friend's home.

Meanwhile, my business came to a standstill. A new brand like mine didn't have a chance in any market without being tasted. With travel restrictions in place, I didn't see how I could sell any wine. Nevertheless, I tried. Nothing could convince the buyers. Restaurants, cafés, and bars across the world were affected by the pandemic. Retailers had enough stock and were cautious when buying more. I broke down one evening and cried myself to sleep. My difficulties were never ending. I wondered what I had done to deserve this.

The following morning, I sat up in bed. My head was still heavy, but I felt a little relieved after all that crying. Thoughts flowed in.

Perhaps I should reinvent how I do business in this new landscape, I thought. The future was ridden with uncertainty, but I had to succeed. Not just for Shloka and myself, but for the dead baby girl who I found on the beach. For Siddamma, who lost her baby to a misogynistic society. For the millions of women and girls who are victims of abuse. For those whose voices are suppressed. For those who feel weak and helpless. I must be their hope.

From that day on, I decided to stop selling wines until commerce bounced back. Instead, I started to speak about my crazy journey that led me to create my brand, Solicantus. Monsieur Alain helped spread the word through his network. Tom Mullen heard about my story through a friend of mine and wrote an article in *Forbes*. Jane Anson interviewed me for *Decanter*. Dhananjay Sardeshpande from *Brews & Spirits* reached out to me. I couldn't believe it.

***

The month of May began, and things were starting to look a little brighter. The hospitalizations and deaths in France reduced. President Macron announced the end of the lockdown, but the borders still remained closed. I continued to write emails to the authorities and prayed for an end to this crisis. Soon, I got wind that France would reopen its frontiers to European countries. *It is only a matter of time before it opens up to other countries,* I thought.

Every two hours, I surveyed my emails. I also searched through my spam to see if Moksh had sent the signed letter. I felt disappointed. *Maybe a message will remind him,* I thought.

"I'm trying to reach you. Let me know when a good time is to talk. Shloka and I are still waiting for your letter," I typed and sent.

He replied, "I'm going to my lawyer tomorrow. Will get back after that."

Lawyer? Why now? Why not just sign the goddamn paper? I dared not ask him. Moksh was seeking advice from his attorney. There was not a chance he would allow him to send Shloka to me. I buried my face in my palms. What was I going to do?

***

By mid-August, the French hospitals were saturated again. People were pouring in with acute respiratory problems. France set a record for the number of new cases reported in a single day. A second lockdown was becoming a strong possibility. In another part of the world, India began relaxing its restrictions. It was as if there was a pattern; when France's cases reduced, India's increased, and when France's cases increased, India's decreased. I felt alarmed. I had to move Shloka before both countries shut down again. It would be a small window. I had to act fast.

I dialed Moksh's number, but there was no reply. Feeling a sense of urgency, I called again. There was no response. I wondered what he was doing. Was he golfing? Napping? Or partying? It had to be one of the three. I called again and let the phone continue ringing until it stopped.

Disappointed, I began to fiddle with the pen on my desk. What if he had changed his mind? I had no time to lose. I called Shloka.

"Please talk to your father sweetly. He needs to sign the document," I said, my voice shivering. I felt horrible.

"I honestly want to tell him how bad I feel about being stuck in this situation. Huh! I wish I was eighteen and could make my own decisions," said Shloka, feeling infuriated.

"Yes, please try telling him, darling. Let's leave no stone unturned."

Moksh finally called back that night, relieving me of my stress. *It must be early morning in Bangalore*, I thought as I picked up the phone.

"Sorry, sweetie. You tried calling me?" he said as soon as he heard my voice.

I wanted to jump to the subject but held myself back.

"Anything urgent?"

"Errr...no, it was just a casual call," I lied.

"Looks like you tried many times. Do you miss me?"

Moksh's comment startled me. There was a long awkward silence before he spoke again. "I don't know about you, but I miss you a lot. Let's forget whatever happened in the past and start afresh."

I felt sorry for Moksh. *Loneliness can be wretched*, I thought. I listened without responding.

"I love you. You're the only one. Nobody can take your place. I'll do everything to make it right this time. I'll move to France, do whatever you want. Just tell me that you want me back."

It was typical of Moksh to try and convince me. I had been fooled several times.

"Moksh, you had all those years to make it right. It's too late now," I said, wanting to put an end to his madness.

Jekyll and Hyde both existed in Moksh. One had destroyed our family. The other wanted to get it back. I would have become a saint if I accepted his offer.

"Life can be a bitch. I know, I've lost you. And now you want to take my daughter away from me."

"The same wife and daughter that you abandoned to be raped or killed on the street?" I asked as anger raged inside me. Every cell in my body hated him. Memories of that terrible night flooded my mind. "You tortured me because I gave birth to a girl! Would a boy have pleased you and your father? It's a shame that you think Shloka is any less capable than a boy."

"Yes, I've made mistakes. I admit it. I realize now what an idiot I was," Moksh said as he wept uncontrollably. "You both are my life. I cannot live without you."

Was he repenting? I closed my eyes. I didn't know. I could only feel sorry for him.

"Moksh, listen to me. We can't turn back time. But we can make it better in the future," I said as I took a deep breath. "I know you feel lonely. But I'm here for you. We still can care for each other as friends."

"Friends, huh?"

"Yes, friends. And you'll always be Shloka's father. Nothing can change that."

"She sent me a long message today. It hurt me so much. She said she never wanted to see my face again. Am I such a bad father? Do I deserve that?"

"Shloka's psychologically devastated, with everything that has happened. She needs time to heal," I said, hoping he would empathize. "She has just stepped into her teens. It's going to be a challenging time for her, as well as for us as parents."

"I understand."

"Then do what is right for her. Set her free."

The line went quiet for a few seconds before Moksh spoke.

"I will, you have my word."

***

It was mid-September 2020. The sun shone brightly as I made my way into Charles de Gaulle Airport in Paris. As soon as I entered the 2E terminal, I checked the display board for the arrivals. Air France flying from Bangalore was on time. Was this really happening? I pinched myself. My business had begun to take shape. People sent emails or called me to order my wines. I needed to work on setting up an online shop to facilitate their purchases. My wine importer in Belgium was very happy with the wines, and she was already planning to put in a second order. Every day I learned something new in the business of wine, like sourcing material for packaging, logistics, prospecting new markets, designing technical sheets, arranging product shoots, and more. Having my brand in stores across the world wasn't a dream anymore—it was becoming a possibility.

And best of all, Moksh had signed the letter, as promised. The French and Indian border restrictions were finally lifted. I had waited four long years for this day. Shloka was nine when I had left India, and now she was thirteen, an adolescent. Everything was set for her. A week prior, I moved into a two-bedroom apartment. *It's going to be a nice surprise for her*, I thought. I had enrolled her in school and bought all her books and stationery. I had even made a list of all her favorite dishes that I was going to cook for her. We would terribly miss Casper drooling on the kitchen floor. He had crossed the rainbow bridge and was now probably watching this moment unfold from heaven.

I went toward the exit area where minors who flew solo were handed over to their parents by the airline staff. The hall was bustling with people. I waited with bated breath. At last, Shloka appeared at a distance. I felt a surge of emotions take over me. I smiled, laughed, and cried, all at the same time. We had made it—we had made it against all odds.

CHAPTER 20
Shloka

Bordeaux, France
June 2025

"How do you feel?" I asked as I brought the water to boil in a pan and put a bunch of uncooked spaghetti into it.

"I've been waiting to turn eighteen since I was a little girl," Shloka laughed as she grated the block of parmesan into a bowl.

I hugged her and kissed her on her forehead. "I can't believe my baby an adult already."

"Huh! I'm not your baby anymore."

It's true, I thought. I was struggling to comprehend how and why that little girl who held my hand to walk was now looking forward to spreading her wings and flying away. In a way, I felt relieved that she had turned eighteen. It meant she could freely travel between India and France without Moksh holding her back in India against her wishes.

"You'll always be my baby," I said, looking at her with great admiration.

Not only had she become fluent in French within the first year of moving here, but she had seamlessly integrated into French society. She made friends, went to school, had sleepovers, had boyfriends, had break-ups, went to parties, and did all the things teenagers do.

"Do you know that we are almost done recording my first song, 'You miss me'?"

"Really? Can you play it?" I asked, with excitement.

She picked up her phone and played the song. I was stunned. I couldn't believe that it was her singing. She was getting better and better at mastering her voice. Just as I had sought vines to heal, she had used music to escape from the trauma of her past. She wrote songs like "I Miss You" and "Back To You," collaborated with international artists like Walt Anderson, supporting lead vocalist of the legendary Grammy Award winning band, Kool & the Gang.

"I can't wait for the world to hear this," I exclaimed.

A feeling of satisfaction came over me. It hadn't been easy being a mother, a father, and a friend to her, all while developing my wine distribution in five countries, launching two other wines under my Solicantus brand, living my purpose of mentoring distressed women and children, and being a voice for abused animals. I felt Shloka and I were moving ahead in our lives, uplifting each other, loving each other. But it was not all rosy. As most parents, I too faced push back, and Shloka, as most teenagers often do, felt the need to rebel. There were always going to be highs and lows, moments of doubt and moments of exhaustion. But each time I was faced with a challenge, I looked back to see how far we had come. One thing was clear—Shloka and I, together with our cats, had built a beautiful life in France, one grape at a time.

Acknowledgments

To my family, whose constant love and support have been my guiding compass. You all have taught me the true meaning of resilience, and what it means to rise above adversity. I carry your love with me every day, and this book is as much yours as it is mine.

And to my loyal dog, Casper, whose love has been my constant comfort through the darkest and brightest of times. Your unwavering loyalty and companionship have reminded me that, love is simple, pure, and unconditional. Thank you for being my silent strength. I miss you everyday.

To my dear friends, whose love, laughter and unwavering faith, has kept me alive. Thank you for being my safe space and for walking with me through the chapters of my life.

To my teachers and mentors, who, through their patience, wisdom, and belief in my potential, have shaped me into the woman I am today. Your guidance has been invaluable, and I carry your lessons with me every step of the way.

To my early editors, Robert Flynn, Patricia Barbe-Girault, Sharon Kizziah-Holmes, Caroline Leavitt. Thank you for believing in the power of my story. Your contribution to my book is invaluable.

To my literary agent, Lindsay Guzzardo. Thank you for walking beside me, holding the lamp and cheering me on when I almost gave up. You are the champion of this book and I could not have come this far without you.

To my editor, Adriana Senior and the whole team of Post Hill Press, it has been so wonderful working with you all. Thank you for believing in my story and making sure my book turns out to be the best it can be. I'm forever grateful.

To my street team, I can't thank you all enough for your valuable inputs and unconditional support.

To Lainey Cameron, thank you for offering me the scholarship to your book marketing course, '12 weeks to book launch success'. It has given me immense confidence and set me up for my author journey. Forever grateful!

Lastly and most importantly, to my dear friend and my book therapist, Samantha Verant. Thank you for showing the path and keeping me company through this crazy journey.

About the Author

Photo by Denis Trapp Photography

Namratha Stanley is a single mother, author, and entrepreneur based in France. She is the founder and CEO of Wine Equation, a merchant company, and the creator of the Solicantus wine brand. In addition to leading her business ventures, she serves as program director at the INSEEC Business School. Passionate about giving back, Namratha mentors women and students, and actively supports children's education initiatives in India. She lives in Bordeaux with her daughter and their two cats.

To learn more visit www.namrathastanley.com or find her on Instagram using her handle, @namratha_stanley_author. You can find her daughter Shloka on Instagram at her handle, @shloka.prst.

About the Author